PSYCHE
and sports

PSYCHE
and sports

edited by
Murray Stein & John Hollwitz

James Hillman • Ronald Schenk • Thayer A. Greene • Thomas Singer
Jan DeVeber Marlan • Brenda Donahue • Elizabeth Retivov
Joan Lamb Ullyot • Katharine Myers • Eric Zengota • J. L. Campbell
Steven R. Heyman • Cathaleene Macias • Ronald Kinney
Margaret Johnson • Jeanine Auger Roose • Carol F. Odell

Chiron Publications ■ *Wilmette, Illinois*

Permissions

Poem, p. 17, from *Duino Elegies* by Rainer Maria Rilke, translation, introduction, and commentary by J. B. Leishman and Stephan Spender. Copyright © 1963 by W. W. Norton. Reprinted by permission of the publisher.

"A Warrior's Creed" © 1982, 1987 by Ralph Blum. From *The Book of Runes*. Reprinted with permission from St. Martin's Press, New York, N.Y.

Illustration of the Queen of Swords from the Pierpont Morgan-Bergamo Visconti-Sforza Tarocchi deck reproduced by permission of U.S. Games Systems, Inc., Stamford, CT 06902 USA. Copyright © 1975, 1984 by U.S. Games Systems, Inc. Further reproduction prohibited.

Photograph of Pictish Warrior, page 119, courtesy of the British Museum, London.

Photograph of the sword bridge from *The Arthurian Legends*, Richard Barber, ed., courtesy of Boydell and Brewer, Ltd., Woodbridge, Suffolk, England.

Photographs on pages 129 and 132 reproduced by permission from Aikika Aikido World Headquarters, Tokyo.

Calligraphy, page 133, from *The Zen Way to the Martial Arts* by Taisen Deshimaru. Copyright © 1983 by Taisen Deshimaru. Used by permission of Dutton Signet, a division of Penguin Books USA, Inc.

Graphs on pages 157 and 158 prepared by Michael Barron, Barron Layout and Design.

Library of Congress Catalog Card Number: 94–28089

Printed in the United States of America.
Copyediting and book design by Siobhan Drummond.
Cover design by Michael Barron.
Cover photography by Siobhan Drummond.

Library of Congress Cataloging-in-Publication Data:

Psyche and sports : baseball, hockey, martial arts, running, tennis,
   and others / edited by Murray Stein and John Hollwitz.
      p. cm.
   Includes bibliographical references.
   ISBN 0–933029–79–9 : $16.95
     1. Sports—Psychological aspects. I. Stein, Murray, 1943–
II. Hollwitz, John.
GV706.4.P66   1994
796'.01—dc20   94–28089
                                  CIP

ISBN 0–933029–79–9

CONTENTS

CONTENTS

PREFACE

This is the second volume in the Chiron series on Psyche and World. In the first collection of essays, *Psyche At Work*, the authors considered the ways in which analytical psychology could be applied to the study and therapy of the modern workplace and other types of organizations. In this second collection, the authors consider the many ways in which the psyche and sport interact and affect each other.

Sport occupies a paradoxical place in modern Western cultures. The sports section of the newspaper usually is placed last, and yet every newspaper contains one and readership often depends heavily upon its interest and quality. Professional athletes are made into celebrities, and yet they can be discarded and forgotten from one season to the next. The image of the collegiate scholar-athlete is the subject of jokes, but the best schools still court players and make money from their performances. A city may be better known for its sports teams than for its politicians or architecture, even though the teams seem oddly ephemeral, fading, closing down, or even traded away to another city.

Despite these ambiguities, sport somehow manages to engage the soul deeply, compelling enormous attention locally and internationally. Through telecommunications, athletic events draw audiences that can number in the scores of millions, vastly exceeding other displays of skill and probably rivaling the almost universal participation in organized religious practices in audience appeal and meaning. Sport has a powerful collective appeal but also an important individual meaning. People require play and derive much satisfaction from it, although many feel embarrassed to be as concerned and obsessed with sport as we often are. To improve the tennis or golf game may take precedence over professional and even erotic interests. Those who play in competition, especially at the elite level, provide a collective spectacle and are also engaged in soul work of their own.

The contributors to this volume address three general issues about psyche and sport. The first is the collective and mythical nature of athletic competition, whose deepest roots are found in religion and the experience of the sacred. From this perspective, modern sport is a ritual container for collective energies. Whole societies can be galvanized around a sports event, turning it into a symbol of collective life. A second group of essays examines the individual's experience of sport, either in the heroic pursuit of mastery or in the phenomenology of being a fan gripped by the numinosity of a sport and its stars. Finally, several chapters are devoted to inquiry into new methodologies and measurement strategies for investigating sports from a depth psychological perspective.

It is the editors' hope that this volume will carry one step further the project of recognizing the psyche at play in the world around us.

Murray Stein
John Hollwitz

City, Sport, and Violence

James Hillman

. . . the most practical advice we can offer to readers is that they had best reconcile themselves to a continuing life with hooliganism in football and elsewhere.
　　　　　　—The Roots of Football Hooliganism

Martial Violence

We are all too familiar with and shocked by the reports, the pictures: Brazilian football stadiums surrounded by moats, chain fences, police with attack dogs; Italian *tifosi* (rabid with typhus); some forty or more killed in Brussels by rioting Liverpool followers; five hundred injured in a race melee at a high school game in Washington, D.C.; and similar stories from Central America, Turkey, Argentina, Peru, China, the Soviet Union, Egypt. When Brazil won the World Cup in 1970, two million people celebrated the returning team: forty-four dead, 1,800 injured. Urban sport spectacles, even local minor contests, result sometimes in deadly violence. This is a worldwide phenomenon.

What does an archetypal psychology say to this? By "archetypal" here I mean ubiquitous, passionate, ever-recurring, inescapable patterns bearing value and religious depth. "Archetypal" also implies "necessary" patterns which govern behavior because they are rooted in psychic life. If the psychic life of human beings is by nature political, following from the premise of Aristotle—*anthropos physei politikon zoon* (man is by nature a political animal), then what necessary and essential political purpose could be served by the archetypal phenomenon of urban sport violence? How might we understand our theme of violence in sports, both psychologically *and* politically? In fact, might it be possible that sports violence provides the very bridge for exhibiting the innate

From the lecture given at the University of Florence, Villa Montalto Hochberg, May 25, 1990 relation, of which Aristotle speaks, between the deepest animal forces in human nature and the life of the *polis*?

To begin with, I shall stake a major claim by extending Aristotle's statement to say that sports belong to the political nature of human being and that inherent violence in sports is therefore also political in significance. Fierce physical contests are neither contingent nor mere accessories and diversions, circuses for the proles and plebs. I want to claim them as inherent components of political existence.

Second, my method for this archetypal investigation shall follow from Jung's famous dictum: "the Gods have become diseases." We no longer look to Olympus—to ancient cults, temples, and statues of the past—for the gods nor to their mythical narratives and dramas. Instead, the gods appear in our disorders, private, of course, but also public. The very first lesson we learn from Oedipus is *not* what Freud taught—a lesson about the private disorder of the erotics of family—but a lesson about the sickness of the city with which the tragedy of *Oedipus Rex* opens and which is the concern of Oedipus when answering the Sphinx and when seeking out the evil that scourges Thebes. Oedipus would save the city. This is his first concern, as I believe it cannot help but be of any depth psychology following from Freud's vision of Oedipus as the basic myth of our field. As well, this concern for the city must be the focus of any psychology of soul since the soul of the individual is located within the wider scope of the *anima mundi*. Saving the city remains the concern of Sophocles at great old age with his *Oedipus of Colonus*, ending that drama by having Oedipus die in a place that blesses the *polis* of Corinth. The Oedipus myth sets the course for depth psychology, not only toward the private sickness of family, but also toward the public sickness of the city. So, by turning an archetypal psychological eye toward urban sport violence, we are continuing Freud's mythical approach, in fact, his Oedipal approach, to psychological disorders.

We are also following Jung by searching out "the god in the disease" of sports' violence. But—which god? The question echoes the standard request put to the oracle in antiquity: To which god or goddess or hero do I sacrifice? For to name the power responsible is already the beginning of remedy (Parke 1967a, p. 871; 1967b, p. 111). To be told the altar at which to lay the trouble "places" and gives a particular significance to the disorder. For the troubles of Oedipus, it was Apollo; for the troubles of Hippolytus, it was Aphrodite; for our troubles in the soccer stadiums, it is Ares (Mars).

That competitive sports constellate the incursions of Mars has long been attested. Even *horse racing*! As late as 1822, the British journal, *The Annals of Sporting*, suggested that spectators go armed to Epsom and Ascot since violence might break out at any time, as, for instance, when a favorite gentleman jockey, having disappointed his followers by not winning, was set upon by the crowd and whipped (Guttmann 1986, p. 68). Look at today's tennis: a doubles match—four men in white on a carefully rectangled ground with white lines, requiring a total of at least fourteen linesmen and judges to keep the decorum and prevent disorder.

Even if Giovanni de Bardi formalized and aestheticized *calcio* in his *Discorso* (1580), earlier writers had called *calcio* a "*battaglia.*" *Gioco della pugna* and other games such as the annual stone fights at Perugia played by hurling rocks, later condemned by Savanarola, attest enough to a wide recognition that Mars indeed was, in earlier Italian times to say nothing of the Roman period, the god in the disorder we now call urban sport violence.

Here we must keep quite clear about two things regarding Mars. He is neither a god of strategy nor of victory. Neither the thought of fighting nor its outcome is his province. Mars appears in the red-faced fury, the intoxicating fever (hence *tifosi*) of actual combat, like a sexual or drug rush, an unstoppable transport to another condition that makes humans passionate about physical combat and addicts them to it, for they are then, during those moments of battle rage, in the embrace of a divine energy.

The epithets of Mars say much about his effects. He was called Mars *moles*, attesting to massive power and his power as a mass phenomenon. He was called *caecus*, blind; and he is also associated with *Nerio* to illustrate his heroic aspect. Other more ancient terms (*Vedic, Avestan*) analyzed by Dumezil that were given to the warriors of Mars were "headstrong young man," "mighty hero," "giant," and also "dancer" (Dumezil 1966, pp. 206–212, 392; Roscher 1965). Words for anger, fury, and killing also belong in this complex.

Although we may have forgotten the gods, they do not ignore us. We are still subject to their archetypal possession. Perhaps, then, the first benefit of this violence is that it forces us to recognize their continued presence, no longer externally in the overt obeisance of our bodies and souls to their rituals, but now as psychological "diseases" in the body politic and soul of the city.

The mythical fact that Mars is always in love with Venus tells of his Venusian component, his Venusian other side which loves beauty as much as battle, as Giovanni de Bardi and his Florentine sportsmen favored and displayed. Just think for a moment about the velvets and silks, brocades and armors, the banners and scarves, the orange vermilions, the scarlets, and the empurpled sleeves worn by the children of Mars, whether in the Renaissance or in any sports event today.

Imagine Venusian love, so sensate, precise and refined, exhibited by the sons of Mars in their care of actual weapons of war, hunt, and sport—the blades, edges, points, teeth, metals, hammerings, and temperings in the variety of knives, swords, spears, pikes, halberds, sabers, battle-axes, skinning knives, rapiers, daggers, and lances that have been lovingly honed with killing intention. Remember the music: the drums and fifes and pipes, the trumpets and bugles, the marching songs, marching steps, marching bands, brass, braid, and stripes. Remember, too, the parades and the legions, the military decorations, the feathered hats and ivory-handled pistols, the medals and honors; and recall the great fortress walls and bastions designed with violence in mind by Brunelleschi, da Vinci, Michelangelo, Buontalenti (Hillman 1987, pp. 123–124).

Even today, as Dunning et al. remark, spiked fences and cages have transformed the majority of British football stadiums into "fortress-like constructions" (1988, p. 235). As well, young fans feel themselves to be defenders of territory at home and adventuring invaders in rival cities.

I ask only that we not forget that Mars governs a great range of the human psyche and human history from the glories of heroism to the assaults of hooliganism. In Florence itself, the Battisterio was originally a temple to Mars; Giuliani de Medici presented himself, after a joust, in the pose of Mars; and the factional fighting between the Blacks and Whites occurred under a statue of Mars.

We may conceive Venus and Mars not merely as opposites, but rather as interior to each other. That lovers fall into the mad fury of Mars does not surprise us. The reverse is just as true, just as evident. The world of Mars enjoys close physical contact, display of body, aesthetic delight in style, instinctual release, passionate impetuosity; all in all, Mars and Venus share a lust for life.

The difference between martial heroism and hooliganism depends largely upon three kinds of discipline: the discipline of beauty, of which we have just spoken and to which we shall return; the discipline of bonding, about which I shall say more toward the end; and hierarchical discipline. These disciplines provide the rituals that can enclose into the human sphere the transcendent infiltration of the godly martial power.

The obessively severe rituals of hierarchy that require instant obedience on the battlefield still show up in the soccer stadium, both in regard to the unquestioned authority of the team manager or coach over the players and in the supreme authority of the umpires and referees over all participants. In sandlot games played by neighborhood children hierarchy is quickly established, a captain emerges. Violent urban gangs enforce strict hierarchical discipline as well. Where Mars is present, so, too, is hierarchy, which suggests that the feminist attempt to dissolve hierarchy to promote literal equality, as if that were the key to democracy, actually invites Mars rampant, disobedient, unordered, and blind. Hierarchy protects the god from his fury. I would even suggest that hierarchical discipline is less a repressive constriction owing to a patriarchal Saturn than it is the *spiritus rector* within the archetypal figure of Mars, whose own violent spirit invents hierarchy to save the god from his blind and wasteful spending in senseless eruptive violence. After all, the gods, as the Neoplatonists insisted, are intelligences. We must assume they know what they are doing in inventing their appropriate requirements.

Some examples may help my point about hierarchical discipline. Both Japanese Sumo wrestling and our Western Olympic sports, fencing and Greco-Roman wrestling, are intensely competitive and physically demanding, calling forth the martial heat of explosive man-to-man combat. Yet the spectators are usually quiet; order reigns owing to elaborate ceremonial discipline. Whereas the Golden Gloves boxing tournaments are noted for violence breaking out in the audience, because, I believe, these tournaments are a kind of democratic free-for-all. Only one side of Mars, his battle rage, has been allowed, neglecting his requirements for hierarchical formalities.

Because the violence, whether heroic or hooligan, derives from divine incursion, it can never be fully explained by Marxist, Freudian, sociological, psychological, symbolic, or structuralist interpretations. We may speak of mob psychosis, of an *abaissement du niveau mental*, of the crowd and its power; we may talk of the revolt of the masses and the impotence of the oppressed classes, of the loss of the father who gives authority and order, of the passive-aggressive behavior fostered by the media, of urban despair and *anomie*, of exploitation and displacement through the commercial manipulation of sports . . . but never can we account for the madness of Mars. For what takes place in urban sports violence is more like what takes place suddenly on the battlefield, and though we call it "hooliganism," this very transgression of all civic norms tells us that what is going on is not simply "sick" but also *mythic*—for where myth now operates most vividly, showing the transcendent power of the gods, is precisely outside of usual reason, in the inexplicable behaviors we call psychopathology.

Testosterone

Mars lives on the Areopagus, his hill in Athens, and he lives in the Campo de Marte *outside* the Roman city. He was always recognized as a danger to the *civis*, and this because he lives inside each citizen's bloodstream, where he is called "testosterone." The virility of Mars is also a phenomenon of the glands. The gods live not only on Olympus, not only in the heavens of myth and the shrines of antiquity; they continue to inhabit our bodies.

Again and again, studies report that the attendees at urban soccer matches are mainly teenagers. This is especially true of the newer, Third World nations where the population's median age is lower than in Western Europe. But even in Cologne, research shows that over half of the spectators at regular matches are 21 or younger and, of course, 88% male. The riots have been called "delayed puberty crises" and even thought about in terms of young males seeking initiation through physical risk.

At the onset of puberty testosterone secretion suddenly increases thirtyfold. The effect of this male hormone is stupendous. In the moose, for instance, the rack of antlers grows to a breadth of two meters in only 120 days. Nearly 90% of the food it takes in goes solely toward its magnificent display of aggressive male pride. Testosterone produces prolonged and intensely exhilarating experiences, a "male high," and it can occasion violence. Testosterone levels are reinforced, not reduced, by violence. No amount of moralist preaching by city elders and sports commentators, or police control, or feminist ideology can affect this natural force, this Mars in the bloodstream. It must be reckoned with. So let us look more closely at the following psychological situations that raise testosterone:

1) Anticipation of a challenge.

2) Competition and success in competition.

3) Increase of status: a successful response to trial.

4) Anticipation of sexual encounter and success in sexual activities (testosterone levels rise before and after sexual activity).

5) Anger.[1]

It is therefore not unexpected that a judgment call perceived as unjust or an unnoticed foul that sets off anger in the crowd will trigger an escalation of fury owing to the increased testosterone levels. And it is not unexpected that, already before a sports event, the anticipation of it prepares for a riot in the bloodstream. Nor should it be surprising that when the game is over, there is no falling off of excitement, and that after a victory, an even higher potential for outbursts exists.

Of these five factors which raise testosterone levels, anger deserves especial notice since it is a major component of sports violence and because anger belongs both mythologically and symbolically to the traits of Mars. Psychology, however, will not help us here, because it too often loses the specific value of anger by clumping it together with hostility, aggression, rage, fury, and hatred. Yet, as the different words show, these states of soul are each different feelings, different behaviors, different significances. Our lack of differentiation of the martial emotions results from a long history, particularly Christian. *Ira* (anger) and *cupiditas* (desire) were long considered the two great enemies of Christian life. *Ira* and *cupiditas* translate into scholastic concepts the primal powers of Mars and Venus, so that in the concepts lies concealed the Christian fear of the pagan gods.

Rather, however, than repress these impulses because they are "pagan," they can be refined. As the amatory arts improve the skills of desire, so sports improve the skills of anger. The coach, for instance, before each game speaks the rhetoric of Mars and unleashes a raging exhortation to impassion his team with the spirit of fight. So, too, the glaring stare of the boxer. A player in every opponent sport must learn, first of all, the skills of anger: how to let it rise, contain it, not "lose" it or "choke." Also, how skillfully to provoke the anger of the opponent so that he or she makes errors and commits fouls. Even solo sports such as golf, downhill skiing, and car racing require the skillful management of anger where the explosive charge upon which successful action depends never crosses over into blind attack. That is, "instrumental" violence used purposefully as a means to an end (as is the

---

[1] I thank Michael Meade for the digest of the testosterone literature.

intention, usually, of hooliganism) must not fall into "expressive" violence—whether the expression is on the playing field, in the stands, or among the police deployed to maintain order (Dunning, Murphy and Williams 1988, pp. 236–238). Mars always strains at the leash of discipline which checks expression for the sake of instrumentality.

When we remove anger from the personal field, detaching it from hostile and aggressive traits, and instead attach it to the archetypal figure of Mars, we can then see its necessity. Mars is the initiator, the beginning—like March at the start of the year, and April, his month, opens (*aprire*) the way, like a butting head of a ram. Anger is the first emotion off the blocks, the spontaneous combustion that originates (*oriri*, to rise) action. How often do the deeper explorations within personal relations start off as angry battles? Disturbing yes, but without anger, with the other cheek turned, there would be no sports at all, not even Ping Pong.

Again, the testosterone factor is not something new. At carnival time in twelfth-century London, young men of the city played ball in the open fields. Senior citizens and local elders spectated the contests, as if to recover their lost youth: "their natural heat seems to be stirred in them at the mere sight of such strenuous activity and by their participation in the joys of unbridled youth" (Guttmann 1986, p. 50).

This "natural heat" (or Mars or testosterone) rises through mere spectating. If this be the case, then sports events are certainly not cathartic (ibid., p. 155). The spectators are more charged afterward than even before they entered the stadium. And so we also see why an entire city is rejuvenated when its team moves toward the Cup Finals. A ritualized revival is in the offing.

In the case of losing we have another picture. Testosterone levels fall when one suffers:

1) Defeat.

2) Humiliation, failure, or loss of status.

3) Denial of sexual access—the Lysistrata phenomenon.

4) Isolation—it is depressing to vital energy to be separated from the body politic.

5) Inescapable punishment.

Thus, the usual formula for reducing male exuberance is cooling off the "natural heat" in a jail cell: isolation, humiliation, and punishment all together.

Since losing lowers testosterone levels and is equated with depression, impotence, and isolation, that is, social anomie, events which can raise testosterone levels favor the communal vitality of the body politic. The testosterone factor is merely another, more physiological, description of what civic celebrations such as triumphal parades, victory arches, brass band military concerts, running the bulls at Pamplona—and soccer matches—have long recognized: a vigorous city must honor Mars.

The close relation between aggressive competition and sexual appetite, which studies of testosterone show, restates, again in psycho-physiological language, the mythological relation between Ares (Mars) and Priapus. You may remember that Priapus, the god of phallic enormity and seminal fertility, teaches the young Ares to dance. Only after he is trained to be a perfect dancer does he become a warrior (Kerenyi 1951, p. 176). Tribal youths in the first flush of puberty must learn hunting dances and war dances so as to make more erotic, aesthetic, and fertile the direct bloodletting called for by Mars. Priapus—besides evoking his Venusian potential—teaches Mars that sexuality shall be *danced*, shall be displayed before women and the community, shall be a beauteous pride prior to violent aggression.

Dance occurs spontaneously. It breaks out. The leap, the stomp, the swivel and sway with arms raised, hands reaching for a high five—all the exuberance after a goal show the martial impulse to dance. Yet, recently the bodily joy expressed by a player after scoring a touchdown in American football has been forbidden and overdoing the "spiking" of the ball subject to penalty.

The following passage is from a recent interview with a British hooligan published in the *Corriere della Sera*. I read it to show that a life without dance, without proud display, without the arts Priapus teaches, leaves to Mars only the imagination of violence.

Gilles, a 26-year-old porter in a large London department store who is about to go to Italy for the World Cup, explains his behavior: Gilles says he is not racist and has never taken drugs, though sometimes he drinks too much. He enjoys "physical confrontation."

"Why does he like physical confrontation?"

This is Gilles's answer: "Because it's lovely to have fear and to overcome fear. And to make a bit of a ruckus. The newspapers go on about our being superorganized. It's not true. The chief of our group gets picked right in the stadium. Whoever is most in form that day becomes chief. Look, I do my portering all week long. I am no one. Maybe in ten years I'll be head porter, if all goes well. I'll still be no one. At the stadium, with my friends, for one day I am someone. You get it?''

There are echoes here all the way back to the *Iliad* and the Bible where captains and heroic chiefs emerge spontaneously according to their form, the martial spirit calling on them at some specific moment.

Spectating

I trust that you will have noticed that I am not making the usual strong distinction between active sports players and passive sports spectators, heaping praise on the first and blame on the latter. That division between players and spectators is psychologically false since the god Mars invades both and testosterone levels rise in both. Watching the match prone on the couch before a color TV in a tenth-story cement apartment nonetheless excites the martial fury; I feel it in my pulse, hear it in my voice, and find it in my behavior toward my fellows and the women who are near.

Moreover, studies show that actual spectators of sports events—bicycling, soccer, tennis, baseball, bowling, whatever—are also those who play sports. The active person is also the watching person; the inactive person neither plays nor watches.

Let me speak in defense of spectating. Nothing more belongs to city life, for a city is the place of spectacle and pageant, the display of the imagination at its most richly complex. Whether in and around the cathedral, the market, the piazza, or in front of the city hall, spectating the performance of others, watching others as players, is a major part of what draws us to cities. For cities are where the great fires take place, the public executions, the new buildings arising, the wedding and funeral processions, the accidents, strikes and demonstrations. To all this the citizen is a spectator, even if today spectating becomes nothing more than an amble through a shopping mall or sitting at a cafe table, "people watching."

The pleasure of watching must not be underestimated. The scopophilia or voyeurism, that erotic flush in the city street, the fantasies released, the speculations derived solely from spectating, are perhaps more the true reason for the flourishing of cities than the usual reasons such as protection, commerce and exchange, communication, culture, industry, opportunity, changing class and so on. Therefore, anything in the schedule of civic events or in the architecture of urban planning that promotes spectating fosters city life and may, moreover, remove spectating from its concentrated focus in sports events.

It has been suggested that New York City, so extremely in debt and with an insufficient police force, should abandon its great parades on holidays, parades which commemorate the ethnic groups in the city, in order to save the expense of crowd control. If, however, my argument holds that an essential aspect of civic life is spectating, then these huge pageants of color, music, and fantasy may actually be more cost-effective in bonding the body politic than sober restrictions. Spectacles satisfy the citizen's need for participation in the civic throng.

The etymology of the word *polis* shows it to mean "throng, crowd, flow, full, many." It is related to such words as *plenus, plerus, plebs, palus, plus* (or overabundance, evermore). It is a Dionysian word. In the midst of the many, packed into the stadiums, individuality melded with thousands of spectators, I am more in and of the city in its root meaning than when I am alone in my apartment behind my locked door. Yet, behind that door, alone, watching the game on TV I am still more a political animal in city life than when not spectating. Again, therefore, whatever promotes throngs and crowds and the temporary dissolution of individualism fosters city life.

Here I need to take an example from American cities. It has been written that the great cities of the United States became homogenized metropolises in the nineteenth century owing to three surprisingly mundane factors. American cities, in their beginnings, were a hodgepodge of ghettos: the wealthy, white, and well-established in their reserves, the older immigrants in theirs, and the newer arrivals from southern and eastern Europe and the so-called coloreds and Asians in theirs. Food, language, ceremonies, holidays, churches, even clothing styles, as well as political loyalties were ethnically determined. These groups did not meld easily. The actual "melting pot," as the American city has been called, came about only when the disparate factions were drawn together in a common *Gemeinschaftsgefuehl.* Education was *not* one of these factors although it is fondly believed that the American democratic, free, public education system did bring unity. The education system arose after the three principal factors which were: first, *public transportation* which allowed people of all sorts to venture cheaply and easily from enclosed neighborhoods; second, the *department store* which attracted people from outlying districts into a downtown where they could jostle and mingle and eventually even fall in love with an exogamous stranger; and third, the *city team*, especially baseball. If the first two, transportation and department stores, encouraged the moving and mixing of bodies, the third, the city team, forged the feeling of the ethnocentrically separated and rival ghettos into a town spirit.

Although spectator hooliganism misuses the city spirit as a rallying banner behind which hides battle lust, the city nonetheless gains thereby. The violence reminds the city that it is a living organism grounded not simply in commerce and culture but in trans-human factors that still demand blood. The violence has many complicating psycho-social factors that it is possible to expose and condemn, and hopefully correct. The basic point I wish to make here, however, is that the source of hooliganism lies neither in eruptive compensation for passive spectating nor in intense civic pride in the symbols of the team.

Ritual

Where then does the problem lie? I have said that urban sport violence cannot be blamed upon the exuberance of team spirit, nor upon passive spectating. I have also maintained that the urban throng fostered by sports events is essential to city life, and I have refused to agree with sociological, Marxist, and other psychological explanations which all too often are used to condemn the phenomenon they would explain.

Instead, I have been claiming that the madness is martial, a divine fury, and that it has physiological constituents which arise in specific situations. In other words, I am saying urban sport violence is an innate, natural potential, belonging archetypally to the human being as political animal and to the city as the abode of this political animal.

I have further been maintaining that hooliganism is aborted ritual. I consider it to be a demand of the god in the populace for recognition and obedience to his power. The martial god in a secular city finds no aegis for his fury. And so, his power dissipates in secular random violence, turning against the very members of his cult, the spectators and fans, who in their unwitting attempt to honor this power only provoke a more stringent repression.

Since we are again on the threshold of the World Cup (1994)

in soccer (football), inviting a divine madness and expecting that "fury and fierce civil strife shall cumber all the parts of Italy" (Shakespeare, *Julius Caesar* III.1), we had better understand something more about young men and their need for rituals, about testosterone, and about Mars. More police, fire hoses, attack dogs, and resorting to flogging serve repressions, but we have learned from Freud that the repressed always returns. Besides, can Mars be repressed? Would we not do better to imagine in terms, not of repression, but of ritual? Turning Mars over to the military, and young men over to gangs, prisons, drugs, and the senectitude of colleges and universities, and testosterone over to motorcycles, pop concerts, and cocaine does not meet the need for ritual. Condemnation does not invite the elders to reflect upon initiation of their younger fellow tribesmen. Rather, these moves abandon youth, even attempt to get rid of it as a "problem." Despite the condemnation and repression, even the murder, of youth by the negligent elders, the "problem" does not go away, manifesting most obstreperously in hooliganism. Hence the righteous concern—and fright—in the elders. They realize that the secular norms cannot hold the divine fury, and that rituals are actually taking place in the gangs, the prisons, the riots, the rock concerts, as if the god, despite the elders, is forcing youth into initiations regardless of their profane and inadequate form.

Societies for centuries have been more concerned with the initiation of their youth—honoring of the "*litima*" (Masai) or violent energy in their young males, the successful channeling of testosterone and the introduction to that god we call Mars—than with almost anything else in their worlds. The preparation of ceremonies and the enactment of rituals constituted the major part of the waking life of most tribal peoples, and initiation went on for years and years, just as ritual was carried into all of life as it was lived, not merely something set apart and called "a ritual." I am not suggesting now, with Rene Girard, that violence is sacred or that it is necessary to the sacred and that the sacred is built from violence. I am, however, suggesting that a more sacred view toward this disorder may honor the god therein and may invite him to reveal more of his deeper intentions with our culture, which treats him as outlaw even as it devotes a preponderant proportion of its industrial potential and export agenda to the service of war.

So I am calling for a turn to Mars with a fresh awareness of his significance as a dominant in psychic life, in civic life. Only that God who brings a disease can take it away. Like cures like. As the Homeric hymn to Ares says:

Hear me,
helper of mankind
dispenser of youth's sweet courage
beam down from up there
your gentle light
on our lives,
and your martial power,
so that I can shake off
cruel cowardice
from my head,
and diminish that deceptive rush
of my spirit, and restrain
that shrill voice in my heart
that provokes me
to enter the chilling din of battle.
You happy God,
give me courage,
let me linger
in the safe laws of peace,
and thus escape
from battles with enemies
and the fate of a violent death.
            [Translated by Charles Boer]

Clinical Recommendations

I much prefer to conclude with the "Hymn to Mars," letting that invitation to the god take its course. As Jung said, quoting an old Latin saw, "whether invited or not, the gods will be present." Yet, as a clinician of the soul, and especially of the soul of the city, who has made a differential diagnosis that our disorder is due to a specific god, I feel obliged to conclude with recommendations for treatment. Treatment begins with recognition of the god in the disease and consists of prescriptions that, we imagine, may more satisfactorily honor the god's intentions.

One: Bear in mind that major civic sports events are dedications of the spirit of the city to the violent force of Mars. They invite Mars to be present, so they must be conceived with solemnity and pageantry: more martial music, banners, songs; more officials, judges, patrons; more parades, costumes, ceremonies. Take a page from Giovanni de Bardi.

Two: Rituals especially for spectators. Do not treat them as sheep, for then they become a mass. Rather, invite them into the arena as participant players in the larger performance. Allow them individual or a small-group heroic entry. Invent a more ritualized *rite d'entrée* and *rite de sortie* so that the god who rules the stadium is contained within the sacred space. Repressive crowd control only becomes necessary once spectators have become a "crowd."

Three: Remember Venus—and not only with cheerleaders and pom pom majorettes. Special prices for women, and special prizes for women's fashion. Dress for the event. Let there be dancing on the field after the game. Display. Beauty.

Four: Less conception in terms of number—the gate, the cost, the crowd—which reduces the spectators to mere "number" and only furthers the anonymity that fosters violence.

Five: More media attention to the public as people, showing off their display, too, to TV viewers. Let TV spot individual women spectators, their clothes, their cosmetics, their hats.

Six: Less humanism. Less translation of the heroes of sport into human terms, as if they were really just ordinary guys with nice little families, who drink milk and eat chocolate, who have smiling wives and drive the same make of car as you. Their role is more than human; as sons of Mars the mystery of their superhuman prowess must be maintained and even ennobled so that they fully become ritual figures, awaking awe, respect, and distance.

Seven: Less monetarial evaluation. The heroes are paid in cosmic figures not because they are so superior to those just below them in ability, but because they are emblems of another world, stars, belonging to Fama, favored by Fortuna. The exalted salary recognizes their otherworldly worth. Their earnings should not be imagined in terms of ordinary mortals.

Eight: Increased competitive intensity in all matches. Sports should always be at the extreme edge of eruption, for the display of managed force, of controlled extremity, demonstrates the capacity of ritual to transform marital violence into martial art. I believe that violence, intensified and formalized at the same time, diminishes the risks of epidemic contagion.

Nine: More hierarchy. A general rule seems to hold in sports: the more hierarchically structured the sport, the more reinforced is the sacred container which keeps the influx of energy within bounds. Hierarchy means rankings, officials, rules, penalties, protocols, captains, divisions—a constant eye for procedural order.

Ten: More aesthetics. A greater appreciation by sportswriters, media cameramen, and citizens of the beauty brought to their city by their champions. Rather than final scores and winners, let us dwell on the "dance" of the game—passes, assists, style, movements. For the game is where the ordinary person is lifted by the epiphanies of physical beauty, moments when Hermes passes, a miraculous turn, a sudden swift impossible save, the whole culture of the plebeian lifted from their seats, lifted by a vision to another dimension by the radiant fire of Mars.

So with these prescriptions, the doctor sits down awaiting the game, once again a spectator.

References

Dumézil, G. 1966. *Archaic Roman Religion*. Chicago: University of Chicago Press.

Dunning, E., P. Murphy, and J. Williams. 1988. *The Roots of Football Hooliganism*. London: Routledge.

Guttmann, Allen. 1986. *Sports Spectators*. New York: Columbia.

Hillman, J. 1987. Wars, arms, rams, Mars. In *Facing Apocalypse*, V. Andrews et al., eds. Dallas: Spring.

Kerenyi, K. 1951. *The Gods of the Greeks*. London: Thames and Hudson.

Parke, H. W. 1967a. *Greek Oracles*. London: Hutchinson.

_____. 1967b. *The Oracles of Zeus*. Oxford: Blackwell.

Roscher, W. H. 1965. *Lexicon der Greichische und Römischen Mythologie VIII*. Hildescheim: Olms.

James Hillman *is James Hillman.*

Ball/Play

Ronald Schenk

There we would stand,
within the gap left between world and toy,
upon a spot which, from the first beginning,
had been established for a pure event.
—Rainer Maria Rilke

All this, when will all this have been . . . just
play?
—Samuel Beckett

As a boy growing up in the Midwest, I would go with my family to church on Sunday mornings. While the preacher was preaching I would sit in the pew entertaining unruly fantasies of all sorts, one of which concerned a ball. In my imagination I would toss the ball to the minister, and he would throw it back. I would lob it up to the choir in the loft, and the choir members would flip it around and then back to me. I would bounce it off the wall and then up to the parishioners in the balcony. The ball would continue around the sanctuary, soaring and falling, rebounding off the wall or going directly to various individuals. It was as if the ball itself "served" to take me out of my subjective consciousness, to gather the community together, and to make a religious event.

Conversely, I had a religious experience whenever I entered a gymnasium or a ball field; I would immediately feel becalmed as if entering a holy place. I loved the warm smell of a waxed gymnasium floor on a winter's night or the fresh smell of the wet, grassy football field on an autumn evening. The geometrical shapes formed by the painted or limed boundary lines gave me a secure feeling. When I would enter this hallowed ground, self-consciousness would fall away, body and mind would unite, and play would take over with a life of its own.

I identified with the ball player as hero and became good enough to make the team at different age levels of competition, even standing out at times. I played in several sports until I reached my level of incompetence in four traumatically unsuccessful years of football at a major college. At this point my interests turned in other directions, and the "ball player" receded into the shadowy spaces of my psyche.

As an adult I had many dreams of athletic events with recurring themes—locating me on game and practice fields, playing different positions each with its own meaning, finding myself in various forms of unpreparedness, usually enduring the wrath of my contemptuous college coach. My career as an athlete was being revealed by my dreams as a failed initiation, a failed attempt at coming into my own as an adult through being a successful warrior, much like the recurring traumatic dreams of Vietnam War veterans (Wilmer 1986). The repetitive nature of the dreams was an indication of my psyche's attempt to work through the trauma. For example, a transformation in my sense of myself as a benchwarming outcast and my usual right-handed way of being in the world was revealed in the following dream:

> College football game. As usual, I am late, can't find all the parts of my uniform, especially helmet and spikes, and I know the coach is angry at me. I grab some books to read on the bench and run out onto the field to join my teammates who are already in the heat of the game. Inexplicably, I wander into the end zone toward which my team is heading. Our team is at the opposite end of the field with the ball and their backs are to the goal line we are defending. Just at that moment, a black, left-handed quarterback on our team by the name of "Farr," throws a pass the entire length of the field into the end zone where I am standing. I am the only one near where the ball is coming down, and there is nothing to do but catch it. In order to catch the ball, I have to use my left hand because my right is holding books. I catch the ball with my left hand, scoring a touchdown. For the rest of the game I feel accepted by my team and the coach.

In another series of dreams, the transformation of the hostile father in my psyche was revealed in changes that occurred in the contemptuous coach. In one dream, he kept a secret garden on the roof over the locker room, in another he had children and a family, in another he wept, and in one he was glad to see me in a place outside of the playing area where we could have a conversation.

The following dream revealed a focus on a new element of my psyche that had to do with lightness of foot, dancing, rhythm, and sensitivity emerging in the midst of an aggressive, goal-directed, authoritarian world.

> I am driving a truck to the team meeting to deliver the film of the team's practice to be viewed by the coaches and players. I am wearing a ballet slipper on the foot which I have on the gas pedal. I am glad that no one can see this slipper. I deliver the film, and it is projected on the screen for all to see. It turns out that the entire length of film is a shot of my foot in a ballet slipper. Apparently the camera, which had been at my side on the seat of the truck, had been going all the time while aimed at my foot. I am very embarrassed.

In a final instance, the difficulty I was having in integrating the ball player of my psyche was depicted by a dream as a split between an ego ideal and the ball player.

> I am at a college lecture being given by a famous teacher. A black man who washes dishes and plays football is in the audience. Throughout the lecture, the teacher complains about the football player being there and at one point tries to throw him out physically, chasing him around the auditorium and even up a rope hanging on stage. Students come to the aid of the black man.

Later in life, I came across two short passages in the work of Carl Jung where he mentions a ball game played by priests as part of a *festum fatuorum* (1954b, par. 460) and ritual ball games played in churches (McGuire 1984, p. 25). With the reading of these notes I remembered my fantasies as a boy in church and started thinking about the ball game and my experience as a ball player in terms of a religious or archetypal process. My renewed thinking eventually took me to the ancient Mayan ball game and associated sacrificial rituals.

In this paper I will explore the underlying religious elements in the ball game, focusing upon the Mayan creation myth, the ancient Mayan ball game, and the ritual of sacrificial beheading that accompanied the game. Finally, I will explore the idea that ball play might be seen as a metaphor or paradigmatic structure for psychological experience itself.

Myth

> *We are merely the stars' tennis balls, struck*
> *   and bandied*
> *Which way please them.*
>
> —*John Webster*

The classic Mayans were a highly evolved culture. They had an astute sense of time and a remarkably precise and complicated calendar. Their architecture was intricately related to the movement of astronomical bodies, and their social system was highly complex. For the Mayans, the ball game was the core of their religious life. Their arch heroes were ball players, and the ball game lay at the heart of their central myth, the Popol Vuh (Tedlock 1985).

> Two brothers, One and Seven Hunapuh, are playing ball one day with the sons of One Hunapuh at a location called the "Great Abyss" on the road to the underworld, Xibalba, "place of fright." The lords of Xibalba are offened by the noise of the ball play and lack of deference to themselves. In addition they become desirous of the equipment used by the ball players. The lords issue a challenge to the brothers to bring their equipment and ball to the underworld to play with them. One and Seven Hunapuh take up the challenge and depart for the underworld. They leave their equipment behind, however, under the roof of their mother's house.

We can see that ball play is located in association with the *underworld*, an abysmal or frightful realm. Apparently the underworld gods have some connection with the ball game; ball play stirs them, and the gods have needs which ball players can satisfy. The brothers leave their equipment behind under the roof of their mother. It seems the brothers are still under the domination of the Mother in a way reminiscent of the fairy tale, "Iron John," another story of initiation, wherein the key to the cage holding the wild man, symbolic figure of vitality, lies under the pillow of the hero's mother (Bly 1990).

> One and Seven Hunapuh start on their journey. After overcoming several impediments, they enter the underworld where they succumb to practical jokes set up for them by the lords of the underworld. They mistake two manikins for gods and burn

themselves on the bench provided for them which turns out to be made of hot rocks. The lords are greatly amused.

The first "road trip" is under way, and the first instance of "bench warming" takes place. "Play" extends to and connects with the underworld, and entrance to the underworld involves play. Practical jokes are a different initiation into the underworld than that of the Greeks, for example, where the gate to the underworld is guarded by a fierce monster, the hound Cerberus.

> The brothers are to spend the night in the Dark House, but they fail to keep their lights going all night. The next day they are sacrificed for this failure and are buried at the Place of the Ball Game Sacrifice. The head of One Hunapuh is placed in a calabash tree.

The ball game has something to do with death. In fact, the Mayan word for ball court, *hom*, is the same as the word for graveyard. Play is for keeps, and what we call "sudden death" is a literal possibility in relation to the ball game.

> Blood Woman, daughter of an Xibalban lord, goes to the calabash tree at the Place of the Ball Game Sacrifice and engages in conversation with the head of One Hunapuh. The head spits in her hand, magically impregnating her. Upon hearing the news of her pregnancy, her outraged father orders her to be sacrificed. She tricks him and flees to the Middleworld where she bears the heroic twins, Hunapuh and Xbalanque.

The severed head, which will come to be associated with the ball itself, has a life of its own. It talks, spits, and engenders. For the Greeks, the head was the seat of the soul (Onians 1951, p. 95ff). Jung speaks of the ancient tradition of the "mysterious head," for example, that of Osiris, and the "oracular head," such as that of Orpheus (1954a, par. 363–373). In alchemy, the severed head was the *caput corvi*, the head of the raven signifying the state of *nigredo*, that is, death, depression, or putrification (Jung 1955–1956, par. 727). The alchemists also thought of the head as the *vas*, the container for the soul (Jung 1944, pars. 116, 376, 517). Many myths depict rolling heads chasing after heroes or heroines before taking their place in the sky as heavenly bodies (Gillespie 1991, pp. 325–330). The severed head, then, is a numinous image with supernatural powers and is associated with soul.

Hunapuh and Xbalanque grow and undergo many adventures as hero twins. They try their hand at farming, but fail. A rat explains why: as the sons of a ball player, they are not destined to be farmers, but ball players. The equipment of their father is waiting for them, hanging under the roof of their grandmother's house. The boys trick grandmother into leaving the house, the rat chews through the rope holding their equipment, and it falls into their hands. The boys sweep out their father's old court, don their equipment, and become the ball players they were meant to be.

"Ball player" is revealed here as a category of identity, a mode, model, or form into which an individual personality can fit: not farmer, but ball player. With mythic god-heroes as ball players, kings and urchin boys alike can identify with the divine through ball playing. The ball and equipment dropping into play is the prototype for the theme of "falling" into play (enacted in the jump ball at the beginning of the basketball game), which will be repeated in the boys' next movement down into the underworld and in the sacrificial ritual of rolling the victim down a stairway to his death.

Once again the lords of the underworld are disturbed by ball play above in the Middleworld. Once again they send a message to the offending players, offering a challenge and directing them to bring their equipment. And once again, the challenge is accepted. Hunapuh and Xbalanque travel to Xibalba, bringing their equipment. Like their father, they overcome the traps set up for them by the lords along the way, but unlike their father, they are not taken in by the lords' practical jokes and survive the first night in the Dark House, setting up the game for the next day. After an argument between the brothers and the gods over whose ball will be used, the lords' will prevails and the play is with their ball. This ball is in fact a skull. After it is served by the lords, Hunapuh hits it back. It turns into a flying dagger which twists about in the air, attempting to kill the brothers.

The argument between the boys and the gods is the prototypical playground argument over whose ball will be used, which serves to get the game under way. The fact that the skull is a ball gives us our first indication of the association of head and ball. We now have the symbolic configuration ball-head-soul for which death serves as a background. This will be the primary image of the ball game mythic ritual.

The boys protest over the use of a ball which is meant to kill them and threaten to leave. The lords persuade them to stay by allowing the use of their own rubber ball as the game ball. The prize for the first game is to be flowers. The brothers intentionally lose this game and then survive the night in the Razor House. With the help of ants, who have stolen flowers from the lords' garden, the boys give the lords their own flowers the next day (the first Rose Bowl parade?), in effect claiming victory over the gods by having made fools of them.

In succeeding days, games between the boys and the lords of the underworld end in ties, and the boys survive the nights in various houses of death—Cold House, Jaguar House, and Midst of Fire. However, in Bat House, Hunapuh inadvertently loses his head to the sharp wing of a bat and it rolls onto the court. Xbalanque replaces Hunapuh's head with a squash carved like a head, and Hunapuh and Xbalanque make a game plan (the first huddle). The game is played with Hunapuh's head as the ball. Xbalanque hits it out of the court and into a grove of oak trees. The lords chase after the head, but a rabbit acts as a decoy by bouncing along as if it were the ball. Xbalanque retrieves Hunapuh's actual head, puts it back on him in place of the carved squash, and pretends to find the ball which is now the squash. When the lords hit the squash, it splatters, and they are again revealed as fools.

This section of the myth firmly establishes the connection between the ball and severed head. We have already talked about the severed head as soul and the autonomous life that it possesses. This sense is reinforced by the image of rabbit-as-ball bouncing through the woods. It seems that the ball as a manifestation of soul has a life or will of its own, an animal life.

The game now transforms into a mystery of challenges and tricks. The lords challenge the boys to jump over a fire pit. The twins, knowing they are meant to die, sacrifice themselves by jumping into the pit. Their remains are ground up and disposed in a river. They then reappear, first as catfish, and then as humans in the guise of actors. The lords want to see the tricks of the actors, and Xbalanque sacrifices Hunapuh by severing his head and rolling it out the door, removing his heart, and then bringing him back to life. The lords are excited by this and want to try. One and Seven Death are sacrificed but not brought back to life. Hunapuh and Xbalanque reveal their

true identities as heroes and arise into the heavens as the sun
and moon.[1]

In summary, the myth of the Popol Vuh provides the ball
game with a fundamental image depicting a religious mystery
having to do with proximity to the underworld, a heroic encounter
of play with the gods, ball as autonomous life or soul, sacrifice, as if
death itself were the opposition or even the goal, and regeneration.

The Game

*Man plays only when he is in the full sense of
the word a man, and he is only wholly man
when he is playing.*
—*Friedrich Schiller*

Evidence exists that the ball game has been played in Central
America at least since 1,000 B.C. (Ekholm 1991, p. 242). The game
had both sacred and secular functions. In its secular form, it was
played for recreation and was associated with gambling for material goods, textiles, territory, and even entire empires. In its sacred
aspect, the ball game was played as a ritual on courts in the center
of religious ceremonial areas. The courts were shaped like the letter "I," generally 6–12 meters wide and 25–63 meters long. They
were surrounded by walls which sloped into the center. There
were markers in the courts themselves, and the walls had rings of
stone placed perpendicular to the court about eight feet above the
floor. The ball was made of rubber, generally having the proportions of a basketball, weighing eight pounds. The players of sacred
games could be kings, specially trained professionals, or captives,
with various numbers to a side—1, 2, 3, 9, or 11. The players were
equipped with pads protecting the knees and arms and, most
importantly, with a stone yoke which went around the hips. The
ball was struck primarily with the hip and also with the buttocks,
elbow, and knee, but not with the hands. From the crouched position of players depicted in Mayan art, it would appear the game

---

[1]Heroes taking their place in eternity is the archetypal theme behind the hall
of fame for athletes. The German god, Wotan, conducted the first recruiting
trips when he went around recruiting heroes for his mythical hall of heroes,
Valhalla.

was played close to the earth. The scoring system was complicated, but the general idea was to keep the ball from hitting the ground on one's own side and to have the ball touch the opponent's ground or touch a marker or ring. A ball going through a ring meant victory for the scoring side, and often the colorful clothing of the spectators would be given to the one who scored.

Perhaps the most intriguing aspect of the Mayan ball game was the sacrificial ritual which accompanied it. It is generally speculated that at the end of the game a beheading was performed upon the losers or those who had been held captive (Schele 1986, p. 243). Images of this sacrifice depict the victim, tied up like a ball, rolling down the stairs of the court to where the beheading takes place. Here the mythical theme of play as play-to-the-death or play-against-death is literally reenacted as evidenced by the rack of skulls placed adjacent to the ball court. Snakes or plants emerging from the headless body of the victim are depicted in Mayan wall carvings, implying a sense of regeneration in the sacrifice.

The Mayan ball game can be imagined in many different ways, each of which provides an archetypal background for contemporary ball games. It served to bring together different components of a community through an event that was out of the realm of ordinary life and that provided community bonding in a sense which Victor Turner calls "communitas" (1969, pp. 96–97). It was a metaphor for combat or war through which kings either celebrated or actually accomplished the winning of territory for their domain.[2] It could also be seen as a fertility ritual marking the boundaries of the seasons, thus the ball game itself would move the culture over difficult thresholds (Gillespie 1991, pp. 330–332). The ball game was a cosmic event in which the king as god or demigod sets the heavenly bodies on their course, depicted in the soaring ball as the rising of the sun into the heavens and the falling ball as its subsequent descent into the underworld. In the Popol Vuh, the appearance of the head of Hunapuh as the ball corresponds with the appearance of Venus in the west, the direction of death.

Finally, the game can be seen as a mode of *initiation* through

---

[2]Our use of warlike terms in football, such as "in the trenches," "the bomb," "the blitz," "captain," "field general," "air attack," and "ground attack" as well as the many allusions to the Super Bowl during the Gulf War by soldiers and politicians, attests to the way that the ball game serves as a substitute for combat.

the ritual acknowledgment of and relationship to the lords of the underworld. In this sense, the ball game becomes the place where death makes its appearance as the final step in the play of life, and where humans have their "close encounter" with the underworld.

The close connection of the ball game with the underworld for the Mayans is revealed in several ways. From the Popol Vuh, we know that the ball game was played in the proximity of the underworld, on the road to Xibalba at the Place of the Great Abyss and in the underworld itself against the lords of death. The ball court thus becomes the gateway to the underworld with the sloping walls of the courts depicting the "jaws of the earth" (Parsons 1991, p. 197). In addition, the wearing of stone yokes around the midriff places the player symbolically half in the middle world and half in the underworld, again a depiction of playing within the jaws of death. Finally, the deemphasis on hands and the sensitivity to gravity in the style of play close to the earth indicates an acute connection to the underworld as opposed to the spiritual heavens (no soaring puerile Michael Jordans here).

Paralleling the emphasis on the underworld are the images of descent and fall associated with the ball game. The twins' ball and equipment drop from the rafters, the twins descend into the underworld to play, the sacrificial victims were rolled down the stairs to their death, and some of the games took place at the vernal equinox. Each of these descents can be seen as reflections of the sun's descent in the west into the underworld.

The Mayans, it seems, emphasized the necessity of loss, sacrifice, and death as manifested in the ball game and its background of mythical images as a central organizing feature of life. In the ball game and its sacrifice of beheading lies the experience of suffering and death that is essential for the life of the soul. The Mayans seem to be telling us that when there is the experience of death, soul is set into play.

Play as Religious Event

> Man . . . is made God's plaything and that is
> the best part of him. All of us, then, men and
> women alike, must fall in with our role and
> spend life in making our play as perfect as
> possible . . . . Life must be lived as play, play-
> ing certain games, that is, sacrifice, song, and
> dance.
>
> —Plato, Laws (vii, 803)

The word *play* comes from the Anglo-Saxon *plega* or *plegan*,
meaning both rapid movement and taking a risk or binding or
engaging oneself. Similarly, the ancient Greek sense of play
included both *paidia*, of or pertaining to a child (improvisation,
freedom) and *agon*, having to do with strife or contests. The common root of several Sanskrit words for play contains the idea of
rapid movement—the movement of wind or waves, shining, sudden appearance, likeness. Likewise the Latin, *ludus*, is founded
upon the element of semblance or deception. Play is fundamen-
tally linked with danger, risk, chance, or a feat to which one is
bound as if by destiny, ritual, or ceremony, as well as rapid movement, deception, or flashing appearance. There is something serious about play, as well as something out of the ordinary, make-
believe.

J. Huizinga states that in play there is something "at play"
which transcends the immediate needs of life, the appetitive, the
rational, the deterministic, but which also imparts meaning to
action. Play is based on a particular imagination of reality as separate from the ordinary world. This world is a borderline realm
"between jest and earnest" (1949, p. 5). It has the quality of freedom, yet it is limited in time and space. In sum,

> we might call it a free activity standing quite consciously out-
> side "ordinary" life as being "not serious," but at the same
> time absorbing the player intensely and utterly. It is an activity
> connected with no material interest, and no profit can be
> gained by it. It proceeds within its own proper boundaries of
> time and space according to fixed rules and in an orderly man-
> ner. It promotes the formation of social groupings which tend
> to surround themselves with secrecy and to stress their differ-
> ence from the common world by disguise or other means.
> (Ibid., p. 13)

Play functions both as a contest and as a representation. "In the form and function of play, itself an independent entity which is senseless and irrational, man's consciousness that he is embedded in a sacred order of things finds its first, highest and holiest expression" (ibid., p. 17).

The pattern which is created through play, however, is disjunctive—one side wins, one side loses. Disharmony is created in the universe, a disharmony reflected in the severing of the head from the body in the Mayan ritual. The French anthropologist Claude Lévi-Strauss refers to this as the "limp" of games as ritual (1973, pp. 460–462). Susan Gillespie considers the "limp" of games as a reflection on the disjunction in time and space of the periodicity of the seasons ensuring agricultural fertility (1991, pp. 332–334). Another way of imagining this disjunction, however, is to consider disharmony as an inherent goal of the play of the world, reflecting a basic mode of being. We want the cosmic order to be symmetrical and harmonious, but the cosmos wants it differently.

The sense of play as religious ritual revealing a "higher order" would parallel Victor Turner's sense of liminality, the condition of being "in between" ordinary and sacred life (Turner 1969, pp. 93–111). Turner refers to Arnold van Gennep's original concept of the *rite de passage* where there is 1) a separation of the sacred from the secular and of the initiate away from the secular; 2) a transition marked by ambiguity and liminality in which the sacred is experienced by the initiate; and 3) incorporation of the initiate, newly informed by the sacred, back into the secular realm (van Gennep 1960). Play as make-believe in earnest would be part of the ludic character of liminality. In other words, play takes place in a sacred ground or *temenos*, outside of ordinary time and space yet maintaining certain factors of the familiar. In play there is "a certain freedom to juggle with the factors of existence" (Turner 1967, p. 106).

Play as religious experience is perhaps best described by Turner when he follows his colleagues Mihaly Csikszentmihalyi and John MacAloon by seeing a factor of "flow" in the player's immersion in the game as liminoid play (Turner 1983, pp. 160–162; Csikszentmihalyi 1990). "Flow" involves the merging of action and awareness in a state of non–self-consciousness. In flow, there is a centering of attention and limiting of conscious focus so that only "now" matters. Ego as mediator between self and other disappears. The player finds a relationship between self, action, and environment in a way that would not have seemed possible in ordinary situations. Flow contains coherent, noncontradictory demands for action and provides clears, unambiguous feedback to the player's actions. Ultimately, flow needs no goals outside of itself. Immersed in flow, the player exists in space and time outside of ordinary reality and in service to a "higher order."

Play as Psychological Event

> *Clov: What is there to keep me here?*
> *Hamm: The dialogue . . .*
> *Clove (imploringly): Let's stop playing!*
> *Hamm: Never!*
> —*Samuel Beckett*

What is this higher order? Huizinga and Turner leave us with play in the ball court as a religious event. From the Mayans, however, we have sensed a different order of play—that of soul set into action. To answer this questions, we now leave play as a religious event located in the ball game on the ball court and move out into the streets where there is a sense of play as psychological event occurring every moment. The psychological sense of play was formulated by Friedrich Nietzsche throughout his work in both content and style—from the ecstatic playfulness of Dionysus, through the playful aphorism as carrier of knowledge, to playful transformation as a foundation for the major concepts of the Overman, the will to power, and the eternal return. For Nietzsche, play became not only the way of associating with great tasks, but also a metaphor for life itself.

George Gadamer (1982) has also explicitly revealed play as a fundamental structure of being (see also Miller 1970, Hans 1981). Gadamer tells us that play is only play when one looses oneself or is forgetful of oneself (in a condition like Csikszentmihalyi's flow and Turner's liminality). Following Gadamer, all play is "deep play," that is, the player looses subjectivity and play itself becomes the subject. Individual initiative and will are compromised by the subjectivity of play itself, as if both the ball and the game had a separate will or life of their own. If we think of this configuration in terms of the ball game, then the court might be seen as the "body" of the game and the ball as the "soul" or "head" of the game (Gillespie 1991, p. 338). Experience takes on a life and will of its own, encompassing the player or "playing the player." In personal relationships between people, for example, the relationship itself becomes an encompassing third entity that is playing through the two participants as a higher order.

Depth psychology, as part of the post-modern movement, contributes to the project of desubjectivizing experience by positing an "other" or an unconscious to which subjective consciousness is related. Carl Jung related how, as a boy, he sat on a rock and wondered if he was a boy sitting on a rock or the rock imagining a boy on top of it (1965, p. 20). Following Jung, we might postulate that we are always in a metaphorical existence, i.e., living through the form of a larger "other." This other can be a perspective, an ideal, a frame of mind, or a mood, which can be imagined in the form of a container such as a god or goddess, a place, a text, and so on.[3] There is a constant tension between our will or subjectivity and that which is living itself through us. The movement of consciousness back and forth between these two sources might be imagined as play, the to and fro of the hermeneutical circle of consciousness passing back and forth between our attempts to try to gain control of life through understanding and awareness of a larger, more encompassing agent *through which* we are understanding. In terms of the ball game, we have intentionality or purpose, as if we were kicking, throwing, or hitting the ball, but the ball itself also seems to have a will of its own in the service of the game or play in which we are immersed.

This situation of "playing while being played with," through a ball that seems to be an object but at the same time has a will of its own, is depicted in the fairy tale, "The Frog King." In this tale, a beautiful princess has a golden ball as a favorite toy with which she plays whenever she becomes bored. As the story goes,

> Now it so happened that on one occasion the princess's golden ball did not fall into the little hand which she was holding up for it, but onto the ground beyond, and rolled straight into the water. (Grimm 1972, p. 17)

---

[3]One example of the "larger than" which we are played by is given by contemporary deconstructionists who would assert that we are played by language. Language then is the movement of play which is permitted by the actual lack or absence of a center or origin of consciousness. Play then is without security, a surrender to the adventure of the "trace," that which remains available to us through the infinite play of signifiers which is language (see Derrida 1978).

The princess seems to have control of the ball until one day it demonstrates a will of its own, eluding her hand and going directly to its own goal. The story goes on to relate how, from the water, a foreign element can now enter her life in accordance with a higher order.

Gadamer tells us that the ultimate goal of play is its own presentation or display; the *mode* of play is its self-presentation. In other words, play or the autonomous body or life, has an inherent *form* of its own. The intention of play is in the revealing of this form. In the evolution of the form or the pattern of the game, there is a self-remembering. When we sense the form of the game, we see ourselves as part of a larger picture. Again, following the example of relationship as a play form which contains the partners in a life of its own, the intention of play would be for the relationship to reveal its form or its body. A hungry child or an angry animal might be that which holds the partners in the dialogue.

The ball game, then, is a reflection of the movement of soul in conjunction with the other, and it is a reflection of our "as if" existence. There is always something going on that we know about, but also something else that we don't know about. We know we are depressed or anxious, but something else is happening as well that is "more than" consciousness—our creativity is emerging or our perspective is deepening.

The ball is a manifestation of the soul's orientation, bouncing or soaring like the rubber ball of the Mayans, now toward self, now toward other. We are always in a game, a world of both freedom and order within a larger invisible world that is constantly evolving from this play. We are always in some sense in flow, in the self-forgetful experience of the game, intending in one direction, but being played in another. As Beckett's character, Hamm, says toward the end of *Endgame*,

> Old endgame lost of old, play and lose and have done with losing . . . . Since that's the way we're playing it, let's play it that way . . . and speak no more about it . . . speak no more. (Beckett 1958, pp. 82–84)

Ball/play, then, is the fanciful spirit of the imaginative mode that soul is always falling into, a "text" that speaks us, an image that envelopes us, an archetype that forms us, or a divinity's domain in which we live. Ball play has its own goal of display, and through recognition of play's form played through us, we re-member ourselves in home-coming. In the words of Rainer Maria Rilke,

Catch only what you've thrown yourself, all is
mere skill and little gain;
but when you're suddenly the catcher of a ball
thrown by an eternal partner
with accurate and measured swing
towards you, to your centre, in an arch
from the great bridgebuilding of God:
why catching then becomes a power—
not yours, a world's.

References

Beckett, S. 1958. *Endgame*. New York: Grove.

Bly, R. 1990. *Iron John: A Book About Men*. Reading, Mass.: Addison-Wesley.

Csikszentmihalyi, M. 1990. *Flow*. New York: Harper and Row.

Derrida, Jacques. 1978. Structure, sign, and play in the discourse of the human sciences. In *Writing and Difference*. Chicago: University of Chicago Press.

Ekholm, Susanna M. 1991. Ceramic figurines and the Meso-American ball game. In *The Meso-American Ball Game*, V. L. Scarborough and D. R. Wilcox, eds. Tucson: The University of Arizona Press.

Gadamer, G. 1982. *Truth and Method*. New York: Crossroad.

Gillespie, S. 1991. Ball games and boundaries. In *The Meso-American Ball Game*, V. L. Scarborough and D. R. Wilcox, eds. Tucson: The University of Arizona Press.

Grimm, the Brothers. 1972. *The Complete Grimm's Fairy Tales*. New York: Pantheon Books.

Hans, J. 1981. *The Play of the World*. Amherst, Mass.: The University of Massachusetts.

Huizinga, J. 1949. *Homo Ludens*. London: Routledge and Kegan Paul.

Jung, C. G. 1954a. Transformation symbolism in the Mass. In *CW* 11:203–296. Princeton, N.J.: Princeton University Press, 1969.

_____. 1954b. On the psychology of the trickster figure. In *CW* 9i:255–272. Princeton, N.J.: Princeton University Press, 1968.

_____. 1965. *Memories, Dreams, Reflections*. Aniela Jaffe, ed. Richard and Clara Winston, trans. New York: Vintage Books.

_____. 1955–1956. *Mysterium Coniunctionis. CW*, vol. 14. Princeton, N.J.: Princeton University Press, 1970.

_____. 1944. *Psychology and Alchemy. CW*, vol. 12. Princeton, N.J.: Princeton University Press, 1953.

Lévi-Strauss, C. 1973. *From Honey to Ashes*. New York: Harper and Row.

McGuire, W., ed. 1984. *Dream Analysis: Notes of the Seminar Given in 1928–1930 by C. G. Jung*. Princeton, N.J.: Princeton University Press.

Miller, D. 1970. *Gods and Games: Toward a Theology of Play*. New York: Harper and Row.

Onians, R. 1951. *The Origins of European Thought*. Cambridge: Cambridge University Press.

Parson, L. 1991. The ball game in the southern Pacific coast Cotzumalhuapa region and its impact on Kaminalijuyu during the middle classic. In *The Meso-American Ball Game*, V. L. Scarborough and D. R. Wilcox, eds. Tucson: The University of Arizona Press.

Rilke, Rainer Maria. 1939. *Duino Elegies*. J. B. Leishman and S. Spender, trans. New York: W. W. Norton and Co.

Schele, L. 1986. *The Blood of Kings: Dynasty and Ritual in Mayan Art*. Fort Worth, Tex.: Kimball Art Museum.

Tedlock, D., trans. 1985. *Popol Vuh: The Mayan Book of the Dawn of Life*. New York: Simon and Schuster.

Turner, V. 1967. *The Forest of Symbols*. Ithaca, N.Y.: Cornell University Press.

_____. 1969. *The Ritual Process*. Ithaca, N.Y.: Cornell University Press.

_____. 1983. Liminal to liminoid in play, flow and ritual: An essay in comparative symbology. In *Play, Games and Sports in Cultural Contexts*, J. Harris and R. Park, eds. Champaign, Ill.: University of Illinois Press.

van Gennep, A. 1960. *Rites of Passage*. Chicago: University of Chicago Press.

Wilmer, H. 1986. Combat nightmares. *Spring*.

Ronald Schenk, *Ph.D., is a Jungian analyst in private practice in Dallas and Houston and author of* The Soul of Beauty *and many articles on aesthetics and psychology.*

The Archetype of the Game

Sports as a Reflection
of Psyche

Thayer A. Greene

For many people the prospect of playing a game has an attraction and fascination which endures through a lifetime. Much has been written of the physical benefit of regular vigorous exercise and also of its emotional value. While such a view is valid, there is much more to playing a sport and being a devoted athlete than simply sweat and relaxation. To play the game, to struggle against a worthy opponent, to seek to gain the victory, and to accept defeat is also a profound psychological experience.

Playing a sport, however, is not the only way that a person can be grasped by the psychic power of the game. Many people are fascinated spectators who love to watch an athletic contest, especially when winning or losing will have significance. Little wonder that a Super Bowl or World Series will gain more attention than a pickup game on the corner sandlot. Yet any game can often catch our attention just by its very nature.

To be an avid spectator is not an unmixed blessing. For most of us there is a spouse and a family to contend with. Many an American husband (or sometimes a wife) carries on a never-ending conflict over time in front of the TV versus emotional availability to marriage and the needs of children. For many avid lovers of the game, the lack of sympathy and understanding coming from family and friends can bring on severe attacks of self-doubt in which they ask themselves whether they are suffering a severe case of psychological immaturity. Is this passion for sports a sign of adolescent fixation which I have been unable to outgrow? Am I reluctant to relinquish a magical world of childhood play and enter into the realistic world of adult behavior? Worst of all, am I committing that most grievous sin of a lack of consciousness? One feels somehow at fault or psychologically regressed when faced with the exasperation of other people who are not themselves lovers of the game. Friends or colleagues may treat this apparent aberration of misdirected energy and enthusiasm with amused condescension or outright criticism. It can even cause anguished reflection and introspection but usually no real change in behavior. Most of us remain devoted players and spectators of the game.

In my own case the experience of self-doubt has been valuable, however, for out of this process of reflection has emerged a clearer vision and understanding of the archetypal roots of the passion and the bond which is shared by countless people who are fascinated with sports. It is that discovery and growing awareness that provides the motivation to present this material. One may ask the question, if a devoted interest in opera, ballet, theater, or film is considered perfectly legitimate and proper, why should a person be embarrassed by a similar love of sports?

This issue is worthy of exploration. To be drawn by the fascination and numinosity of the game or contest is a profound religious and psychological experience. One cannot explain this phenomenon by reducing it to childhood feelings and dynamics, although they clearly play an important part. The most common term to describe an ardent supporter of a particular team is to call him or her a "fan." Being a fan is very serious business. It demands the sacrifice of much time, considerable money, continuing anxiety and tension, and very frequently a great deal of heartbreak. If you have the misfortune by dint of birth or destiny to be a Boston Red Sox fan, you are assured of endless heartbreak. Of course, it could be even worse. You could root for the Chicago Cubs! No one in New England will ever forget the sixth game of the 1986 World Series when the ball trickled through Bill Buckner's legs or the playoff game of 1978 with the Yankees when Bucky Dent hit his windblown home run. Such is the inevitable suffering that comes with being a fan. It is the shadow side of joy and celebration which victory brings, allowing grown-up people to hug each other in delight and dance in the streets. The clue to this agony and ecstasy is to be found in the root meaning of the word *fan*, probably short for *fanatic* which stems from the Latin word *fanum* which means "belonging to the temple of the god of that place, being inspired by the local divinity" (Walker 1980, p. 53). To be a fan, therefore, is to be a worshiper.

What might be the judgment of a cultural anthropologist from another planet upon observing the American landscape for the first time? Passing over our great cities, such an observer would look down upon great oval arenas and stadiums containing beautiful green spaces covered with geometric patterns of lines. He would see massive crowds of people moving in and out of these stadiums with what appeared to be a scheduled regularity. Looking more closely, he would also discover opposing groups of individuals moving back and forth in apparently meaningful patterns across the geometrically lined green spaces, each group wearing a different colored uniform. Such an extraterrestrial anthropologist might wonder what manner of ritual behavior is this? What sort of religious rites are being so loyally and regularly celebrated by such multitudes?

Knowledgeable sports fans will surely remember some of the great ritual events of recent sports history. Consider, for example, the 1980 Olympic hockey game between the United States and Russia. David did not face more difficult odds against Goliath and yet this American team of talented amateurs fresh out of college astonished the nation, the world, and most especially the Russians by defeating a team of older, more experienced professionals. The drama and excitement of that remarkable victory drew millions of spectators who had never before watched the game of hockey being played.

Those who love the game of tennis will remember that famous final at Wimbledon between John McEnroe and Bjorn Borg which went to five sets in over four hours of play. The fourth set was won by McEnroe in an 18-point tiebreaker, some of the points lasting for more than a minute of play with the championship hanging on almost every point. Every swing of the racquet carried with it the potential for victory or defeat. In such moments, there is an archetypal energy and excitement shared by those who play and those who watch.

For baseball fans, the sixth game of the 1975 World Series between the Boston Red Sox and the Cincinnati Reds is considered one of the greatest games ever played. The lead moved back and forth through the first nine innings as one dramatic play followed another until finally in the twelfth inning, already after midnight, the Red Sox won when Carlton Fisk hit a home run that landed in the screen only four feet inside the foul pole. A more recent World Series game won with a dramatic home run was the first game of the 1988 World Series when Kirk Gibson of the Los Angeles Dodgers limped to the plate on two injured knees that prevented him from running and proceeded to hit the ball out of the park so that he could hobble around the bases to the roar of eighty thousand people. That particular moment was compared by many writers and observers to the climactic scene in the baseball film, *The Nat-*

ural, which ends with a home run that is archetypal in its effect and meaning.

One of the most thoughtful books about the history of sports and the American sports experience in particular is entitled *From Ritual to Record*. The author, Allen Guttmann of Amherst College, comments on the enormous high that many of us get from playing in or watching a close and exciting contest. He writes, "In sport we can discover the euphoric sense of wholeness, autonomy, and potency which is often denied us in the dreary rounds of routinized work that are the fate of most men and women" (1978, p. 157). The fact that so many of us have been powerfully affected by great moments of great contests reveals that there is psychic energy being activated in an intense way in the sports experience. We are dealing with more than a game for children. Jung spoke of the archetypal layer of the psyche from which emerges the collective imagery and mythology of our humanity. It can be argued that the game or contest touches that archetypal layer and therefore evokes from many people a numinous quality of feeling and experience that is religious in the broad sense of the term.

The roots of our contemporary sports enthusiasm go back in time over many centuries. My first personal encounter with this fact occurred during a trip to the Yucatan Peninsula in Mexico. Located there are the large and well-preserved ruins of the Mayan Toltec city of Chichen Itza. You will find there a ball court, resembling very much a modern athletic stadium and measuring 272 feet long and 119 feet wide. Two large stone rings are placed twenty feet above the ground in the center of the longer sides of the stadium. A soft rubber ball had to be batted by some part of the body, but not thrown, through the ring. The game played seems to resemble a mixture of soccer and basketball.

Essential to understanding the significance of this game is the fact that the ball court was always part of the most sacred space. It adjoined the Temple of Warriors and was decorated with bas-relief emphasizing the religious significance of the ball rites, especially those having to do with the human head. Those who actually played the game were of noble cast and probably were priests. There were seven on a side.

Professor Guttmann describes the mythic background to the game in these words:

> Behind the game itself was the myth of twin brothers whose names appear in various transliterations. The brothers left their mother's house in order to challenge the gods of the

underworld in a game of football (actually soccer of sorts). They lost and paid the mythically predictable price of defeat— death. The head of one brother was placed in a tree, where a young girl happened upon it. From the mouth of the head spurted a stream of seeds which impregnated the girl, who removed to the house of the twins' mother where she bore children. They grew to manhood and challenged the gods at football and, again predictably, won. Whereupon the heads of the twins rose to heaven and became the sun and the moon . . . . The archeological evidence for this sun-moon myth can be found in more than forty ball courts which have located in an area stretching from Arizona to Guatemala and Honduras. Considered as symbols of the heavens, the ball courts are invariably within a temple complex. (1978, p. 19–20)

Guttman then goes on to comment on the outcome of the game and its consequences for those who participated. He writes:

Whether the losing players or the winning ones were sacrificed is unclear, but we can safely assume that the requirements of the contest qua contest doomed the losers rather than the winners. In either event the archeological evidence is quite clear that the game was literally for life or death. Each of the six reliefs at Chichen Itza shows the decapitation of a player. (Ibid.)

I would add that such dramatic information gives a whole new meaning to our casual use of the term "sudden death overtime."

The ball court at Chichen Itza dates back to the ninth century A.D. but the game of ball is much, much older. Pictures of ball playing have been discovered in Egypt dating from the eighteenth century B.C. In that early time of agricultural development, the ball appears to have represented fertility, the life-giving principle, not unlike the myth of the seed-pouring head just mentioned. The playing of the game of ball was therefore a sacred fertility rite which activated the life principle and the renewal of the earth. Modern sports have lost this sacred connection with earth but the excitement and passion which stirs large crowds of spectators is living proof of the extent to which the playing of the game continues to provide an archetypal source for the activation of the libido.

Much later these early fertility games were taken over by the Christian Church and converted to Christian uses. The ball became the symbol of the resurrection and was associated with Easter observances, thus remaining a rite associated with the coming of spring. The first reference to such a ball game in the Church dates from 508 A.D. in the city of Naples. The evidence clearly indicates that the games were ceremonial, took place within a sacred edifice, and had a religious or spiritual purpose (Watkins 1913, p. 103). We have later evidence that ball games were played in the medieval churches of southern France from the eleventh to the fifteenth century. The passing or throwing of the ball was often accompanied by a dance moving in a circular pattern after which the priestly players returned to the chapter house for a sacred meal. In the sixteenth century, however, at the time of the counter-reformation, the Catholic Church banned the playing of ball as frivolous and insisted that the energies of the priests be redirected to something more edifying (ibid., p. 95).

No discussion of the origins of sports and the game would be complete without attention to the Olympiad in ancient Greece, especially since more than one billion people around the world have watched the Olympics in the last few years. The exact history of the origins of the Olympic Games is unknown and in all likelihood never will be known. It is clear, however, as Professor Guttmann writes, that the athletic events were "held in order to persuade the god to return from the dead, to reappear in the form of a new shoot emerging from the dark womb of the earth into the light of day" (1978, p. 22). We see here again the themes of death, renewal of life, and fruitfulness. Scholars suggest that defeat in an athletic event was a symbolic substitute for sacrificial death. Victory was, therefore, the victory of the god over death. Mortal men who were victorious in the Olympic Games were treated as heroes, both regal and divine, and were crowned with a spray of olive like the wreath of Zeus himself. Upon the victor's return to his native city, he was dressed in royal purple and drawn by white horses through a breach in the wall cut specifically for his triumphal return. In many cases, he was worshiped after death as a hero, not because he was successful hero, but because he had once been a god incarnate (Corford 1962, p. 221).

Although there was a slow but progressive professionalization of athletics in ancient Greece, it was in the Roman Empire that we see the ubiquity of athletic professionalism. This is not surprising since the Romans had a very different attitude toward athletics and games. They believed in physical fitness for the ulterior purpose of waging war. The only athletic events which seemed to have interested them were the fighting events for which they used commercially employed professional gladiators and slaves. There was little or no voluntary offering of one's strength and energies to compete in the service of a god. In many ways, our modern professional sports are closer to the Roman than the Greek model. Most of us are not aware that both Socrates and Plato were victors in the early Greek games. One would hardly have found them in the Colosseum in Rome competing as gladiators.

Turning from the past to our own age and culture, one can observe both similarity and contrast. Our sports stadiums are jammed with people. Television and radio provide a never-ending supply of athletic events to follow. The majority of Americans are involved in some sporting activity as either participant or spectator. Records are carefully kept. Gambling is a pervasive form of sports-related activity. Certainly our level of enthusiasm is at least as great as that of the ancient Greeks two millennia before us. The archetypal power of the game has lost none of its impact upon the collective human psyche. But there has also been significant change. Professor Guttmann makes this observation:

> Whether or not one considers the passions, the rituals, and the myths of modern sports as a secular religion, the fundamental contrast with primitive and ancient sports remains. The bond between the secular and the sacred has been broken, the attachment to the realm of the transcendent has been severed. (1978, p. 26)

Guttmann goes on to say that the Greeks had no athletic records in our sense of the term.

> The very notion of quantified achievement is probably more compatible with the standards of a secular system than with one closely oriented to the transcendent realm of the sacred .... When qualitative distinctions fade and lose their force, we can turn to quantitative ones .... Once the gods have vanished from Mount Olympus or from Dante's Paradise, we can no longer run to appease them or to save our souls, but we can set a new record. It is a uniquely modern form of immortality. (Ibid., p. 55)

In contrast, for the Greeks, comparing Olympic performance from one Olympiad to the next seems to have been a matter of indifference. In fact, their stadiums varied in size and so did the distances of their competitive events. The emphasis upon exact quantification appeared in the eighteenth century and is closely associated with the scientific and experimental attitudes of the modern West.

What do we find when we examine the very nature of play itself? Guttmann states that "play is autotelic." In other words, it is its own purpose or goal. "Pleasure," he writes, "is in the doing and not in what has been done. One might say that play is to work as process is to results" (1978, p. 3). Scholars make a distinction between two kinds of play. One stems from the Greek work *paidia* meaning "spontaneous play." The other is drawn from the Greek word *ludens* meaning "regulated, rule-bound, organized play," namely the game (Callois, quoted in Baecheler 1979, p. 188). Guttmann argues that the games symbolize the willing surrender of absolute spontaneity for the sake of playful order.

The French scholar, Roger Callois, provides the following interesting definition of particular elements which together constitute the experience of the game. 1) The game is free. Playing the game is not obligatory or coerced but is a voluntary act of participation. One can recognize how quickly a game ceases to be "fun" when this element is missing. 2) It is separate. That means that it is circumscribed within particular limits of space and time which are defined and fixed in advance. Quite simply, you cannot change the position of the goal posts or the length of the game in the middle of it. 3) It is uncertain. That is, the outcome cannot be predicted in advance but emerges from the play itself. Consider here the United States hockey victory in the 1980 Olympics. 4) It is unproductive. The outcome of the game is not something to be made, bought, and sold, but rather the emergent consequence of the playing of the game. The attitude of someone like George Steinbrenner of the New York Yankees or the late coach Vince Lombardi of the Green Bay Packers stands in dramatic contrast to this point. 5) The game is governed by rules that are made up. In other words, the rules of the game stand outside any other rules and constitute a second reality. One can observe this in the behavior of children making up special rules to play a special game and also in the decisions of such ruling boards as those of professional baseball and football which are empowered to change the rules of the game.

It is worth noting that there are many games which are not contests and many that are. Leapfrog, for example, is a game but not a contest whereas basketball is a contest. There is a Japanese game called *kemari* in which no one wins and no one loses. Instead the players act out their sense of universal harmony. Contrast such an attitude with the Greek roots of the word *athlete* from *athlos*, meaning "contest" and *athlon* meaning "prize." In so-called war games we see an example of contests which are not games in any historical or psychological sense (Guttmann 1978, pp. 5–6).

In his classic book, *The Savage Mind*, the cultural anthropologist Claude Lévi-Strauss discusses the relation between game and ritual. Both game and ritual are played, he argues, but ritual is a "favored instance of game," remembered because it is the only one which results in a particular type of equilibrium between the two sides (1966, pp. 30–32). Games have a disjunctive effect, he contends. They end in establishing a difference between individual players or teams where originally there was no indication of inequality. At the end of the game as contest, there is a distinction of winners and losers. Ritual, in contrast, is the exact inverse. It conjoins, that is, brings about a union or organic relation of two initially separate groups. The purpose of such a ritual game is that everyone can pass to the winning side. Lévi-Strauss cites the example of a tribe in New Guinea which plays soccer until both sides reach the same score. This is treating a game as a ritual.

Louis Stewart, a San Francisco analyst, discusses play and games in terms of affect and emotion. He states that,

> play generates internal tensions of disequilibrium, polarized dimensions of success and failure, acceptance and rejection. This is a feature of structured games which inevitably evoke strong emotional reactions in the players. The play of childhood is often interrupted by emotional outbursts that cannot be contained in the play itself and lead to "hurt feeling." As children mature, those tensions may be contained for longer and longer periods of time and are even transformed into aspects of the game itself. (1986, p. 187)

To sum up Dr. Stewart's thesis briefly, he argues that play and games provide a channel for the transformation of negative affective experience and the release of imagination. An individual can learn how to deal with early experience of loss and defeat by participation in games which reconstellate the affect but provide an archetypal and social container for transformation.

Dr. Ray Walker, a Jungian analyst in Connecticut, supports Dr. Stewart's thesis. He believes that the athlete is part of the adolescent tribal stage of development.

> The collectively enacted ritual of athletics is justly celebrated to the degree that it contains and channels into a process the fiery and murderous libido which let loose, is war itself. Ath-

letics here recognize law or rules as super-ordinate to libido, and thus yoke the human animal to community and culture. (1980, p. 55)

Consider how the language of sports has influenced the language of politics, business, social and individual interaction. Concepts of fair play, recognizing necessary boundaries, winning and losing, equal opportunity, the worthy opponent, and such all have their roots in the archetypal psychic structure of the game. Affect and libido are contained and brought under conscious ego control through such conditioning.

So far this review has included the historical, religious, collective, and psychological origins of sports. Let us turn now to the individual, personal, and intrapsychic dimension. Personal and professional psychological experience has made it clear that there is an introverted and imaginal dimension to sports and the game. Years ago in the early period of his training analysis the dreams of a training candidate repeatedly presented the imagery of the game of baseball as a central theme related to his analytic process. The training analyst was perplexed by this phenomenon. His introverted orientation had no interest in the game of baseball for its own sake but his analytic instinct sensed that this repeated dream motif was significantly related to the individuation journey of the extroverted sports enthusiast who sat before him.

The analyst's extensive knowledge of alchemy finally provided a bridge of understanding. Baseball, after all, is played upon a field called a diamond, an image familiar to alchemy denoting the center, the Self, the source, and the final opus. What's more, the batter's task is to make a successful journey against adversity, which begins at home plate, circles the bases, and returns home to complete a quaternity and change the score from zero to one. There are, moreover, rules to be observed, boundary lines to provide limits, and umpires to demand that the whole effort be accomplished with integrity. The analyst helped the dreamer to understand and appreciate that if Jung's personal myth was alchemy, perhaps some aspects of his own myth were expressed through the images and the archetypal structure of a game such as baseball.

A lengthy clinical practice presents one with many sports dreams from patients. More frequently they have come from men than from women and from active sports participants than from those who have no interest. Almost no sport is excluded—golf, tennis, handball, hockey, soccer, basketball, football, baseball, track, many more—even croquet! Each game has its own rules, equipment, physical movement, and requirements of skill and therefore its own character and meaning. Tennis, for example, is a totally different game than golf. It requires a different temperament and psychology. Golf is essentially a contest with oneself which demands great control, precision, and skill to find the center, namely the cup, on all eighteen holes of the course. The eighteenth green always adjoins the first tee so that you end where you began after making a circumambulation of the course.

Tennis, in contrast, requires an opponent whose strokes one cannot control or even anticipate. One must constantly react to the unexpected and maintain a high level of intensity to engage with a human "other" who stands on the opposite side of the net. The interplay of these opposites is the fundamental pattern of the game.

The capacity to appreciate these distinctions is critically important for understanding what a dream is seeking to portray and what the ego needs to learn from the particular sport image. Some years ago a man who had been an excellent college athlete and whose life has since been characterized by frequent changes and disruptions, shared the following dream: "I was at bat in a baseball game and swung at a pitch. The umpire called it a strike and I protested. Then on the next pitch I hit the ball to right field but the right field foul line had not been marked off clearly enough. I also couldn't tell where the baselines were. I needed to get to first or second to be safe." Since this man was not my analysand but gave permission for the use of the dream, the only appropriate comments would be to note how clearly the issue of distinct and defined boundaries is represented by the imagery of the dream and to wonder why one would protest a swinging strike. This dream, one suspects, had immediate and painful relevance for the life situation of the dreamer. Individuation requires such psychic boundary lines if one is ever to circle the bases safely and return home to oneself.

Another man with a strong critical father complex which required him to make constant demands upon himself to prove his competence and manhood had a brief dream in which he dribbled a basketball through several opposing players, leaped up for the basket only to discover that the basket had been lowered three feet and did not require such a leap. One could argue rightly that such a radical change in the objective structure of the game suggests that the dreamer's conscious father-bound ego drive is hiding an unconscious need for life to be easy and less rigorous. That was certainly the dreamer's view! An alternative perception of this particular dream, however, is that the unconscious went so far as to change the rules of the game in order to compensate a one-sided ego attitude.

A man who had been a baseball pitcher in his youth had a brief dream in which he was pitching a baseball toward a batter and catcher at the plate. Then abruptly the image changed and he became the catcher receiving the ball he had just thrown. In order to interpret such a dream, one needs to appreciate the difference in the function and activity of a pitcher and a catcher. In baseball, the pitcher is the initiator of the action of the game. Play begins over and over again with every pitch. In that sense, pitching provides an excellent image for the expression of yang energy in the psyche. It gets things going. It activates. It provokes. It catalyzes. By contrast catching what the pitcher throws is a receptive and responsive mode which captures more nearly the yin experience. What the dream indicated was that the dreamer was developing a potential capacity to experience a balance of these complementary polarities through his ego.

In the late 1960s, at the height of the so-called hippie movement, a young man age twenty-eight who had been a college and professional football player sought therapeutic help. He had an IQ of 160, was gifted in many fields including music and psychology, but was a college dropout. When he began therapy, he was heavily into drugs, blocked in the creative use of his considerable talents, working as a bartender when he worked at all. There was about him such a sense of waste of ability by a man who sat on the sidelines of his own life potential. Over the course of two years of analysis, he had many remarkable and illuminating dreams which produced gradual but discernible change in his psychic process. Then shortly before he ended his treatment with a much improved life situation, he had the following dream: "I am sitting in a seat at the topmost level of a large athletic stadium such as the Los Angeles Coliseum. Down in the center of the field is a closed circular ring like a boxing ring where two men are about to begin a contest which is a mixture of boxing and wrestling. I am fascinated and drawn to this event so that I begin to descend the many steps of the stadium and then walk across the field until I am looking up into the ring at the two contestants about to begin. As I look closely, I am surprised to see that each of them has my face." Here was a man who had become disengaged from his own creative life, sitting as far away from the struggle, the agon, of his own existential self-encounter as one could sit. Now finally the ego was being drawn by a compelling energy within this archetypal and collective setting to become personally and actively engaged with himself. Within the defined boundaries of the boxing ring he can no longer remain a collective and passive observer. One is reminded of the counsel of Krishna to Arjuna in the Bhagavad Gita that he can no longer hold himself outside the battle but must risk himself in the struggle of the opposites. Jung also recognized that life demands the engagement and involvement of the embodied ego. Only after that has occurred can the ego appropriately experience its own transcendence by the Self.

A painfully amusing dream was brought in by one man who entitled his dream "The Lost Souls Olympics." It went as follows: "I am a finalist in a tournament of losers who play a poorly organized sport called 'Wall Ball,' where people stand in a furnished room and hit Ping-Pong balls off a wall to each other; the object of the game is to just keep returning the ball. No serious athlete has any interest in this sport. The people who play it, hate it. They play it because it is the only thing people so poorly qualified can play. The opponent in the dream hits a 'banana ball,' one so poorly hit I just have to let it go to win the game. The opponent is black. The spectators in the room groan 'banana.' However, I compulsively swipe at the ball, just touching it as it falls to the ground, thus snatching defeat from the jaws of victory." Here we see the recurrent theme of winning and losing, victory and defeat, acceptance and rejection. The dreamer is in fact a bright and successful college administrator who had been a fine athlete in school and college. At the unconscious level, however, we find a very different picture. Caught in the compulsive pressure of winner-loser psychology, he manages to find a way to fail in the contest with his dark shadow. What is revealed is an underlying feeling of incompetence and inferiority hiding behind an impressive persona of outward achievement.

Finally, consider the dream of a woman struggling to come to terms with an extremely sadistic animus problem and to free her feminine center from a life-long oppression by rigid patriarchal values and performance expectations. "A group of people, mainly men, are playing tennis in a concentration camp. I am standing with my tennis racket near the electrified fence. The ball comes my way. I put my racket up to stop the ball and bat it back, aware that a lot seems to be riding on my skill. I tick the ball with my racket and it goes over the electrified fence. The people playing are shaking their fists at me. Evidently the Gestapo commandant had arbitrarily said, as the ball flew over me, that if I slammed it back, the players would be freed." Here we see the archetype of the game totally divorced from the spirit of play or service to the sacred. It has become a rigid and demonic method of control and bondage which exerts terrible performance pressure upon the dreamer's ego. In an active imagination following the dream, she first explored the sadistic power drive of the commandant, then the compulsive and driven quality of the ego. Finally she became the tennis ball and this is what emerged: "I have gotten out of that deadly game, the sadistic compulsion under which it is played. If you don't win or satisfy the commandant, you are taken out and shot. The best players are kept alive to play the camp officers. I can't stand that kind of pounding. At last I am free to bounce around or maybe find a little boy to play with me spontaneously and take me at night and put me under his pillow. If you think I am going to let you slam me back into that game, you are crazy! I can't stand the pressure."

The archetype of the game can be a vehicle for the growth of the ego and even of the soul through a process of genuine psychic transformation. Equally, it can become the instrument of sterile, compulsive rigidity and the loss of our common humanity. The decisive factor, as always, will be the level of our consciousness.

References

Baecheler, Jean. 1958. *Suicides.* New York: Basic Books.

Corford, F. M. 1962. The origins of the Olympic Games. In Jane E. Harrison, ed., *Epilegomena to the Study of Greek Religion and Themis.* New Hyde Park, N.Y.: University Books.

Guttmann, Allen. 1978. *From Ritual to Record.* New York: Columbia University Press.

Lévi-Strauss, Claude. 1966. *The Savage Mind.* Chicago: University of Chicago Press.

Stewart, Louis. 1986. Affect and archetype: a contribution to a comprehensive theory of the structure of the psyche. In *The Body in Analysis.* Wilmette, Ill.: Chiron Publications.

Walker, Ray. 1980. The athletic motif. New York: C. G. Jung Foundation.

Watkins, John M. 1913. Ceremonial game playing and dancing in medieval churches. *The Quest* 4(1–4).

Thayer A. Greene, Ph.D., is a graduate of the C. G. Jung Institute of New York and a faculty member of the New York Institute. He is a Jungian analyst with a private practice in individual and group psychotherapy.

Baseball as the Center
of the World

A Condensed Jungian Guide to
the Psychological Experience
of Baseball Fever

Thomas Singer

*Cartoons in Collaboration with Stuart
Copans, M.D., and Mitchell Rose*

Cartoons originally appeared in *A Fan's Guide to Baseball Fever* (Mill Valley, Calif.: Elijim Publication). Used here by permission of the authors, with new text.

Fans as Idiots?

It is easiest to think of sports fans as idiots parked in front of the boob tube, unable to relate to anything but blind aggression in the most passive way. It is equally convenient to classify sportspeople as fixated in the eternal youth phase of development. But fans and players alike have a much deeper experience of symbolic play than one might imagine if one is bound by these facile stereotypes. There is passion, drama, and depth in sports even when it is exploited by then insatiable greed of bored contemporary man seeking heightened experience, money, and fame as rewards for his play. For example, if one thinks of a baseball game as a living symbol and the fan as a central participant in its dynamic unfolding, it is not so crucial that consciousness be at center stage for the symbol to do its work—namely to bring vitality and meaning into everyday life.

One way to evoke the psyche at play is through play itself. In that spirit, it is possible to look at the suffering baseball fan through the insightful eyes of depth psychological cartooning— i.e., the psyche playing at the meaning of play. Or, is there meaning in the madness of an insatiable sports junkie?

Possession

Baseball fanatics are like creatures possessed. They live for the game and everything that surrounds it—statistics, media bombardment, trivia, memorabilia, oral history, nostalgia. This state of arousal is known as "The Fever," and millions of people suffer it and are occasionally renewed through it. One can think of it as a huge national complex and, depending on one's attitude toward collective life, can view it as gross pathology or marvelous creativity or both. As with most complexes and addictions, Baseball Fever is repetitive, autonomous, remarkably resistant to consciousness, and especially antagonistic to psychological interpretations. It comes and goes as it wants in the course of an individual's life, sometimes remaining dormant for decades only to reassert itself through T.V. or radio as one turns 80 in an old folks' home.

Distraction

The Fever can interfere with every aspect of one's life and has protean symptomatic manifestations. Many wives (and some husbands) have lost their spouses to the most treacherous rival—sports addiction. In fact, for many people, their most passionate and deepest feelings are lived through their involvement with a player or team—a kind of ongoing active imagination through which all sorts of psychological phenomena are experienced.

Magical Practices

Primitive, even atavistic, modes of perception, behavior, and thinking are activated in the fan's wish to see his (her) team win. Fans are prone to terrible mood swings, compulsive behavior, social withdrawal, obsessional thinking, magical practices, paranoid delusions, and terrible bouts of nostalgia and baseball melancholia.

Witchcraft

Levels of emotional experience normally forbidden in daily life find easy expression in the fan's unbridled hatred, sadism, gloating, ridiculing, and murderous rages.

Descent

The baseball *nigredo*—loss, hopelessness, despair, destruction—is an annual event for almost every fan. And these are people who in every other aspect of their lives are able to mobilize a host of impenetrable defenses against otherwise dreadful feelings.

Transcendence

Blessedly, there are defenses against baseball loss. They range from statistical analysis to disillusionment to intellectualization. A favorite of the Jungian fan is transcendence—to rise above it all by seeing the wondrous delight in grown men at play.

"So home is the goal—rarely glimpsed, almost never attained—of all the heroes descended from Odysseus. . . . If baseball is a narrative, an epic of exile and return, a vast communal poem about separation, loss, and the hope for reunion—if baseball is a Romance epic—it is finally told by the audience. It is the Romance Epic of homecoming America sings to herself." A. Bartlett Giamatti

Fan-in-Exile

What fuels this national madness? The former president of Yale University and commissioner of baseball, A. Bartlett Giamatti, located the origin of the Fever in the longing for home. He saw us all as modern-day Ulysses, exiled in time and space from our native soil, yearning to round the bases and head for home—a return to our origins. Baseball thus concretizes what Western man has been seeking for three or four thousand years.

Tribal Spirit

The Fever is not just an individual experience. It is also a collective or tribal possession. The baseball team bears the tribal spirit of the community. The team becomes a personal totem, a family totem, and the town totem—a source of hope, inspiration, pride, reverence, awe, or scorn depending on whether the spirit (and the standings) are moving in the right direction or not. Fans identify with the totem as an incarnation of the gods, and it is usually symbolized in animal form on banners, caps, and uniforms. They worship the totem and by its spirit are bound together in a most intimate manner to other members of the tribe.

Fate of the Region

The performance of the team becomes a direct incarnation of the fate of the individual and the tribe. Because of this profound identification, elaborate mythologies begin to build around the players and teams of destiny.

Eros

And, on a more human scale, fans are bound together in a collective spirit of Eros that is rarely shared in more formal places of worship.

Mass Hallucinations

Occasionally, one finds oneself in direct contact with the archetypal realm. Individual, tribe, and team are joined together in a mass hallucination or altered state of consciousness that the uninitiated can neither see nor believe. This is akin to the collective vision reported a few thousand years ago when the chief shrine of the ancient cult of Aesclepius was moved from Greece to Rome. A huge crowd watched in awe as a 100-foot-long snake—the chief god of the cult—slithered out of the temple it was abandoning and made its way down to the boat that was transporting it to Rome. Worshipers at the temple of baseball have reported similar phenomena.

Shadow Projection

Of course, the archetypal experience of the baseball fanatic is not always sublime. Sufferers of the Fever are particularly ripe for shadowy seizures and quite capable of behaving like monsters when they project everything devilish onto their hated rivals.

Sacred Time

When the Fever grips the entire community acutely, the experience of time shifts dramatically. In this heightened state, a kind of delirious excitation takes hold in which every moment of every game grabs the fans as if it is the first and only time in the history of humanity that such an event has happened. In the language of theology, the ball game becomes a "once-and-for-all event." The World Series becomes the Alchuringa Dreamtime of the baseball universe and fans experience a *participation mystique* in the moment of creation.

Meaning of Life

At this intensified spiritual peak of the Fever, what happens to the team becomes a "life-and-death event"; the outcome of the contest is at the center of all meaning to the devotee (and the guru). Bart Giamatti wrote, in *Take Time for Paradise*.

> If there is a truly religious quality to sport, then it lies first in the intensity of devotion brought by the true believer or fan. (1989, p. 23)

Late in the season, every game becomes a cosmic struggle in which all the natural and mystical forces of the universe are brought to bear. The importance of these games for the true fan is matched only by the suffering of Christ or the temptations of Buddha.

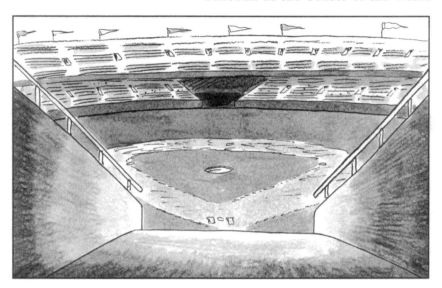

Taoist Flow

It is no accident that the first game of baseball was played on the Elysian fields in the late 1800s. Play requires a sacred place and a freeing up of the psyche and body for player and fan alike. That's why people still sing:

> Take me out to the ballgame, take me out to the park—Buy me some peanuts and Crackerjack, I don't care if I ever get back, for it's root-root-root for the home team, if they don't win it's a shame, 'cause it's one-two-three strikes you're out at the old ballgame.

The mandala of the ball field puts one in touch with the natural rhythm of life, a sublime state of being at ease that is all too rare and even sweeter for that reason. On a soft summer day when everything is exactly where it belongs, Baseball Fever allows the fan to become one with the relaxed crowd, the green grass (or even the Astroturf), the warm sun, the blue sky, and the handsome players. All weave together in a seamlessly integrated dance of perfect balance. The harmonious feeling that accompanies this easy flow of human in tune with nature can only be described as serene. Baseball Taoists will tell you that a single experience of it lasts a lifetime.

Transformation

If the fan suffers deeply and truly enough, drinks the feverish possession to its dregs, personal and communal transformation is possible and life is renewed. The transformation is different at different stages of life, suiting the natural development of the ego and self. As a child, the Fever gives birth to the image of oneself as a hero or heroine, able to go forth into the world and slay the dragon if not the Mets. In the middle years, one can recapture youth, initiate children into the spirit of the game, and find new meaning in community participation. And, if the Fever burns long enough and is suffered deeply enough, a very salutary outcome is a transformed spirit—a wise old fan of baseball—a truly philosophical soul. This rare bird has been around long enough to embrace all phases of the game, including the most bitter rivals. He and she just love the game and through it, life.

Reference

Giamatti, A. Bartlett. 1989. *Take Time for Paradise: Americans and Their Games*. New York: Summit Books.

Thomas Singer, *M.D., is a psychiatrist in private practice in San Francisco and chair of extended education for the C. G. Jung Institute of San Francisco. He is the author of* Who's the Patient Here: Portraits of the Young Psychotherapist *and* A Fan's Guide to Baseball Fever, *with Stuart Copans and Mitchell Rose.*

Hockey and the Sacred

Sport as a Bridge to the Self in the Individuation Process

Jan DeVeber Marlan

. . . by affixing the attribute "divine" to the workings of autonomous contents, we are admitting their relatively superior force. And it is this superior force which has at all times constrained men to ponder the inconceivable, and even to impose the greatest sufferings upon themselves in order to give these workings their due. It is a force as real as hunger and the fear of death.

—C. G. Jung, "The Relations Between the Ego and the Unconscious"

Introduction

This presentation begins with the rather extraordinary premise that the sport of ice hockey, one of the most fast-paced, aggressive contact sports ever developed, is a unique form of religious expression. It posits further the likewise extraordinary notion that fanaticism, as a form of sacred possession and experience of the numinous, is a bridge to an archetypal experience of Self in the individuation process. Material from a case study is offered to explore further the interpenetration of hockey and religious metaphor in a description of the emergence of what Jung called animus. The archetypal nature of this figure is explored, as well as the dangers implicit in the ego's identification with an archetype.

Sport as Religious Metaphor

The notion that sport and religion have a link is not a new idea. It is based upon historical evidence which suggests that primitive men and women believed sport and games to be gifts from the gods, and thereby sacrificially enacted in homage to them, to ensure the revival of nature in spring after the winter and the renewed growth of vegetation (Brasch 1970, p. 4). Examples of this are the Mexican Zuni tribe, who played games because of frequent droughts, convinced that these would magically bring rain; the Makah Indians who, as whaling season approached, played a primitive form of field hockey with a ball and bat made of whalebone; and the Wichitaka tribe, on the Red River of Oklahoma, who played a sport similar to field hockey which symbolically enacted the contest between winter and spring, with the triumph of spring, thereby ensuring the renewal of life and growth. Certain Eskimo tribes had similar seasonal games to retain the presence of the sun. Originally, then, sport served as an expression of ritual practice and fertility magic, suggesting primitive people's need to remain in the grace of their gods to ensure survival. It was from such primitive magical enactments of faith that sports are believed to have evolved.

The association of games with religious practice continued from early times well into the classical period in Greece:

> games had a sacred character for the Greeks, and brought a man into contact with the gods, and this explains why they were always held under their tutelage in the most sacred sanctuaries: Olympia, Delphi, Nemea, the Isthmus. (Yalouris 1979, p. 9)

The Olympic Games, for example, which began in 776 B.C., were held in the temple of Zeus and were originally played in honor of him. Over the passage of time, such contests came to be secularized. They appear to have separated in function from religion to become events engaged in purely for pleasure, enjoyed for their own sake as sources of amusement and excitement. But have sports really lost their archaic underpinnings in religion, or do they, in a somewhat obscure way, remain as essentially bound up with the religious function as they were in antiquity, but for different aims? The derivation of the word *sport* may provide a clue: it is a shortened form of *disport*, meaning "a diversion and amusement," from the Middle English *disporten*, rooted in Latin *des porto*, meaning "to carry away." The extent to which one may, in fact, be carried away to heights of ecstasy, transported to new levels of energy, via either participation in or observation of sports activities, is a topic of considerable interest to a variety of writers who seek to express their felt belief in the link between the functions of sport and religion.

Novak (1967), one such writer, notes that religions share particular elements and structures with sports which suggest a common function: they are organized around ceremonies, in which a few surrogates perform for all; they channel very human experience (danger, contingency, chance); they operate in sacred time and sacred space (consecration of certain places, days, hours, cycles, rhythms); they demonstrate heroic ideals to emulate. Sports may, in this sense, serve for modern men and women the function of religion:

> not only are the rituals, vestments, and tremor of anticipation involved in sports events like those of religions. Even in our own secular age and for quite sophisticated and agnostic person, the rituals of sports really work. They do serve a religious function: they feed a deep human hunger, place humans in touch with certain dimly perceived features of human life within this cosmos, and provide an experience of at least a pagan sense of godliness . . . sports drive one in some dark and generic sense "godward." (Novak 1967, pp. 19–20)

The athlete, for Novak, may function as modern-day priest, insofar as others (the observers) live through him: as he dons his uniform, he is in effect donning priestly vestments; in his athletic contest, he sacrifices himself, and thereby sacrifices for others, which is a priestly role. He behaves like the gods, the chosen ones who "act out liturgically the anxieties of the human race and are sacrificed as ritual victims. The contests of sports . . . are Eucharists" (ibid., p. 132).

For Giamatti (1989), the religious nature of sport is articulated as a seeking for immortality (through ritual or record making), but he primarily urges a vision of sport as a means of self-transformation, of being taken out of the self. One's immersion in the experience of sport is "a moment when we are all free of all constraint of all kinds, when pure energy and pure order create an instant of complete coherence" (Giamatti 1989, p. 35). At that moment, when pulled to our feet by what we perceive, we are "pulled out of ourselves. . . a moment . . . when something . . .

ancient, primitive, primordial takes over . . . of fully playing as the gods must play" (ibid., p. 35).

This description of the engagement of energy involved in sport, whether as participant or observer, has been echoed by many who feel themselves transported by their experience. Sports generates a play of arousal and affect that has been variously described as ecstatic, inspired, or impassioned, and even more, as sacred or transcendent. We are momentarily taken out of ourselves, can vicariously live through another, and can live or die as they live or die; and shortly after, go back to being ourselves. This is the ecstatic experience. It no doubt applies to many if not all sports or encounters with sports. But it is perhaps no better exemplified than by the fascinating, arousing, and always controversial sport of ice hockey.

Hockey as Religious Metaphor

As one of the oldest games known to us in its various forms, it is not surprising that hockey's origins are attributed to a number of different sources. It has been suggested that hockey derived from prehistoric man's delight in stick-and-ball games, which embrace both his instinctual urges to hit something and his magical beliefs in game as a religious rite for survival purposes. Another tale of its genesis is the creation myth of the Wichita Indians, which included the idea that hockey was first played because of the earliest surgical operation, that is, that primitive man somehow produced the objects of the game out of his own body, the ball from his left side, and the stick from his right, and immediately began to hit the ball with the stick. Soon afterwards, other men were created who learned how to play from him, divided into two groups (i.e., the first hockey teams), and set up the first game (Brasch 1970, p. 176). Another story is English in origin and suggests a primitive ritual turned to a game:

> On Hock-tide or other occasions, the burnt skull of a sacrificed beast was bandied through the streets of northern villages. That became the puck in hockey; and since there was a taboo against touching it, shepherds' crooks were utilized as sticks. The original objective was home, the player's family garden;

but secularization reversed the goal, which became the opponents' cage. (Guiness and Hurley 1986, p. 116).[1]

Ice hockey probably first originated in Canada in the nineteenth century, but there are several divergent accounts of it. One story concerns a group of French explorers in 1740 who happened upon a group of Indians chasing a ball across a frozen river. As they swung wildly at the ball with curved sticks, often missing and hitting a player, they cried out "ho ghee" ("it hurts") and the word *hockey* allegedly came from this, not to mention the game itself and its original violence (Considine 1982, p. 213). Others attribute the word to the French word *hoquet*, the curved stick or shepherd's staff, an interpretation that relates also to the English burned skull story. Later versions of its origin attribute the first game to English soldiers and also to students at McGill University. Whatever the truth of its natural origin, hockey appears to be a sport with legendary ritual and tribal underpinnings. But what could be so religious about this rough competitive sport that it inspires the present writer its selection to exemplify sport's religious metaphor?

Consider the following scenario: Sixteen thousand people, dressed in a variety of colorful sacred garb bearing images of a peculiar symbol, file ritually into a domed amphitheater, anticipating that their spirits will soon be uplifted by being present while a particular energy is generated in a shared celebration of the ordered ritual about to take place. It is the appointed hour (ritual time) and the appointed place (ritual space).

The celebrants of this peculiar rite solemnly begin to emerge, also garbed in ceremonial dress, and heralded by communal chants and incantations from the anticipating multitude. The highest priest appears first, evidenced by his ritual implements: the familiar, heavily decorated crown and scepterlike wand. He enters his sacred place, engaging in a private ritual praxis of his own, repeating a sacred sequence of carefully orchestrated prayer movements.

The ceremony is about to begin. A hush comes over the amphitheater and sacred preparatory songs are offered in oblation to the spirit that rules this strange celebration, infusing each participant and each observer with an energy for the enactments that are to follow. In such a moment, participant and observer may even become one, so fully are the commitments of each.

---

[1] I am indebted to Josephine Evetts-Secker, a Jungian analyst in Calgary, Alberta, for this reference.

For these are the gods! The people chant certain ceremonial slogans, as they raise their cups in salute to the beginning of the ceremony. It is a powerful one, in which enormous personal agony and joy are ascribed to the seemingly insignificant sacramental occurrence of a small dark object being projected beyond the high priest's control into the hungry mouth belonging to his oppressor.

The ceremony is orchestrated as a predictable sequence with only a few mystical surprises, until its denouement. Perhaps it is transcendence! Then all are thrilled and feel a rush of exhilaration, the victory propelling each to heights of ecstasy; but sadly, all too often, the ritual fails, with a pall of mourning descending over the hoard as they file in silence from the sacred place, to await the next scheduled ceremony.[2]

This is an image of a hockey game. Perhaps the goaltender—as high priest—is recognizable to the reader. But if not, it may be helpful to allude to his strange ritual dress—his mask and stick as miter and scepter—and to his private goaltending rituals as ceremonial prayers to invoke the gods of hockey to deliver a win or to bind his almost overwhelming anxiety in having, as former goaltender Jacques Plante once observed, the only job in the world in which, when you make a small mistake, a red light comes on behind you and eighteen thousand irate people shout "Stupid—get the bum out of there" (Hunt 1972, pp. 3–4).

The game itself is probably recognizable to the reader. Perhaps it can be imagined as a container for religious energy, which in contemporary culture has all but divested itself from the more traditional bounds of church and temple and has been seeking an expression of itself. It does suggest a communal fervor, an experience of transcending of the personal, lifting above the everyday common goal.

Contemporary culture possibly hungers for this container. Ken Dryden, a former professional goaltender, alludes to this in a book he co-authored with Roy MacGregor (1989). He implies that hockey could be described as a most profound expression of the Canadian soul, that it serves, in outland Canadian frontier provinces, the function of a binding community metaphor, that which pulls people together (Dryden and MacGregor 1989, p. 15), the town rink functioning for all the world as the community cathe-

---

[2]See Michael Novak (1967, p. 173) for the inspiration behind this particular description, a piece by Childe Herald from the *Rocky Mountain Herald*, 1955.

dral. But the implication of this description of hockey in Canada may be more universally true; in effect, it suggests that sport may be imaged in the function of religion.

One might ask the obvious question: how has hockey come to carry the religious function when so many religious traditions assumedly provide still viable and useful containers for the sacred? How is it that so many have been drawn into the observation of the religious via sport? (I need only cite the popularity of Monday night football, let alone the many and diverse amateur, college, semi-professional, and professional sports teams that can bear witness to the enthusiasm of their followers in support of this contention.)

The Loss and Reemergence of the Sacred

C. G. Jung (1933b) stressed the importance for each individual person of coming to terms with one's personal experience of a religious outlook on life, observing that the lack of this was, in fact, what led to many of his patients' illnesses. The healing function, he believed, came from being connected with the numinous reality of the divine. Jung contended that for modern man traditional religion no longer carried an adequate link to the experience of the sacred.

Stein (1985) has noted that Jung's treatment of Christianity attempted to return to awareness elements of the shadow that were repressed or split off. Jung believed that what was evil—symbolized by the devil and relegated to the shadow—needed to be reintegrated into the Christian perspective in order to approximate a more whole (i.e., containing the opposites) vision of religion and soul. According to Jung, then, traditional Christianity did not understand the darker side of the psyche (devil, instinct). For Jung, spirit and instinct (mind and body) need not be separate, and the recovery of the reality of the psyche in our time involved rediscovering the importance and meaning of the instincts and honoring them, as opposed to the more familiar Christian perspective of disavowal.

What this essentially implies is that instinctual elements, such as aggression, sexuality, and body, in terms of Western Christian religious perspective, have been slowly over time relegated to the realm of the unconscious. By virtue of the laws of psychic energy and compensation, it is apparent that what has been so radically repressed should eventually find a means of expression, and thereby make its way into consciousness.

Jung was aware of this as early as 1910 and stated as much, albeit in a rather radical and exaggerated manner, in a letter he wrote to Freud in that year. He was speaking about the importance of revitalizing a feeling for symbol and myth and stated the necessity:

> . . . ever so gently to transform Christ back into the soothsaying god of the vine, which he was, and in this way absorb those ecstatic instinctual forces of Christianity for the *one* purpose of making the cult and the sacred myth what they once were—a drunken feast of joy where man regained the ethos and holiness of an animal. That indeed was the beauty and purpose of classical religion, which from God knows what temporary biological needs has turned into a Misery Institute. Yet how infinitely much rapture and wantonness lie dormant in our religion, waiting to be led back to their true destination! A genuine and proper ethical development cannot abandon Christianity but must grow up within it, must bring to fruition its hymn of love, the agony and ecstasy over the dying and resurgent god, the mystic power of the wine . . . only *this* ethical development can serve the vital forces of religion. (Jung 1973, p. 18)[3]

The ecstatic instinctual forces he mentions appear to be the very elements with which contemporary Western religion has lost touch, and, not altogether surprisingly, it is the elements of instinct, passion, and ecstasy that find their way into the experience of sport. Perhaps sports, such as hockey, carry these lost elements of the divine, and thus offer a means of expression of their unconscious dimension.

The sense of hockey as an expression of instinct via its bodily and aggressive confrontation is not difficult to see. Neither is it difficult to imagine sport as a container and expression of passion and ecstasy, as we consider the involvements of it participants and observers. That hockey might also contain disguised sexual elements is a bit more obscure. Yet one need only reflect upon the jargon of hockey to discover its sexual undertones. Consider, after

---

[3]Jung, in later life, commented on the exaggeration and inflation of his perspective at the time in his life that this letter was written, although the point he was making was worked over in many ways in his later work, particularly in *Modern Man in Search of a Soul* (1933b) and in his later writings on religion and alchemy.

all, that it is a game in which the ultimate activity is expressed as "shooting and scoring," with its central thrust being to "bury the puck deep in the net." Anyone listening to a play-by-play announcement of a game will hear repeated references to the "creases," the "box," the "rebound," "forechecking," "backchecking," "pokechecking," "holding the stick," and "pulling the goalie," not to mention such phrases as "come up big," "come down the slot," "take the body," and "put it through the five-hole," let alone "he slammed it in" (the puck into the goal, that is). It is, I believe, a game incontestably permeated with sexual imagery and innuendo.

The implications of the idea that instinctual and ecstatic elements in the unconscious reemerge in sport, and particularly in hockey, are enormous and far-reaching, and therefore difficult to demonstrate. One way to examine them here is through a case example, which offers a direct report of how the metaphor of hockey came to serve one person's individuation process. In keeping with Jung's notion that all theory-making may essentially be a personal confession, the following is the subjective experience of the current writer and all subsequent interpretations and amplifications derive from it.

The Image of the Goaltender in the Individuation Process

The series of images and experiences which emerged over the course of my analytic experience the last four years are, I believe, useful in articulating the symbolic connections between sport and religion insofar as they reflect a passionate involvement in the sport of hockey and one of its figures, an involvement that borders on a kind of divine madness (the emergence of Dionysian energy). In addition, this material details the emergence and development of the animus as well as the phenomenon of fanaticism as possession by an archetype. Jung's notion of mana personality has relevance here as well, as possibly connected to the notion of charisma, i.e., how one person can draw another into projective identification or *participation mystique*.

In order to arrive at a place where these ideas can be explored, it is first necessary for me to present the material as it evolved. Thus the following is an account—perhaps like a personal myth—

which delineates the appearance and development of the figure of the goaltender.

Ron Hextall, Dionysus, and Me

Like the mythic god Dionysus, giving no warning of his coming, a goaltender named Ron Hextall first came into my life about four years ago as an inner figure in a dream in which I found myself standing by the side of a hockey rink. In this dream, I somehow wanted recognition from Hextall, but he had no interest in me and turned instead to my husband (a Jungian analyst) who was behind me. Hextall acknowledged his presence with genuine interest and affect, much to my frustration and disappointment.

At the time I hardly knew who Ron Hextall was, let alone had much overt interest in him. I knew that he was the goaltender for the Philadelphia Flyers and had, the year before, won the Vezina trophy as the NHL's best goaltender and the Conn Smythe trophy for the most valuable player in the Stanley Cup playoffs, although his team lost the Stanley Cup in the final game. What I did know of him was through my son's interest in him. I believe I had only seen him play once, and that was on TV.

For my son, Brandon, however, the sun rose and set on Hextall. My son was at that time an 8-year-old Mite-level goaltender, and Ron Hextall, whose vibrant style and breathtaking skill captured his admiration, was his hero. He copied his movements and gestures, his style of roaming from the net (when he could barely skate); he wanted a shirt like his, a stick like his, in short, anything that would make him feel that he had incarnated his hero. At the time, I found this idolization and imitation cute and had ordered my son a miniature Hextall shirt to copy his idol. But at that time all my affect toward Hextall came through Brandon.

My husband and I had only recently become interested in hockey at all, through the influence of my son's enthusiasm for the sport, which he had begun to play the year before. My dream also came at a time when I was just beginning my own Jungian analysis, with no clearly defined thoughts of ever training to be an analyst, which makes the first Hextall dream a rather startling initiation of a process of revelation which was only later to become clear to me.

There began a rather profound series of Ron Hextall and

hockey dreams which eventually numbered more than thirty over a three-year period. Who was this figure, I wondered, and why had he come into my soul? At the time, I might add, I was rather startled to find him there, first of all because I barely knew of him, but mostly because he seemed in some ways to be a most unlikely figure to appear in my evolving dream process as a professional woman approaching mid-life. Why Hextall? I asked at that time. It's a question that I've continued to ask myself over the years of my involvement with him. Eventually, one thing became absolutely clear: he had a reason for being there.

Hextall, in the dream, wanted nothing to do with my son, but with "the Jungian analyst" (my husband) behind me. Years later, as I entered my own Jungian training, I recognized a teleology, a prospective function, present in the original image, as if the Hextall figure, from the moment of his appearance, knew what *he* wanted from *me*. But I had not the slightest idea of this at the time.

I dreamed about him several times before my first significant affective connection to the literal man emerged. This came during a playoff game between the Flyers and our team, the Pittsburgh Penguins, in the Stanley Cup divisional playoff series of 1989. Hextall may have had the worst game of his life that night, playing to a psyched-up crowd of 16,000 avid Penguin fans who were taunting him to fall apart. Ten goals later, he was pulled and replaced by his backup goalie and then sat on the bench. The crowd went wild, chanting his name in mockery, like some kind of tribal incantation before the kill. I recall feeling tremendous ambivalence, as I both wanted the Penguins to win, while I experienced deep sadness and compassion for this vibrant young man who had mysteriously caught my interest and now seemed injured and crushed.

Some enigmatic sacred fire was ignited for me that night in this experience. As I paced sleepless around my room, I was obsessed with thoughts of compassion for him, thoughts which I felt driven to express, but for which I could find no vehicle. I shared these feelings with my husband, who seemed to understand that some deeply felt inner issue was gripped in this. It was actually he who came upon the idea of writing to Hextall that night, as a means of beginning to unravel what symbolic significance he was beginning to have for me. I sat up most of the night writing a very long letter, detailing the strange way in which my interest in him had begun and my inner work with him was evolving. I somehow wanted him (the literal person) to know. It wasn't enough for me that he was a figure of my unconscious.

The following day I decided to send the letter to him care of the Flyers and eagerly awaited the reply I expected would come. No one had ever written such a letter to him, I reasoned; he would understand, be moved by my sympathies, and respond appreciatively. I also later read and discussed the letter with my analyst, who encouraged my attempts to activate whatever image was there and to find whatever means possible to give it expression. Sadly, though, the letter was never answered. I continued to wonder if he ever received it, and if so, what he thought of it. I felt a bit sorry for him, receiving such an odd and emotional attempt to connect with him, a communication that had an air of both fanaticism and desperation to it. Perhaps someone who screened his mail mercifully saved him from it.

Nonetheless, the dream about Hextall shortly after this was a very powerful one in which his affect toward me changed to one of openness, genuine warmth, and connection. Walking with him in the labyrinth of hallways under a rink, he suddenly turned to me and kissed me, a kiss marked by the infusion of a liquid substance into my mouth. Walking with him later outside the rink, his left biceps caught on fire and I was desperately trying to extinguish it. The infusion of his substance was at this point real and palpable to me, the fire of his influence almost all consuming.

A series of dreams followed of repetitive attempts to communicate with the Hextall figure by word or letter, which were unsuccessful, as if I could now not get the inner figure to respond to me any more than the outer one. These dreams constantly rehearsed the questions: Did he get my letter? Did he hear my story? He appeared momentarily in dreams, offering a momentary hope, then just as enigmatically dissolved or disappeared. Encounters were planned that failed in the end. I despaired at times of ever "knowing" him.

My obsession with him grew by leaps and bounds over the following months. I began to collect photographs and articles about him and to talk incessantly about him, as if he were as real and palpable an influence on my life as an intimate family member. I began to collect film clips of interviews with him, which I watched and studied with an intense desire to know who he was, to see what his "real" personality was like. When no answer to my letter was forthcoming, the imagistic inner Ron Hextall responded in an active imagination as I wrote back to myself, struggling to understand who he was and what it was I needed to hear from him. I knew that I wanted his acknowledgment, his interest, and his acceptance of me.

I think my friends thought I was crazy. My language changed, accommodating inflections of his speech and expressions I had heard him use in interviews. My obsession with talking about him spilled over from my analysis into my relationships with friends and acquaintances, who treated me in a rather pathetic way, tolerating my lunacy and seeming to be always trying to encourage a new subject. Somewhere around that time I had a dream of Hextall in which I was inside his mask looking out through his eyes. This is what I felt Jung must mean by being in the grip of an autonomous complex.

Shortly after this, I began to imitate him through a burning desire to play hockey, which I actualized by buying all my own equipment and joining an adult learn-to-play-hockey program, comprised of seven women and twenty-seven men. My husband bought me, through a distributor of player's former equipment for collectors, Ron Hextall's actual hockey socks, which I wore when I played, feeling that I now had embodied him. Oddly enough, I took a player position, fearing to be a goaltender. Some of this was wisdom, considering I was playing against adult men with far greater skill than I had. The culmination of all this was in donning my son's equipment to play goaltender for his birthday party, this time against ten-year-old boys (more my speed!). I wanted to know what it felt like to *be* Ron Hextall, and I had as far as was humanly possible, taken that up in a literal attempt to live him.

The power of this image has been almost overwhelming, reaching almost lunatic proportion in my obsession with both the literal and figurative Hextall. As he evolved in my dreams, a different energy began to be constellated in the outside world, and what slowly evolved for me was a desire to train as an analyst. When it came time to write my admissions essay for the institute, I found myself telling the story of my goaltender, who carries for me the creative power of this different, more masculine energy with its eruptive shadow aspect. It became clear to me that standing on the side of the rink was no longer where I wanted to be. And as literally I joined the ranks of hockey players, in my inner life I knew that it was time to be in the game.

The risk that brought in the external world involved my decision to train as an analyst and my subsequent shift of the inner creative energy once wrapped up in my son as the carrier of my animus energy and then in the Hextall figure, now out into the world in my own creative application. But when I was accepted for training in the spring of 1991, I secretly felt that Ron and I had made it!

For five months after that, there were no further dreams of Hextall. I wondered if he was assimilated into my psyche and would reflect on him from time to time in an almost nostalgic way. But when I began training in the fall, he did appear again in a dream, so there was more to gain after all. And again, the image was the agony of the difficulty of making a connection. We apparently weren't done with each other yet!

Then a subsequent dream opened a new vista to the experience: I finally am in proximity to him on the ice, and my appreciation of him is received. He then emerges after the game from the locker room wearing a distinctive soft yellow-gold-brown turtleneck sweater. It was a color I had come to associate with images of a newly emerging Self energy from several previous dreams in which umber-colored spaceship structures and yellow-gold flowers had appeared. Hextall now "wore" this color. In the dream, we have dinner together; we've become friends. He then takes me to show me his house (which I had searched for in dreams for years). As my journal of the dream states, "my sense was that now we are truly known to each other, no longer estranged. He will call me to spend time together when he is in town; we are really friends. I feel deeply gratified and finally connected to him."

Four days after this dream, I traveled to Philadelphia to see a game and was finally able to meet Ron Hextall in person. I briefly told him some of this story, which no doubt puzzled him. I did learn that he had never received my original letters. For me, meeting the literal man was a revelatory experience, a recognition that what he had carried for so long had far less to do with him than with me. This was a tremendously important affective awareness which probably allowed the *participation mystique* (of the intermingling of our two psyches) to go into dissolution.

Not long after this encounter, I dreamed one of the last dreams of Hextall: that he was being traded to New Jersey. A year later, he actually was traded, donning the "new jersey" of the Quebec Nordiques. But that was not the emotional message of the dream, which I believe rather reflected a deeper sense of the movement of the energy away from this figure into new and subsequent figures, which began to appear shortly thereafter and who have continued to reveal and evolve further aspects of myself.

The Goaltender and Dionysian Energy

All in all then, who was Hextall? Was he an image of my animus energy? Or of my slowly evolving Self process? Through much reflection, I have begun to understand the projection of my inner masculine energy onto this fiery, intense, and emotional man whom I had witnessed, until finally meeting him, only in images, both inner and outer.

What's the meaning of the image of a goaltender in the psyche of me as a professional woman? First of all, the goalie is arguably the feminine position in hockey if there is one: as guardian of the gate, deciding who or what gets in or through its crease, deflecting the aggressive, phallic dimension of the game—therein lies some of the potential for the feminine identification with this figure in hockey. Yet Hextall is a goaltender who plays the game in an exceptionally phallic way: as one of the best stick handlers in the NHL, he comes far out of the net and, with his large goalie stick, plays the puck with almost the agility of a third defensemen. His capacity to move around the goal with speed and alacrity is exceptional, so that he in no way represents a passive stasis but the active phallic feminine. He is the one who can let in what he wants or turn away the essentially masculine striving (scoring) dimension of the game with an equal kind of power.

And what of his aggressiveness? Ron Hextall is a goaltender who is known for his superb and breathtaking agility, for his creative and risky roaming from the net, and for being the only goaltender to score a goal by shooting the puck the length of the ice (he's done this twice). At the same time Hextall is known for his fiery aggression, usually enacted in defense of his teammates, which has lead to some slashing incidents in which he has received multiple game suspensions. Given this, he has been accused by the media for some time of being unstable, having a dual personality—calm, intelligent, and sensitive in his off-ice demeanor while eruptive and passionately losing his temper on the ice. This anomaly in his character, while earning him much public disdain, has no doubt fueled the activation of his image in my own personality. I have both an on-ice and off-ice Hextall, to which my family and friends can attest.

Somewhere in the exploration of this image, it occurred to me that the manifestation of Hextall is an experience of the myth of Dionysus infecting my own life. In speaking about Dionysus, Hillman (1972) has noted:

though he is male and phallic, there is no misogyny in this structure of consciousness because it is not divided from its own femininity . . . female is not added to or integrated by male; rather, the image shows an androgynous consciousness, where male and female are primordially united. The coniunc-tio is not an attainment but a given. (Hillman 1972, pp. 258–259)

My sense of the melding of the masculine and feminine in the epiphany of the goaltender image is paralleled in this understand-ing of Dionysus.

Dionysus is a god who is known for his comings and goings, and his unexpected ways of appearing and disappearing. My dream experiences of Hextall have been like this: he comes when he wants to, receives what he wants, and leaves when he wants. Just as the women followers of Dionysus felt in rapture of him as a god, my experience of the Hextall image suggests an immersion in the presence of the divine, both being in awe and unable to affect much toward him. As Dionysus did inspire people to madness and heights of passion and ecstasy, so has the image of Hextall at times consumed my life by what has seemed to be lunacy. The wish to merge with him has felt more than once to be on the order of madness, of being swept away in the grip of an archetype, a kind of sacred possession.

Dionysus is the god who came as a mask, and with his goalie mask, Hextall is certainly the quintessential masked figure. I have a photograph of him in my office with his mask lifted that I've always been particularly intrigued by, as if my wish is to unmask him, to understand what lies in the essential nature of his being underneath the facade of the goaltender. The accouterments of the goalie—the stick, the heavy pads, the goal mask—do have an almost religious quality to them, not unlike the bishop's garments, miter, and scepter. In a certain sense, Hextall can be thus seen as a religious figure, both as carrier of the numinosum and as serving the function of religion: *re-ligio*, "a linking back," here as a bridg-ing to the archetypal experience of Self.

Dionysus is a god who animates all of life and whose followers participated in a mystical form of ecstatic experience. He is a god of immanence and transcendence at once. While we think of most gods as transcendent, above us and unreachable, Dionysus was also a god of immanence who was somehow more real and palpa-ble and knowable. He therefore stands for the knowing of the unknowable. The mask presents a face that is knowable, yet it is also what conceals; thus it is both the knowable and the unknowable at the same time. It is the simultaneous experience of revelation and concealment.[4] All of this I feel amplifies the essential feeling of the Hextall energy as it evolved in my process of individuation: he hid, evaded, and kept me intrapsychically drawn toward what seemed unreachable but eventually came clear as the teleological project of the evolution of career direction and integration of split-off aspects of the Self.

In summary, then, the experience of the Hextall figure is not unlike the emergence of the archetypal pattern we would refer to as Dionysian. According to Jung (1944), "the Dionysian element has to do with emotions and affects which have found no suitable religious outlets in the predominantly Apollonian cult and ethos of Christianity" (June 1944, par. 182). It is, in a sense, a return of the very aspects that we previously examined as relegated to the shadow of Christianity and Western religion: the body, aggression, sensuality, passion, and ecstasy.

Fanaticism and Possession: The Animus and the Charismatic Other

There is another obvious entry into the material outlined above, and this concerns the extent to which it reflects the possible danger in the ego's identification with an archetype. Jung (1933a) cautioned against the dangers inherent in identification with an archetypal content from the unconscious as leading to a kind of inflation that may weaken consciousness. Such an identification with unconscious contents can appear as fusion (or possession) with an image different from the ego's: the ego thinks it is other than itself.

The fanaticism that overwhelms the followers of rock stars, politicians, actors, and other public figures fits this portrait. What

---

[4]This, incidentally, parallels Jung's understanding of the symbol:

> Every psychic product, if it is the best possible expression at the moment for a fact as yet unknown or only relatively known, may be regarded as a symbol, provided that we accept the expression as standing for something that is only divined and not yet clearly conscious . . . every psychological expression is a symbol if we assume that it states or signifies something more and other than itself which eludes our present knowledge. (Jung 1921, par. 817)

is primarily going on in such an experience is that the "fan" projects an archetypal content (for example, hero or savior) onto the star, who is then believed to embody the projective content literally. Jung referred to this as "mana personality" (1928, par. 374–406). Novak, in speaking of the power an athlete can carry for his fans, describes this phenomenon in a particularly poignant way:

> Athletes are not merely entertainers. Their role is far more powerful than that. People identify with them in a much more priestly way. Athletes exemplify something of deep meaning— frightening meaning, even. Once they become superstars, they do not quite belong to themselves. Great passions are invested in them. They are no longer treated as ordinary humans or even as mere celebrities. Their exploits and their failures have great power to exult—or to depress. When people talk about athletes' performances, it is almost as if they are talking about a secret part of themselves. As if the stars had some secret bonding, some Siamese intertwining with their own psyches. (Novak 1967, pp. 31–32)

What Novak is describing here, I believe, is the projection of an archetypal content and the subsequent immersion in it (identification with an archetype) which blurs the boundaries between ego and Self, and self and other. The danger is that this creates an illusory reality, in which the ego can imagine itself to be really and directly connected to the object of projection (as I did at times with Hextall), or inversely, feel the infusion of the other into one's own personality (possession), which can eventually result in overidentification with an object of projection (as in my imitation of Hextall's speech and mannerisms and in becoming a hockey player). These are the consequences of unintegrated projection which remains literal.

The emergence of what Jung has called animus or anima is always experienced in projected form, whether onto a literal person (falling in love) or via a symbolic encounter in dream or imagination (as an inner figure). The more numinosity there is in the experience, the more closely it approximates what Melanie Klein and others have referred to as projective identification, which parallels the concept Jung borrowed from Levy-Bruhl called *participation mystique* (i.e., the lack of differentiation between self and object, between the ego and its projective content).

In this sense, the Hextall experience has been for me what could be described as an encounter with the numinous power of the animus archetype, inasmuch as it is an archetypal reality which calls forth specific elements of the Self (frequently, but not always, contrasexual attributes) that are first projected outward, and thus personified. In his original understanding of anima/animus, Jung (1928) discussed it as a "function complex" whose purpose was to serve as a bridge to the unconscious. Gradually, as its energy was freed from projection and intergrated into the personality, according to Jung, it no longer appeared in a personified form, but instead became the function of relationship with the unconscious (Jung 1928, par. 339). There is a way then in which animus energy, when intergrated, becomes available to the personality as the functional bridging capacity of the transcendent function.[5] This was, for Jung, accomplished through the mediation of a symbol, and it is clear that the image of Hextall has been such a transitional mediating symbol.

As an endnote, it might be interesting to posit just what it was about Hextall—or any charismatic figure—that can draw such energies to itself. Is it aspects of power, position, and status that fascinate (fasten-ate) our energies and engage our fantasies? Or is it perhaps due to an ego lack one needs to compensate through an inflationary identification? Or is there, in actuality, some rare and wonderful, as yet undefined, enigmatic energy that emanates from such a figure, drawing others to itself with an invisible magnetism? This is not unlike a return to the archaic nineteenth-century images of Mesmer, animal magnetism, and invisible fluids. Yet it is possible that returning to this original, once too literal, way of imagining would now be a fruitful way of reflection about the nature of connection and relation. After all, as Jung so poignantly indicated, for every projection there is generally some "hook" in the outside world (1946, par. 499). An investigation of the nature of charisma might, at another time, begin here.

Conclusion

Hockey has been and is for me a very gripping metaphor, one that transcends even the Hextall experience. The power, the sense of

---

[5]The original idea behind this thinking came from Peter Mudd, a Jungian analyst in Evanston, Illinois.

identification with one's heroes, and the ecstatic energy that can be present when this sport is played can be understood as a nearly transcendent experience. Anyone who has ever fallen victim to a passionate investment in how a team does or in the outcome of a competition will immediately recognize this dynamic. It is the stuff of agony and defeat, of triumph and exhilaration. It has an effect upon the spirit that has moved droves of people to seek out these experiences again and again, often at tremendous cost and personal sacrifice. The recollection of the religions of antiquity in this description is obvious. The issue is the reclaiming of the spirit. For me, it is particularly profound to see that, in the appearance of a constellation like Ron Hextall, psyche has taken the lead.

References

Brasch, R. 1970. *How Did Sports Begin? A Look at the Origins of Man at Play*. New York: David McKay Co., Inc.

Considine, T. 1982. *The Language of Sport*. New York: World Almanac Publications.

Dryden, K. 1983. *The Game*. New York: Penguin Books.

Dryden, K., and R. MacGregor. 1989. *Homegame*. Toronto: McClelland and Stewart, Inc.

Ellenberger, H. 1970. *The Discovery of the Unconscious*. New York: Basic Books, Inc.

Giamatti, A. B. 1989. *Take Time for Paradise: Americans and Their Games*. New York: Summit Books.

Guiness, G., and A. Hurley, eds. 1986. *Auctor Ludens: Essays of Play and Literature*. Philadelphia: John Benjamin's Publishing Co.

Hill, G. S. 1992. *Masculine and Feminine: The Natural Flow of the Opposites in the Psyche*. Boston: Shambhala.

Hillman, J. 1972. *The Myth of Analysis: Three Essays in Archetypal Psychology*. Evanston, Ill.: Northwestern University Press.

Hunt, J. 1972. *The Men in the Nets*. Toronto: McGraw-Hill-Ryerson Limited.

Jung, C. G. 1921. *Psychological Types*, CW, vol. 6. Princeton, N.J.: Princeton Unviersity Press, 1971.

———. 1928. The relations between the ego and the unconscious. In *CW* 7:123–304. Princeton, N.J.: Princeton University Press, 1966.

———. 1933a. A study in the process of individuation. In *CW* 9i: 290–354. Princeton, N.J.: Princeton University Press, 1959.

_____. 1933b. *Modern Man in Search of a Soul*. New York: Harcourt, Brace, and Co.

_____. 1944. *Psychology and Alchemy*, *CW*, vol. 12. Princeton, N.J.: Princeton University Press, 1953.

_____. 1946. Psychology of the transference. In *CW* 16:267–321. Princeton, N.J.: Princeton University Press, 1954.

_____. 1973. *Letters*, vol. 1 (1960–1950), G. Adler and A. Jaffe, eds. Princeton, N.J.: Princeton University Press.

Jung, E. 1957. *Animus and Anima*. Zurich: Spring Publications.

Koltuv, B. B. 1990. *Weaving Woman*. York Beach, Me.: Nicolas-Hays.

Lewis, I. M. 1986. *Religion in Context: Cults and Charisma*. Cambridge, England: Cambridge University Press.

Novak, M. 1967. *The Joy of Sports*. New York: Hamilton Press.

Otto, W. F. 1965. *Dionysus: Myth and Cult*. Dallas: Spring Publications.

Sansone, D. 1988. *Greek Athletics and the Genesis of Sport*. Berkeley, Calif.: University of California Press.

Stein, M. 1985. *Jung's Treatment of Christianity*. Wilmette, Ill.: Chiron Publications.

Yalouris, N., ed. 1979. *The Eternal Olympics: The Art and History of Sport*. New Rochelle, N.Y.: Caratzas Brothers.

Jan DeVeber Marlan, *Ph.D., is a licensed psychologist in private practice in Pittsburgh, Pennsylvania, and a diploma candidate at the C. G. Jung Institute of Chicago.*

The Way of the Warrior

One Metaphor for Individuation

Brenda A. Donahue

Martial Arts: Body and Alchemy

About eleven years ago, I was told that I had to have a spinal fusion. My lower back was arthritic, congenitally malformed, and periodically the bones would become misaligned, creating muscle spasm and shooting pains that moved down both my legs. I could not walk to the bathroom and had to remain flat in bed while on anti-inflammatory and pain-relieving drugs for two to three weeks at a time. When my doctor told me that I needed surgery, I was teaching in an internal medicine residency program and was able to do extensive research on postsurgical complications following the type of surgery I was supposed to have. Since the incidence of chronic pain following the surgery was high, more than forty percent, I decided to seek out an alternative to stabilize and strengthen my back. My orthopedic surgeon was willing to help me with anti-inflammatory medication and frequent checks to make sure I would not create more damage. Together we worked at identifying which muscle groups needed to be worked. After a long and fruitless search for a program which would help me, my children suggested that I come to their martial arts school. They were sure that there I could be helped to strengthen my back. I went with them and, to my surprise, I was helped to heal my back without surgery.

For a long time, I hated it. I was forty-three years old, I had not exercised since high school, and my back hurt. When I entered the door of the school, my personal was stripped away. I was no longer a wife, a mother, or a professional woman with standing in the community. My children stood ahead of me in the school and knew more than I did. I became a beginner, a clumsy beginner. My body, which had become molded, sculpted, and armored from years of sitting or walking, began to change by practicing movements that created pain in my back. No one felt sorry for me; no one coddled me; I was there to confront the woundedness in my body and to begin slowly to change it. I was given the tools, the rest was up to me. After one month of practice, it was clear to me that the tools would work and that if I could persevere, I would avoid the dreaded surgery.

Learning to make pain an ally rather than an enemy is probably one of the most heroic things I have ever done. To push myself slowly and mindfully into the painful movements needed to create the physical changes necessary to build up the muscle and to free the joints and ligaments in my back was a challenge. If I pushed too hard or too far, I was in so much pain that I wasn't able to move or sit without a brace. My fear of pain had to be transformed from the image of a dreaded enemy into an appreciated ally and teacher.

The way my martial training began and still takes place is through work with the physical body in movement or in stillness. There is little verbal explanation as to why certain movements are done, or what their effects throughout the body will be. The orientation is toward the physical, and the learning is through experience. Very few words are used in the practice room; respect is shown for the teachers through the traditional bow. Competitiveness is allowed only with oneself, and tournaments and abuse are not allowed. It is said that the forms are so powerful that someone could be injured accidentally, so while students practice with each other, it is never in a competitive or a destructive way. Fighting is only to protect one's life.

As it became clear to me that my back was being healed, I had to develop within myself a sense of play in order to find ways to make a needed and dreadful experience challenging and interesting. I pretended that I was entering a sacred place each day, where I would have an adventure and learn from all my experience. Whatever happened there was valuable and something from which to learn. As I practiced this way on a daily basis, I learned balance, coordination, speed, timing, and the ability to relax into pain in order to hold a position; an attitude of being with all of my inner experience began to develop within me in a way I had not known ever before. My practice took place in an atmosphere that appeared to be solely dominated by an aggressive and heroic form of the masculine, but my body said something different. It said that I was experiencing something deeply feminine and rooted in nature, cycles, and the primordial. The sense I had was similar to that of being pregnant. The goal belonged to nature. My work was to do what I could to support and balance what was naturally taking place.

I was emotionally and mentally captivated by my experience. My dreams indicated that something powerful was happening, and I couldn't understand what it was, other than that it was an encounter with something archetypal for which I had no name. One night, I dreamed that as I was practicing, the old Grand Master (I have never met such a person) and his wife invited me to walk outside in the forest with them. They were dressed in brocade robes and seemed to be quite royal, yet very comfortable to be with. They taught me many things as we walked, and I awoke crying because I felt so loved by them, and I felt pain because I could not remember the things they had taught me.

I knew that I had experienced an encounter with the old wise woman and old wise man and that somehow my martial arts practice was important and linked with knowledge that was as yet unconscious for me. What touched me most about the dream was the feeling of being deeply loved and cherished by these figures. It is that feeling of love which has infused my practice and give me the strength to continue.

About three years after I began my practice in martial arts, I was fortunate enough to meet Harley Swift Deer, a twisted hair elder of Cherokee and Irish descent and head of the Deer Tribe Metis Medicine Society. The twisted hairs are members of a medicine society that twists together knowledge from many different tribes. Knowledge is added to the general body on the basis of whether or not it works or can be applied. From Swift Deer's knowledge, I developed a lens through which to view my martial arts experience. One of the basic concepts that I learned is the idea of "orende."

Orende is twisted hair word for the psychokinetic force carried in the outer part of the body. It is the energy that makes a substance what it is. The highest level of this energy for people is considered to be a 10. Human beings, according to these teachings, are the only beings who have a free will, which enables us to move orende up and down the scale. Rocks with an orende of 2, plants with an orende of 3, and animals with an orende of 4 are complete and are thought to be fully in harmony with the purposes of nature or sacred mystery. All humans are said to be incarnated with an orende of 10, which drops during pregnancy and birth process and then slowly builds up again. Orende increases or decreases from a dynamic interplay of several factors: the physical, emotional, mental, and spiritual, and the quality and degree of relationship with what analytical psychology identifies as the ego, the environment, and the Self. If the mother is spiritually, physically, mentally, and emotionally stable, safe, nurtured, and supported during the pregnancy and birth process, the orende of the child remains high. If the child is welcomed and parented in an environment that is balanced in these areas, then the orende of the child remains high. To the extent that the physical, emotional, mental, and spiritual energies of the child are supported and nourished, the orende of the child remains high; to the extent that the environment negatively impacts these same aspects, the orende drops. As orende increases, wisdom and knowledge are thought to increase.

Persons are differentiated from human beings on the basis of their orende. A person is not considered to be human until he or she has an average orende of 5, and enlightened human beings are considered to have an average orende or 8, among all four aspects. Orende levels fluctuate because of the dynamic relationship between the factors mentioned above and because these factors shift accordingly with the challenges of life. In Jungian terms, the development of orende is like the process of containment of energy that emerges as the ego-Self axis develops. With this concept in mind, I looked back over my training in martial arts and saw that I had never worked to develop my physical orende, and my exercise had impacted me emotionally, mentally, and spiritually.

Orende is energy and all energy is thought to be related to the four cardinal directions. Each direction works with energy or orende in a different way and relates to a different aspect within a person. The way the energy works is considered to be the power of the direction. The aspect of the person that works with that energy is considered to be a shield that is young or old, masculine or feminine (Loomis 1988) (fig. 1 and fig. 3).

The south is the direction of water; it carries the emotional aspect of human beings, and in this direction energy is given away in order to create balance. The north carries the element of air; it is the mental aspect of human beings and balances through receptivity. The west is the direction of earth and the human body; in the west, the energy from the north and south poles is received and contained. The west pulls mental and emotional energy into itself, the way a magnet attracts iron fillings or the way that an unknown something within a crystal causes it to form itself in certain ways. In analytical psychology, the west would be considered the place

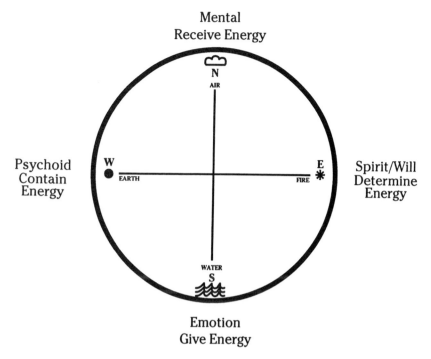

Mental
Receive Energy

Psychoid
Contain
Energy

Spirit/Will
Determine
Energy

Emotion
Give Energy

Figure 1

where body and image are intertwined, and I have substituted the word *psychoid* for the Native American word *body* in the west.

> The idea of the psychoid unconscious was first put forward by Jung in 1946. His formulation has three aspects: it refers to a level of, or in, the unconscious which is completely inaccessible to consciousness. It is neutral in character being neither wholly psychological nor wholly physiological, but being both. . . . [The psychoid] embraces the two poles (image and body) and can be experienced and comprehended through either. (Samuels, Shorter and Plaut 1986, p. 122)

The east is the location of the sun or fire; it is the direction of spirit or "will." In this direction balance is achieved by determining or defining the movement of energy through action.

The concept of the powers of the four directions became a way for me to reflect on my martial arts practice. One of the first forms that I practiced to heal my back was a series of eighteen movements which face cyclically in each of the four directions. I practiced only this series of movements for about three years. I would move slowly, smoothly, and sometimes hold each of the eighteen positions for as long as a minute. Many of the positions were painful to move into and difficult to hold. Even so, as I practiced, I began to love this form that was my teacher, and I was told it took an enlightened master a whole lifetime to perfect these movements. In my secret heart, since I had no English word to call it, I named my teacher "tree form," after the trees which are so rooted in earth, so strongly reaching for the sky, and yet bending and swaying with the winds of change.

It was this series of movements through the four directions which healed my back and taught me how to make pain a friend (see fig. 2). It is difficult to put my physical experience into words and easier to use imagination to make the transition from body to meaning. Imagine a body that is twisted into an uncomfortable posture with iron bands holding that body in place for many years. Imagine the bands being removed. The person would have to be taught to move again, to develop the muscles that had been neglected and to relax the muscles that had been overdeveloped. The person would have to relearn movement. In a psychological sense, analysis does this with relations between the ego and the unconscious that are blocked or rigidified and need to be freed. In a physical sense, "tree form" did this for me, and in the doing my orende was raised.

From what I understand, in the twisted hair tradition the teachings of balancing the energies of the four directions are considered to be a legacy from the matriarchy and have their roots in feminine experience. In these teachings, the balance achieved is considered to be dynamic rather than static and always changing in response to the demands and challenges of life or nature. When one works dynamically with these concepts, it is said that one is dancing the wheel. Tree form taught me to dance the wheel physically. In a sense, physical movement and conceptual experience are quite removed from one another, and I had difficulty making meaning come from my physical experience of marital arts training. For me, the concept of balancing the shields, which is the human experience of the energies of the four directions, gave me a way to make meaning out of something that seemed deep and quite mysterious. I began to think of myself as dancing the wheel and of my need to make meaning as a dance that was mental, rather than physical.

When life presents a challenge, the north-south axis becomes

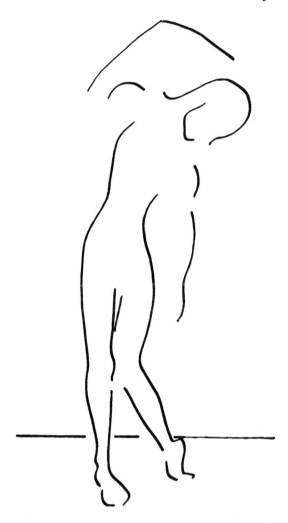

Figure 2: *Tree Form, one position of eighteen*

activated. Emotions flow and are received along with other impressions by the mind. At the same time, these energies are held by the psychoid dimension. To the extent that energy flows along the north-south axis, the west holds or compensates and, with introspection, transforms (see fig. 3). Images and physical responses are produced in dreaming and fantasy life which compensate and complement the movement of energy along the north-

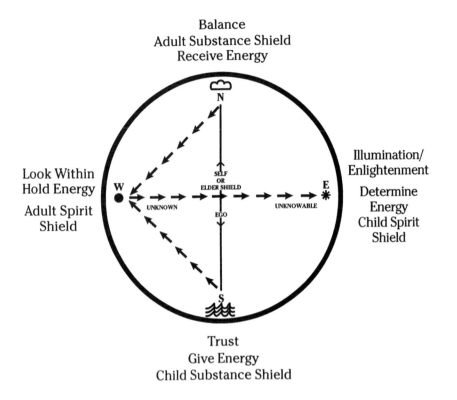

Balance
Adult Substance Shield
Receive Energy

Look Within
Hold Energy

Adult Spirit
Shield

Illumination/
Enlightenment

Determine
Energy
Child Spirit
Shield

Trust
Give Energy
Child Substance Shield

Figure 3

south axis. The psychoid reality of the west holds and stores the north-south energy. What is produced is disease, nightmare, and dreaming. If the energy is allowed to flow in the north-south axis, transformation of energy (which can be as simple as reflecting on the nightly dreaming) is distilled spirit or will. Will is considered to be a human faculty which can determine energy movement and behavior in harmony with the purposes of the Self. It is the link with the unknowable or nature.

I have placed the Self in the center of this wheel. As orende is increased in each of the four directions, the ego-Self axis develops. In the south is the child substance shield containing all of the experiences in a person's life encoded on themes of feelings. If emotions are released and given away, trust in the Self and a child-like innocence develop as orende increases. In the north is the adult substance shield. As orende increases the person becomes more receptive mentally and more balanced. The north-south shields are part of our material reality, and in the sense that they have been or are a part of that reality, they are said to be known. In the west is the adult spirit shield. It is considered to be contrasexual to the material gender (Loomis 1988). A woman has a little girl shield in the south, an adult woman shield in the north and an adult man shield in the west. A man would have the opposite. As orende increases, the function of the adult spirit shield is to lead a person to look within and discover the unknown or, in other words, to assist in the development of introspection. In analytical psychology this shield would be considered the anima or animus. In the east is the child spirit shield. It is also contrasexual to the material gender. In the case of a woman, it would be a little boy; for a man, a little girl. Its function is to lead the person into a relationship with the unknowable or sacred mystery. As orende increases in the east, illumination and a progression toward enlightenment occurs. In the center of this wheel is the elder shield, with the ego. The elder shield is imagined by the twisted hairs as the old wise woman and the old wise man. It is considered synonymous with what analytical psychologists call the Self. Its function is to nourish and to support a relationship between the person's ego and each of the four directions. The elder shield supports the development of the ego-Self axis.

The process I am describing can be understood by looking at a tree. The tree faces four directions simultaneously. It is impacted and changed by the environment, and there is within it something indefinable which makes it unique and yet similar to others of its species. That indefinable something is spirit, and it develops like a fetus does in pregnancy. However, the actual tree does not possess an ego. The ego in a person can be the observer, the humble worker, or the clinging tyrant. It can cooperate with or obstruct nature. It is the ego that has a connection with each of the four directions. As spirit or will is distilled, the ego assumes the position of a servant. The higher Self (the "as above") is dynamically related to the ego (the "so below"), and the function of the ego is the process of accommodation and assimilation (McCann and Pearlman 1990, p. 7).

When accommodation to and assimilation of change cannot take place, orende cannot increase. Orende can be raised by balancing the four directions and distilling spirit, or it can be frozen or dropped through a constant reactive or victim stance toward the world. The person goes inward through self-castigation and depression (self-victimization) or looks outward and blames others for their problems (projection). The ego swells and is subjected to touchiness, moodiness, and mental noise. It falls victim to a horde of feeling tones and rigid thoughts and gradually becomes unable to relate to the higher Self or to others. It is helpful, when thinking about lowering orende, to return to the wheel and use it to clarify how energy is bound in each of the four directions (fig. 4).

Lowering orende in the south takes place through dependence and attachment to the patterns of thought, feeling, and behavior learned in the family of origin. There is little true emotion that flows in response to the present moment; rather, feeling tones exist with or without stimulation in repetitive and predictable patterns. When this is the case, emotions are held; they are received from others or they determine behavior. Orende in the south increases by freeing one's own emotional energy through mental receptivity, through changing the physical patterning of the feel-

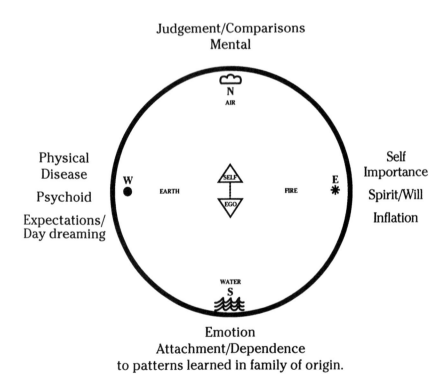

Figure 4: *Lowering of orende*

ing tones which are held, through habit, by the body. It is also raised through a feeling connection with and a reflection upon dream images.

In the north, orende is lowered through judgments and comparisons (fig. 4). Judgments occur when we limit our own or someone else's experience or set up a standard norm that defines what we or others may or may not receive mentally. Comparisons occur when we limit ourselves or others by a set of external standards. Others are labeled as primitive, unsophisticated, heretics, or any other label that makes our mental standards or our group's mental standards better than or less than another person or group. To increase orende in the north, one needs to stay focused in the now, to receive emotions as they are experienced, to learn to be flexible with our belief system and see not only our own point of view but to try to develop the ability to perceive reality from another point of view. Studying what others have felt and thought and questioning our own experience in this light, learning about ourselves, our symbology, our heritage, our myth, about all that goes on within and around us with wonder and curiosity raises orende. Keeping the mind an open cup and learning to receive rather than give, hold, or determine mentally will develop orende in the north.

In the west, orende is lowered through organic disease, self-abuse, daydreaming, and expectations (fig. 4). It is easy to understand how disease and self-abuse lower orende. The lowering of orende through daydreaming or expectations is more difficult to understand. Daydreaming, or what analytical psychologists would call passive fantasy, keeps one removed or mentally and emotionally separated from being present in physical reality. One is only present in fantasy. Energy is held but not transformed because there is no introspection, and therefore no conscious connection with what is going on mentally and emotionally. On the other hand, expectations hold outer reality frozen and lower orende through a projected form of containment. When expectations operate, the holding or containing function is transferred to an environment or to a person who is expected to perform the containing function, for example, "If only he (she, they, it) would change, I could improve my life." In this way, something out there becomes the container, and because it cannot contain, transformation cannot take place. When the nature of the psychoid realm is not embraced but is given away, or received without reflection, or when it determines behavior with no reflection, looking within has not been developed. Raising orende in the west comes through a conscious relationship with fantasy and image, and/or certain kinds of physical training such as martial arts. A reflective relationship with the unknown reality of the psychoid realm releases energy and allows it to flow through the body in a contained and vibrant way rather than being held unconsciously in patterns that create a depression of energy (lowering of orende).

In the east, self-importance or inflation lowers orende (fig. 4). Inflation is a state in which something small (the ego) has appropriated to itself the qualities of something larger (the Self) and hence is blown up beyond the limits of its proper size. There is no ego-Self axis because there is no spirit. This axis develops, or not, to the extent that spirit is distilled. The human spirit, as it is distilled, has a relationship with the unknowable or, as the twisted hairs call it, the sacred mystery. And paradoxically, the human spirit is the child born from the relationship of the ego to the Self (see fig. 3). In the twisted hair teachings, maturity or human being-ness is indicated by the existence of the ego-Self axis, with the ego related to the Self. Spirit is thought to be located in the body (just a little below the navel) in these teachings, and it is spirit in the east that develops in the mature human being from a distillation that naturally occurs from balancing the other three directions. The tension that creates the dynamic movement of the three directions and the distillation of spirit is the ego-Self axis at the center of the wheel. When the ego is identified with the "as above" by appropriating the authority of the old wise woman and the old wise man to itself or projecting this authority out onto figures in the environment, there can be no movement within the wheel.

When there is no movement within the wheel, the conscious attitude is rigidified and the normal process of compensation that exists between the ego and the unconscious is lost. The person becomes more and more neurotic. Another way to say this is that when orende is being balanced in the south with the giving of emotions, in the west with the containment of energy through introspection in the psychoid realm, and in the north with the mental energies being receptive, will or spirit in the east must develop. But when the ego is in an inflationary state and identified with the higher Self, there is a blockage in one or more of the other directions. When we hold, receive, or determine only with our emotions, we are out of balance. When we give, receive, or determine only with our body or our images, we are out of balance. When we give, determine, or hold only with our mind, we are out of balance. To the extent that we are out of balance in one direction, the other directions try to compensate. Being out of balance is directly related to lowered orende levels and immaturity.

> Childhood is innocent but it is also irresponsible, hence it has all the ambiguities of being firmly connected with the archetypal psyche and its extra personal energy, and at the same time being unconsciously identified with it and unrealistically related to it . . . the basic problem for the adult is how to achieve the union with nature and the gods with which the child starts, without bringing about the inflation of identification. (Edinger 1973, p. 11)

Working with the concept of raising or lowering orende through the proper or improper use of energy is an ancient concept, yet it is a powerful way to express the idea of individuation or normal development into a human being.

As spirit or will is distilled from a balancing of the other three directions, orende is increased. The person becomes a mature human being, capable of truly moral behavior and humble demeanor, accepting, not avoiding, the shadow. The reason for this is that when emotions flow and the mind is receptive, one cannot deny one's darkest secrets or highest aspirations.

In martial arts training, the body provides a container where ego and shadow meet and the tension of that meeting is held. Special movements, developed over generations, cleanse the body and refine its energy. Psychologically, one's laziness, pride, greed, competitiveness, and other shadow components bubble up and come to mind when these special body positions are held or moved through. This process is very difficult to explain because the experience differs from individual to individual. What I think is happening is that body is compensating for the conscious attitude the way a dream does.

Different movements evoke different responses, just as different dream images evoke different responses. Gradually the student learns to pay close attention to the way the movements are being experienced and to work with different movements at different times. It is also important to have a teacher who can observe the student's movement and know which forms of movement would be most helpful for that person to practice at a given time. After my back became stronger, I was allowed to begin to practice forms that would increase my strength, endurance, and flexibility. One of these forms was called ocean form and was developed by linking human movement with the movements of the ocean (see fig. 5). The ocean was considered to be one of the strongest, most

Figure 5: *Ocean Form, one position in a form that is five hours long*

powerful forces of nature, and therefore very martial. As I began to practice the form, I began to feel in tune with a yielding, receptive, watery form of being that replicated a soft, fluid motion that was now high, and in the next breath low, exploding upward, then imploding inward, like the waves on the surface of the ocean. Underneath the movement, an immutable, deeply peaceful, ever-changing force within my own being connected me with life, just as a drop is a part of the ocean. The drop changes, it is never lost, it is always a part of and never the whole of. The discipline required to perform each movement accurately and then weave the move-ments together smoothly creates a sense of allowing or cooperat-ing with the reality behind the movement.

Nothing in the world is softer or more yielding than water.
But, for wearing down the hard and strong,
there is nothing like it.
That yielding overcomes the strong
and softness overcomes the hard
Is something that is known by all,
but is practiced by few.
(Ni 1979, p. 94)

Repetitive practice of ocean form frees my emotional and mental energies and allows me to become more flexible, receptive, and introspective. I feel deep peace as I concentrate on moving accurately and smoothly through this form. The need to focus attention fully on the position of the body, whether in motion or in stillness, forces me to let go of egocentric concerns and stand within the still point of the present moment. This experience seems to me to be a form of meditation that lessens the danger of inflation and allows a natural and balanced increase in the orende, rather than increasing orende only in the north-south (mental-emotional) axis and leaving out or fighting the psychoid and spiritual realities of human experience.

As I began to feel younger, healthier, and more deeply in touch with all of my experience, I became increasingly puzzled about what was happening to me. I began to look for the roots of martial arts in Chinese history and found them in alchemy, a discipline common to both East and West and connected with meditation. In the East, the emphasis was on body, longevity, and the elixir of immortality; in the West, the emphasis was on transmuting base metal into gold. Both, I think, deal with the archetype of individuation, both are related to an experience of psychoid reality that creates a balance through introspection and facilitates the development of the ego-Self axis.

In Chinese Taoist (alchemical) thought, a person refined physical energy through progressive stages into spiritual energy that was deeply aligned with the Tao. This took place through ongoing effort in physical training, diet, emotional discipline and meditation . . . . The ongoing effort was considered to be a state of being, a process, rather than one single moment frozen in time . . . . Rather it was seen as deeply related to the cares and concerns of everyday life . . . . The goal of this ongoing process was an ever-increasing union of opposites . . . . There is an inner light in all of us, only we do not see it until we have

> refined and purified our body . . . . When we do, it will not only
> be brightness on brightness but also yin and yang combined.
> (Deng Ming Dao 1991, pp. 22–23, 312–314)

In martial arts practice, the body itself becomes a mandala. The earth of the body and the air sustaining it are inseparably linked. Movement of the body through the forms creates an awareness of breath and the need for air. Breathing patterns are often quite specific for the particular form being practiced and make the bodily movements more difficult to perform but at the same time deepen the experience of the movements. The breath (air) combined with movements (earth) creates burning (fire) in the muscles and heats the body until sweat (water) is produced. In olden times, these operations blackened the belt and the clothing used for practice, which is how rank was earned. The center of the body, just below the navel, is where the breathing takes place and it is thought to be the place from which all movement originates. I have learned from Swift Deer that this is the location of will or spirit. The movements of the body trace a mandala that moves out from this center. The body was not ignored in Western alchemy, but the experience of it seems to be less physical and more subtly connected with image.

In Western alchemy,

> Paracelsus attributes incorruptibility to a special virtue or agent named "balsam" . . . . it is produced by a "bodily operation." The idea that the art can make something higher than nature is typically alchemical . . . . "In the first place, the impure animate body must be purified through the separation of the elements, which is done by your meditating upon it; this consists in the confirmation of your mind beyond all bodily and mechanic work." In this way "a new form is impressed" on the impure body. (Jung 1942, par. 170–172)

Here, although the emphasis is on the image, I believe that the process being described is the same. Over and over in the alchemical treatises, the four elements of air, earth, fire, and water are mentioned as the substances transformed and transformative, leading to the transmutation of the base metal into the pure gold. The difference is in the way the psychoid reality is reflected upon: East transforming through an experience of body and West transforming through an experience of image. (For an in-depth look at the historical development of alchemy, see Cooper 1987 and Johnson 1974.)

As I explored the similarities and differences between Eastern and Western alchemy, I began to understand that the archetype of individuation was the root of my intense captivation with my martial arts practice. Unaware, I had stumbled upon this archetype manifested through physical movement, rather than image. Jung used the term *individuation* to describe the process "by which a person becomes a psychological 'in-dividual,' that is, a separate, indivisible unity or 'whole'" (Jung 1939, par. 490). He speaks of the process of individuation as if the existence of a potential wholeness were always present, and the process itself as a knitting together of what already exists (Jung 1951, par. 278). It seems to me that what Jung is describing combines disciplined focus with yielding and letting go, like a heart beating—open and being filled, then contracting and expelling its contents. This alternating experience of focus and yielding is what moving through the martial arts forms is like for me. They work together and cannot exist apart.

Jung links Ares, the Greek god of war, with the individuation process itself and uses Ares and the word *individuation* interchangeably. Certainly the word *Mars*, the Roman counterpart of Ares, is etymologically linked to the word *martial*. He says:

> Ares, accordingly, is an intuitive concept for a preconscious, creative, and formative principle which is capable of giving life to individual creatures . . . and as such it plays an important role in the purification of the natural man by fire and his transformation into an "Enochdianus." (Jung 1942, par. 177)

The Enochdianus to which Jung refers is an aspect of long-lived Melchisedek who was considered to be a prefiguration of Christ. Jung connects Ares with the body and the affective-instinctual nature of human beings and implies that the Ares energy is the container or theme of the alchemical opus and supports the transformative processes associated with the work.

Ares really is an appropriate presiding deity, because balancing the mandala of the body in daily practice is difficult. The mind, the emotions, the body, and the will are often at war with one another. And so I was delighted to find the god of war named in alchemical thought. The movements I practice are more than 1,500 years old and are the products of generations of study by enlightened masters who came to terms with this war between the mind, the emotions, the body, and the will and learned how to raise orende through refining the physical body. The movements are hard to perform and correct position is often so painful that it can only be entered into a little at a time, a real battle. One gradually learns to yield to the transformative power of the movement, which acts much the same way the symbol does. Self-importance withers in the face of basic organic experience.

Daily practice of these highly specialized movements is challenging and provides an experience of individuation at a totally different level. Pushing the body just past the point of endurance, shaking and burning when holding a position yet concentrating to hold that position, moving when it feels as if there is no more breath to move, relaxing into pain rather than fighting it, continuing on in the face of weakness, laziness, mood swings, and fatigue, and learning from mistakes are all metaphors for the lessons learned in the practice room, lessons that each of us have to learn daily from the challenges that life gives to us. In a physical way, these are the experiences of individuation, and I have come to a deeper awareness of them from the war between my physical parts. Ares is activated in the separation of the elements of my being; mindfulness, endurance, patience. and introspection allow these parts to recombine in greater purity. To set aside a time, three or four days a week, and a sacred space where these lessons are heightened willingly creates an experience that seems to me to be similar in many ways to Jungian analysis. In analysis, we learn to go into the unconscious (the unknown) and come into relationship with our contrasexual aspects. In Western alchemy, there is a sense of cooperation and union between the masculine and feminine, and a union of body (yin) with mind (yang) in Eastern alchemy.

In the Native American pipe ceremony that I have learned from Swift Deer, the pipe is "married" by inserting the masculine stem into the feminine bowl. The entire pipe ceremony is a celebration of the relationship between Great Grandmother (form) and Great Grandfather (image) and their lovemaking which produces sacred mystery. It is sacred mystery which dances all of creation into being and imbues all of creation with its awareness. It is this union of form and image in the psychoid realm that creates our spirit, our enlightenment. How different this is from our own patriarchal mythology. In the twisted hair teachings, there is no hierarchy of power, no lordship or dominion, no casting out into a vale of suffering. There is balance and value in all of life, for all of life is imbued with spirit. In these teachings, it is thought that as orende increases in the human, the vibrational rate of the person increases until it is more and more in harmony with the purposes of sacred mystery. This is a poetic way to think about individuation.

If Ares is the principle underlying individuation and war is a male-dominated pastime, how could I be having bodily experiences that feel deeply feminine? What does the martial mean in martial arts? Why is the twisted hair word for warrior the same as that for priest or priestess? What would Ares (Mars) have to do with the individuation process? The answers to these questions are embedded in the twisted hair teachings. The relationship between the complementary energies of form, body or matter (the feminine), and image (the masculine) is central to the individuation process. That process is sacred and needs protection and nourishment. That is why the word for warrior in the twisted hair teachings does not have gender and is synonymous with the word for priest/priestess. It is the warrior within each of us that facilitates the development of the ego-Self axis by confronting the outer or inner tyrants that disturb or disrupt that process.

Individuation requires a space which is protected so that self-reflection can take place and self-awareness can develop. It requires being present in the now and implies developing the quality of mindfulness. It requires a disidentification with the persona used to relate to the outer world so that one can develop an inner orientation and learn to be receptive to one's own experiences in the present moment. The twisted hairs refer to this process in a very musical way: they call it dancing your sacred dream awake, and in order to do this one must be a warrior, a priest/priestess. It is the warrior within us who leaps into the unknown of the present moment.

One of the ways I have found to amplify and summarize this experience is a poem written by a fourteenth-century Samurai warrior. It is called "A Warrior's Creed."

I have no parents: I make the heavens and earth my parent.
I have no home: I make awareness my home.
I have no life or death: I make the tides of breathing my life and death.
I have no divine power: I make honesty my divine power.
I have no means: I make understanding my means.
I have no magic secrets: I make character my magic secret.
I have no body: I make endurance my body.
I have no eyes: I make the flash of lightning my eyes.
I have no ears: I make sensibility my ears.
I have no limbs: I make promptness my limbs.
I have no strategy: I make "unshadowed by thought" my strategy.

I have no designs: I make "seizing opportunity by the forelock" my
  design.
I have no miracle: I make right action my miracles.
I have no principles: I make adaptability to all circumstances my
  principles.
I have no tactics: I make emptiness and fullness my tactics.
I have no talents: I make ready wit my talent.
I have no friends: I make my mind my friend
I have no enemy: I make carelessness my enemy.
I have no armor: I make benevolence and righteousness my armor.
I have no castle: I make immovable mind my castle.
I have no sword: I make absence of self my sword.
(Blum 1982, p. 60)

References

Blum, Ralph. 1982. *Book of Runes*. New York: St. Martin's Press.

Cooper, J. C. 1987. *Chinese Alchemy*. Wellingborough, Northampton-shire: Aquarian Press.

Deng Ming Dao. 1991. *Scholar Warrior*. San Francisco: HarperCollins.

Edinger, Edward. 1973. *Ego and Archetype*. New York: Penguin Books.

Johnson, Aued Simon. 1974. *Gold: Historical and Economic Aspects*. New York: Arno Press.

Jung, C. G. 1939. Conscious, unconscious and individuation. In *CW* 9i:275–289. Princeton, N.J.: Princeton University Press, 1959.

_____. 1942. Paracelsus as a spiritual phenomenon. In *CW* 13:109–188. Princeton, N.J.: Princeton University Press, 1967.

_____. 1951. The psychology of the child archetype. In *CW* 9i:151–181. Princeton, N.J.: Princeton University Press, 1959.

Loomis, Mary E. 1988. Balancing the shields. *Quadrant* 21(2):35–50.

McCann, Lisa, and Laurie Ann Pearlman. 1990. *Psychological Trauma and the Adult Survivor*. New York: Brunner/Mazel.

Ni, Hua-Ching, trans. 1979. *The Complete Works of Lao Tzu*. Los Angeles: College of Tao and Traditional Chinese Healings.

Samuels, A., Boni Shorter, and F. Plaut. 1986. *A Critical Dictionary of Jungian Analysis*. New York: Routledge & Kegan Paul.

Brenda Donahue *is a member of the Chicago Society of Jung-ian analysts. She has a private practice in Oakbrook Terrace,*

Illinois, and holds a second-degree black belt in Chung Moo martial arts.

The origins of Chung Moo martial arts can be traced to China before the Han dynasty. The tradition and knowledge of more than fifteen centuries was brought to the United States in the 1970s by Chong Su Nim, Iron Kim, 8th generation master.

Figure 1. The Queen of Swords

Swordplay

Elizabeth Retivov

I walked up the rickety dark stairs of an old unremarkable building on the back streets of New York. The fumes of the car repair garage below fueled my anxiety and trepidation. A woman in her middle years, a bit overweight, I was well aware of how I looked and what ostensibly got me there—a curiosity sparked by a chance article on aikido, a Japanese martial art, and an inner nettlesome and often renegade tomboy. This and additional concerns caused me to question seriously what I was doing on these pitched stairs.

As I entered the dojo, I was unprepared for my response. Coming out of the dark, I was dazzled by the clear sunlight, the spare white walls, and the white canvas matting. My eyes were pulled to a recessed alcove at the end of the hushed room where they were held by the calm and burning eyes of an ancient man with a wispy gray beard, Morihei Ueshiba, the founding father of aikido.

In the hush, all was alive. I watched the students in white uniforms, some with black *hakamas*, kneel in orderly rows and wait attentively. The sensei entered. Bowing. Heads to mat. To the Master. To the sensei. The sensei to the students. And so the practice began.

I was in love, and I could not escape the inevitability of that in which I felt myself so powerfully caught. Lightning had hit, and I was on fire.

As it splits the dark sky and strikes the fecund earth, lightning is the first sword—insisting light into primal dark; printing brilliant patterns that crackle indelibly across the vast sky of mind. Unlike the experience of the constant stars, or the predictably fluctuating moon, or the propitiated certainty of the ever-renewing sun in his daily course and night-sea journey, white lightning hits, dances, severs, rivets, pierces, slashes, burns—inspiring holy fear and wonder. Naked blades of lightning like the naked steel blade of the sword, revealed in a flash from the secret dark hilt, startle the heart. Blood runs when lightning runs across the sky and strikes, and when the sword dances, thrusts, and cuts.

Entering

In my still-stiff white workout uniform, I am now on the practice mat. Awkwardly, I am learning to roll my body forward and to fall backward from a standing position, to move obliquely in relation to my partner who is attacking me with full intent to hit. The first lesson of the warrior it seems is about being round, moving softly yet firmly—and letting go. Paradox materializes. A lifetime of body armoring is threatened.

I feel exhilarated, alive—but also clumsy and ridiculous. I'm aware that I certainly am not "a natural." As I set out on this unknown enterprise, my mind flashes warning lights. I know these kinds of experiences cut into deep internal structures. They betoken places of initiation and sacrifice. Given my passion, which in spite of all my fears is driving me forward, I muse on the cautionary tale of Semele. She could not wait for the god-child of passion, Dionysus, to ripen slowly to term in her womb. Instead of staying to listen to the subtle inner processes and husband the slow incubation, she became possessed by the desire to behold the unmediated countenance of the godhead, Father Lightning Flash, Zeus himself. Zeus warned her. She insisted. In the flash of his splendor, she was holocausted. She touched a holy thing outside the protections of a sacralized space. Death can result when the unprepared, uninitiated self is exposed to the powerful and potentially destructive energy of the life force itself. I am warned. It is here in this deep threat that I find the entry point, the opening into the energy circle of lightning.

Lightning, the Create manifesting from the Uncreate and, according to Plutarch, the originator of all life: "the heavenly Phallos fertilizing the primal waters with its primitive energy" (Nichols 1984, p. 285), is the archetypal opener. It traces a white calligraphy of life and death against the darkling sky. As Jung notes, lightning signifies

> a sudden, unexpected, and overpowering change of psychic condition.
> "In this Spirit of the Fire-flash consists the Great Almighty Life," says Jakob Böhme. "For when you strike upon the *sharp* part of the stone, the bitter sting of Nature sharpens itself, and is stirred in the highest degree. For Nature is dissipated or *broken asunder* in the sharpness, so that the *Liberty shines forth as a flash.*" (Jung 1950, par. 533–534)

The fire-flash, like the sword, breaks asunder the stone, the fixed and rigid parts of ourselves, and in the opening of the darkness of stone to light, severed from Nature, we begin to see. This swift opening to light, or consciousness, is rent violently as in the manner of lighting and of the sword. The "Liberty" is yet in flash form, in potentia. We must suffer further operations, like the sword itself in its forging, if we, like the finished and living sword, are to have balance, weight, and truth when singing through the air to the goal.

As the sculptor surveys his stone for flaws, he finds the fault line. Along that line will be the opening that will split the stone but not smash it. With a single blow, clean like a sword stroke or lightning thrust, the stone is opened. So begins the liberation of the inhered form of that unique stone. Under the listening hands of the sculptor, the slow, hard, careful chiseling gradually brings the stone to its destined end, wherein the potential form is released, stroke by stroke. As the stonework unfolds, the sculptor, in the rhythm of movement and rest, inhale and exhale, systole and diastole, opens herself and enters into the unfolding rhythm of the stone's life. In this way the stone and the sculptor unite. So, too, unfolds the individual struck open to the individuation process.

As the earth's stone undergoes a rebirth at the hands of the sculptor, so the mined metal of the sword comes to shape in the carefully tended fires of the swordmaker, moving through black to red to white. The woman who forges her sword must, in a parallel process and with slow, hard, careful work, also temper her lightning energy from black to red to white like the sword which she would claim and carry.

In aikido, although there is regular practice with wooden swords, the sword is seen as an extension of the hand-blade, the edge of the palm and little finger, the whole of which is the blade through which the circulating *ki* (*chi*) or invisible life force extends. To begin to help focus this energy, my teacher often repeated the thought that when practicing with the sword, practice as if you have none, and when practicing without the sword, move as if you have one in hand. This caveat continually reminds me that my relationship with the inner sword is the subject of the practice. In the play of the seen and the unseen, the "is" and the "is not," each motion can become a sword cut, and each cut potentially carries the lightning-sword energy, enfolding spiritual authority and temporal power.

My task is to keep kindled and to refine the light and power of the "spirit of the Fire-flash." Pointing to the moon does not thus become confused with the moon. This is my reference point when I yield to the magic of the aggressive power of a hard punch. There is a deeper magic. I begin to intuit that energy when I hold that power inside. There it pools in the furnace that is deep in my abdomen to dance me mercurially like lightning—a shape-changer, yet the inner power endures, sealed in that inner vessel, the alchemical *athenor*, the belly's *hara*.

To see advanced swordswomen proud and powerful as the male warriors on the mat strikes deep into the labyrinthine darkness of my female patriarchal conditioning. Out of the blackness other new thoughts began to shimmer into form. I don't have "Liberty shining forth as a flash" (Böhme) and am not free and liberated until I know how to strike and to cut. To say I am a woman who knows how and is willing to kill, shock. Death is the truth of the warrior's sword, and it can teach how to live in the timeless moment of life evanescent. A further thought expands in my mind. In carrying the sword of compassion to spare or to slay, I carry empathy's opposite, her correction and her balance, her natural partner. Taking up the living sword to travel a warrior's path delivers that knowledge of compassion, the skillful means which spontaneously, like hair growing, knows when to slay, when to spare. In liberating compassion the immediacy of living is established.

The warrior, when pressed to stay in the service of a "lord," may or may not choose to lend her sword and life to the endeavor. She is a free agent, made independent by means of her sword knowledge and the sword oath she has sworn: "Before the Lady of Stars and by her Holy Fire I swear—I will never be false to the Truth that is within me; I will deal justice to my enemies and keep faith with my friends. And if ever I dishonor lord or kindred of the blade I bear, may it turn against me and may my ghost forever wander without comfort in the dark" (Paxson 1984, p. 199). She and her sword, listening to the inner high priestess, choose when and where they will journey.

In the second half of my life, the path of a swordswoman who can cut cleanly, beyond conscious thought and from the source of her being, is an image as compelling as union with any lover was in my younger years. In the dance of the sword, self, sword, and other unite in a movement that is as ancient as time itself, as "advance and retreat and around again . . . the stars circle the heavens and the fires leap and fall . . . her senses encompassed her enemy—(she knew) he was part of her as she was part of the burning air, the fire, the stone on which she danced" (ibid., p. 198). One moves into the rhythm of life herself. There in the sword, freedom is redeemed.

The Jungian individuation process can be characterized as a series of initiation points within a larger spiral pattern. The evolution of the swordmaster is one pattern or model for this process, during which the self, like the recombinant metal of the sword and the swordswoman who would claim it, is in a parallel process tempered to life in the successive firings. Thus, to live the prospective function is to move forward with the Life Force, guided by a notion that there is a series of increasingly complex and potentially deadly initiations to be accomplished. Each initiation on the path will rotate consciousness to such a degree that a different perspective and relationship to the world and self will be launched, generating its own values, laws, and sensibilities, usually at swords point with the previous course. Initiation is a sword of self-sacrifice that leaves the old orientation, with which one was previously identified, dead and that is experienced as a deathlike suffering.

The trajectory of the developing sword consciousness and the various points of initiation and transformation can be viewed as a pentagram or five-pointed star, which holds and binds the "Fire-flash" (Böhme) as it gradually tempers in the sacrificial furnace of devotion, practice, and discipline. Each point of the star sets a new direction for the woman on this path and marks a critical initiatory way station. These critical junctures can be imaged as different warrior mentalities, all of which are immanent within us.

Out of the original primal light, which is simultaneously fecundating agent, source, and path, is born a warrior force like that of Cuchulainn the Celt. Gripped in an all-consuming "warp-spasm," he evokes and unleashes "the earth magic of full thunder, the tellurian electricity housed in the blood which flows . . . and stains (the earth) like a draught of wine" (Durrell 1990, p. 138).[1] The next point in the pentagram, requiring a volte-face in a vertical thrust upwards, is carried by the image of the knight-hero Lancelot, who binds himself to the stern Guinevere, Arthur's warrior queen of the Courts of Love. Then comes the long horizontal transverse—a veritable dark night of the soul—to the realm of the likes of the legendary aikido master Ueshiba, who at any moment is ready and can best a younger armed samurai buck with but a fragile fan.

Last, before the final reunion with the source and physical death, is the location point of the sage, who has realized the internalized sword, which is crystallized into a manifestation of the living light: Böhme's "Liberty shining forth." This is visualized in the image of Ueshiba, who is now weaponless. He kneels in prayer, suffused and illuminated by the light source. In this pentagramatic model, the warrior-sage occupies the same low ground as the Celt. However, he returns to live in the tellurian world a totally changed and different man. He lives as a part of all, in the thick of life, yet "alone," not caught in the past nor drowned in the present nor bedazzled or worried by the future. Humbly, in the marketplace of life, he lives the sword of life and death, moment to moment in the eternal now.

To reform and refine the raw bloody sword power into the sword of the gods and the stick of awakening, one must homeopathically put oneself to the sword. Like the knight Sir Lancelot,

---

[1]In *The Tain*, the hero Cuchulainn is seized and transformed by the "warp-spasm" which runs through his body. It turns him into a "monstrous thing, hideous and shapeless, unheard of" (Kinsella 1970, pp. 150, 151). In this "seized" mode, larger than life, he drives out to kill his enemies.

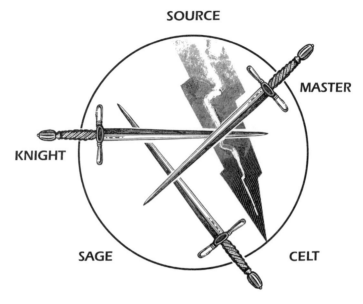

SOURCE

MASTER

KNIGHT

SAGE

CELT

Figure 2

who elects to crawl on his hands and knees across a deadly sharp sword bridge to rescue his queen, the swordswoman also will resolve to undertake the "sword bridge." She will begin to learn to sacrifice her own blood, not another's, when she struggles like this knight to make the passage to the fearful land of the dead to retrieve another aspect of self. To cross the razor-thin bridging paths from the point of the Celt, to that of the knight, and on to the master and to the sage, she paradoxically offers her blood in multiple small acts of willing and voluntary self-sacrifice. So is the sword power polished and refined.

A vignette from the classic sword movie series, *Samurai*, cuts to the essence of the swordswoman's path. The hero, played by Toshiro Mifune, at this point still a rough-and-ready Celt fighter, easily swept up into the Celtic "warp-spasm," cockily walks into the small shop of the master sword polisher, whose faded sign reads: "Souls of Samurai Polished." The sword polisher, a most unprepossessing old man, one who has perhaps attained the sage realm of the pentagram, asks, "How would you like to have this polished, sir?" Mifune replies, "Sharp enough to cut." The old man replies, "I decline. Read that sign out there. I polish the swords of samurai, not sharpen murderous weapons. I won't bother with killers disguised as swordsmen." The wild fool leaves home thinking that he could so easily be a samurai. He is ever ready in his cowboy mentality to slash open whatever offends him. In limitation (in this case, the more advanced outer "other" who says, "I decline") begins the transformation to the warrior who knows that her sword reflects the degree of discrimination she has attained in her mind and in her soul and in her body.

The game of imitating the play of the god's Vajra-thruster (Indra's thunderbolt and the Buddhist scepter: invincably hard and sharp-cutting as a shining diamond and empty as space) as it unfolds in the practice and discipline of aikido patterns an inner operation, analogous to the workings of the individuation process, which unites in a unique tapestry the many opposing strands of dark and light. In line with this weaving of opposites, the goal in this masculine sword discipline is paradoxically to learn receptively, to understand and align with the intuited broad play and dance of the *chi* or life force (which in active sword form follows learnable trajectories—much like a body language of the I Ching). Moreover, the ritual practice of aikido is a ground on which children and women and men of whatever weight, strength, age, position, wealth, or beauty are able to join mind, body, and spirit so that the flow of this light and shadow can be brought to bear in one's daily life.

The basic structure of the practice, like the basic cycling pattern of the monomyth of humans (Campbell 1968, p. 30), namely, birth, death, and rebirth, is threefold: entering, blending, and leading onward to new ground and a new situation out of which a new action or entering birth develops. This threefold structure is the means by which basic instinctual energies like aggression, violence, and power shape to consciousness and are transformed through the vehicle of "sword bridge" sacrifices. The structure of the practice is a vessel wherein the passions of powerful and potentially destructive affects can transformatively become the creative energy to pilot us forward moment by moment along the many sacrificial bridges we may be called upon to traverse.

To *enter* is to move out of the line of direct attack while entering into the maelstrom of the attacker's negative energy sphere. One enters by not meeting the oncoming force head on. One then *blends* with this powerful, potentially harmful drive so that it moves along the rim of one's centered circle. It is joined and so becomes neutralized. From this position, extending the energy out, the swordswoman *leads* the now united self-and-other to the new end she designs. This is the practice, again and again. Entering: a birth and a beginning. Blending: a death, a negation of the unique self. Leading: a rebirth, a new position, uniting self and other into a new configuration. This threefold flow is contained in all the techniques (*katas* or forms)—one of the simplest of which, *irimi nage* (literally, the attacked enters)—is known as the "twenty-year technique." To move softly into the turbulence of the tumult with effortless power takes at least twenty years to practice and to perfect, although a beginner from day one can still drop an opponent with that move. But she will not be lightning. This requires the discipline coordination of mind, body, and spirit.

Feminine yin receptivity is the warrior's correct attitude to masculine yang attack. The required warrior response to the lightning's thrusts is to parry with that sword which unifies the movement of the active masculine drive with the flowing and circular feminine flow. The conjunction of these opposites is built into the basic cruciform shape of the sword itself. Lightning dances and plays with lightning: entering, blending, leading—birth, death, and a rebirth; again, and again, and again, until one finally experiences the soul of the triune play of life.

I First stepped out onto the practice mat like the naked Celtic warrior, dressed in fierce and colored body tattoos, phallus exposed, only a waist cingulum to hold the weapon. The energy of the first of the swordthrusters, the Celt, fueled by the flames of magic, ritual, and righteous rage, directed my attacks and the attacks I received in return. A puppet dancing on lightning's strings, with the wild and untamed berserker sword power of the gods in my hands, I fired violence, which begot violence. The Celtic flame is uncontained and burns wildly in the eyes and in the circulating blood. To kill the enemy; to claim and display his severed head, the jewel of power, is the goal. Like the Celt, I was gripped in the heady blood drive to behead, to cut the other dead.

As S. Nichols comments:

> Lightning has always been experienced as a symbol of divine energy—a numinous force emanating from God. It represents naked power and illumination in its most primitive form. It comes from heaven to touch (our) lives directly without the mediating influence of the magician and his wand, the emperor and his scepter or the pope and his crozier. (1984, p. 285)

It is with the help of the Celtic warrior that one can image the illuminating sword power of the gods as it first comes numinously

Figure 3. *Pictish warrior, water-color by John White, ca. 1590.* **From** Celtic Mysteries, *John* **Sharkey** *(London: Thames and Hudson), plate 29.*

to humans in its most instinctive and unregenerate form in the combative desires to kill, to overpower, to gain advantage, to conquer. I, like Cuchulainn in the realm of the Celt, touch archetypal aggression:

> The warp-spasm seized Cuchulainn, and made him into a monstrous thing, hideous and shapeless, unheard of. His shanks and his joints, every knuckle and angle and organ from head to foot, shook like a tree in the flood or a reed in the stream. His face and features became a red bowl . . . his mouth weirdly distorted . . . and fiery flakes large as a ram's fleece reached his mouth from his throat. His heart boomed loud in his breast like the baying of a watchdog at its feed or the sound

of a lion among bears. Malignant mists and spurts of fire . . .
flickered red. (Kinsella 1970, p. 150)

In a situation such as aikido, where aggression and violence are
not suppressed or split off but, on the contrary, are the subject of
study, the protective floorboards are quickly ripped up to expose
the fiery furnaces of the depths. As a woman, it is a relief to find a
sacred arena where the flood of my rage can burn and in the burning begin to shape spirit.

The sword is not a primitive weapon. A culture, and by parallel an individual, must be developmentally ready and sophisticated enough for the possible transformation processes that
sword-making sets into motion in the culture and in the individual
psyche. Sword-making requires a knowledge of metallurgy and is
a product of the more culturally sophisticated "fire" knowledge.
Metallurgy intervenes into the womb of earth to wrest forth the
stones, the seeds, earth's children, which will be subjected to the
calibrated fires of the *athenor*, the new and artificial womb of
man.[2] The metals thus extracted are then further forged to
become the swords which are duly reverenced, acknowledging
their holy origins from the mother earth. They are highly personal
weapons and, in the mystique of the sword, are considered living
beings—each unique and uniquely named with a virtue and wisdom independent of the temporal owner, the sword's powers living on after the original owner is dead. Such are Charlemagne's
"Joyeuse," Odin's "Flame," Arthur's "Excalibur," the Zen monk
Takuan's (1573–1645) "True and Wondrous Sword of Tai-a," a
mythical sword that gives life to all things, friend and enemy alike,
and, more humorously, one samurai's "Clothes Rod."

As the sword holds the spiritual power of the gods made manifest, they were not for the use of the common man, but the warrior
elite and those of priestly or royal status, trained and initiated into
the sword's mysteries. Fittingly, swords are seen to

shine and discharge lightning bolts. They grow and shrink at
need, they make the owner invisible, they give him the power
to travel over long distances, and they run blood when he dies.
Heroes pierce rocks with them, splinter arrows in flight, and
create hills and springs by striking the earth. (Cavendish 1970,
p. 2746)

---

[2]Eliade explores this notion in depth in *The Forge and the Crucible* (1962).

Today most of the world is committed to a philosophy of action ruled by the mystique of this power of weapons. Consequently, it has divided into multitudinous closed and armed camps. Right or left, guerrilla or establishment, ghetto, third world, world powers, corporations, single individuals—common men as well as kings—all embrace the deadly violence of the sword without the developed self-control that training and initiation imparts. This highly active "outer" orientation toward the enemy brings the one-sided West, in particular, to a crisis in which we may simply self-destruct. Loosed from our archetypal roots, which provide a metaphysical orientation and consciousness, forge a connection with the polar dimensions of the psyche, and thus set a limit on aggressive behavior, we Westerners become the depopulated lands, sere and dry, unable to support new life. Our "riches" multiply into ever-rising mountains of dead discarded garbage. To rebalance the sword requires an in-depth inner journey to retrieve and revive its godly and sacred origins and thus renew its transformative potentials.

Working at the forge, refining the black ores through the molten red to the white heat which is then cooled and hardened, one comes to know the soul of the sword and the path it imposes on a life.

The story of "The Sword of Yraine" tells how the novitiate Shanna comes to choose the sword and in the process bind herself to the warrior goddess Yraine, Lady of Stars. In the service of this most ancient of goddesses whose rich lineage traces back to Ishtar and beyond, the heroine, Shanna, becomes an initiate as she claims the sword which is bestowed by the warrior goddess in whose womb the sword is fired.

> Shanna's eyes returned to the blade, like a sword of fire in the torchlight—the steel blade of a warrior that she had never yet held in her hand. But she had seen enough swords to know that this was a good one. She wondered what great warrior's body (this robber) had taken it from. It would cut cleanly; there would be pain like a bright blossom in the mind, and then—the embrace of the Goddess . . . There was an integrity to that steel that transcended the wretchedness of the lout who bore it. He should not have it, she knew, for he cannot understand its soul. (Paxson 1984, p. 192)

As I continued on the path of this practice, tumbling a man twice my size and half my age with my "sword blades," eyes soft-focused, back erect, I felt the power of this magical force of the warrior goddess, alive and energizing, begin to circulate. Entering the dojo is an experience of entering a temenos, a sacred ground of practice, wherein the endless repetition and movements begin to enter and rewire the instinctive electrical pathworks of the body. Upon entering, one bows. After changing into the requisite white practice uniform, one bows again before stepping onto the mat, to Ueshiba—the embodied spirit of aikido. Barefoot, kneeling on the mat, one bows yet again. To the sensei, to one's partners, and again upon leaving the mat. *Dojo*, the "place of enlightenment," is derived from the Sanskrit word *bodhimanda*, that place where the self or the ego undergoes the transformation into the egoless self. In the temple of my practice, the imprisoning ego is forced to loosen its hold and open to the powerful energies of the old warrior goddesses, who bring a strict new morality to bear. Through this lens, I am to see my opponent as myself and the world as my mirror of truth. Bound in this dance of union, there is immediate feedback in my every move as to the nature and degree of my level of harmony with myself, my partner, and the world. In the swirl of the wild activity on the crowded mat of the dojo, I am responsible for the well-being of both my partner (the "enemy") and myself while at the same time "letting go" in the full circular movement of martial play.

The Celt energy eventualy begins to soften. The impact of the bowing and the other repetitions of practice pierce new pinpoints of light into the dark body paths. There is a transpersonal force that transcends my ego which is being physically activated and acknowledged every time I step onto the mat. I start to carry this new body knowledge out into the world at large. I am moving about the streets of New York with a new confidence, my "sword" sheathed and at my side. To consciously own and bear the responsibility of this ancient powerful energy, particularly as an older woman, gave the world a new sparkle and dance. Like Shanna, I was taking back from the "robber" and for my own use the sword whose soul I now saw and honored. Heroic deed and efforts become less of a psychic necessity as the sword is carried openly, responsibly, and respectfully. The renegade shadow and cowboy mentality is held to the rule of the sword. If the sword is used physically, it exterminates; if used psychically to cut through the matter of mind, it initiates and evolves.

As in 17th-century Japan, bands of outlaw swordsmen run amok in our current culture. Gangs and corporate raiders share the same plundering ethos. This ravaging energy courses along unchecked in Western cultures. Disconnected from the sword's cosmic dimension, which provides a vertical point of contact between the lower human and the upper divine worlds, violence will rule in the instinctive drive to power. Women, in particular, having eschewed and depreciated the sword, are now called upon to reclaim and honor the art and rules of arms, which are under the banner of the old warrior goddesses whom we have abandoned to the dark realms of the unconscious. (It is important to note that Cuchulainn received his sword knowledge from a woman.) We women must be capable of countering these soul robbers who run as freely and unchecked in the outer world as they do in our own inner worlds. For the Japanese, the sword symbolizes courage and strength and is one of the three treasures (the other two being the mirror of truth and the jewel of compassion).

Images in an archetypal form, in this case, the pentagonal star, hold and bind powerful affect and shape it ritually into a path of ever deeper and more complex initiations that can channel and lead the ego and self into synergistic play rather than destructive and plundering opposition. The progressions of the image, like notes in a scale, can, within a form, flow forward and backward to create themes and shape a complex structure. Lightning, Celt, knight, master. These are the notes of the scale's progressions up and down and around, which then create the fivesome themes of transformative swordplay. I enter into the possession of the kingdom of the warrior by imitating and playing the human images that are relevant to this particular kingdom—Celt, knight, master, sage. I find there the swordswoman's inner path. Imaginally, as I play, I shape my reality forward; firing and tempering the jewel of courage and strength.

In aikido, as in life, punches are not pulled. One must learn to strike another person with conviction, cleanly with the blade of *ki*—the life energy extended out. One usually works with a partner, taking turns in the roles of the attacked, the *nage*, and that of the attacker, the *uke*. To not hit sincerely is to deprive the partner of her practice. I can only be as good a *nage* defending myself as I am an *uke* who attacks with the intent to hit. There is no separation—you are both attacked and attacker. When watching those most proficient at aikido in the ever-moving lightning warrior dance, the observer cannot tell the attacked from the attacker. The play of opposites continuously unfolds.

Whichever image of the pentagram's form that I play takes me into the domain I desire to inhabit, that of the warriors, and thrusts me into that dance. A true strike at another or a strike received presents me with all the inherent possibilities of that reality: Celt, knight, master, sage. Bound within image, form, and the threefold rhythm, instinctive aggression has the potential to become the light of the awakening holy spirit as it is finally manifested in the realm of the sage.

Ever moving to achieve dancing the circle, I am gripped by the breathtaking elegance of the advanced warriors who become the sword. I realize that the now-identified and known Celt has to be sacrificed to move deeper into the pattern of this energy flow.

I find love again, but the love, as in the Arthurian courts of love, is now different. It is love in renunciation for the other. The fascination of the sword is used not to terrorize but in the service of devotion. The other truly must become my partner, whomever she (or he) may be and on whatever human level she presents herself to me. This matters deeply if I am to achieve elegance. Head smashing, hard throwing, and wrist wrenching must be killed. The desirousness of the power win becomes a death-in-life.

Blending

In the Celtic culture, the druid priests, kings, and warriors dominated. The feminine force, although profound, acknowledged, and propitiated, had no earthly physical representative as important as these figures of the patriarchal masculine (Kinsella 1970, p. xiii). The physical and earthly queen force cannot be born until the linear masculine admits and consciously develops the feminine notion of path or journey; receptive, open, beginningless, and endless. The masculine notion that life is a particular place or destination—winning advantage over and conquering—must give way. A major possibility for human evolution is then freed to evolve. To understand the limitations of victory is to curve the energy that flows toward death back into life, and in particular, into the life of the heart. Thich Nhat Hanh observes: "If the human species has been able to make any progress, it is because of our heart of love and compassion" (1990, p. 45). To penetrate into the wild and uncivilized forest of death requires the sword of love.

This significant human discovery must be realized first in the soul and through the sensual realm, before the spiritual. This soul development can be contemplated, for example, in the image of Sir Lancelot and his burning desire for the elegant and very earthy Guinevere, Arthur's warrior queen and priestess of the Round

Figure 4. *From* **The Arthurian Legends,** *Richard Barber, ed.*
(London: Peter Bedrick Books, 1988), p. 53.

Table. Guinevere is not a common adulteress as she is usually
portrayed, but a warrior high priestess in the ancient lineage of
Ishtar (Goodrich 1991, pp. 150–174). It is this earthly queen who
initiates Lancelot into the inner mysteries of the sword. Lancelot's
many adventures under Guinevere's tutelage are intended to
focus the energy on interiorizing the instinctive sword and turning
it toward the sword of psychical evolution. The tale of Lancelot
risking death to cross the deadly sword bridge to rescue Guinevere
from the land of the dead, the depth of psyche, points the narrow
way forward along this sword's edge of death and transformation.

Guinevere, virgin in the antique sense of the word, is Lancelot's heart-life and soul. The awakened "Guinevere" awareness
begins in the appreciation of a beauty, elegance, and form that
cannot be possessed but only known. This separates a Lancelot
from his fellow knight-in-arms, Gawain. Gawain, in stepping into
the journey of the riddle: "What does a woman most desire?"
(sovereignty), strides forward in acknowledging the separateness
and inherent value of the feminine. However, Gawain undertakes
this adventure to save the life of his king, Arthur. Lancelot goes to
save the very life of the queen herself. Gawain, in the sword bridge
adventure with Lancelot, further demonstrates that he has not yet
developed psychologically far enough to withstand a journey to
the land of the dead to retrieve his "Guinevere," the living femi-

nine force, which finds coinage for humankind as a whole in Lancelot's valuation and self-sacrifices. Zimmer remarks: "By releasing Guinevere, the feminine, life-giving principle, the highest symbol of the chivalrous love and life of the Round Table, life force in its visible human incarnation, the knight, Sir Lancelot, would break the hold of death upon the soul, that is, would be the restorer of our immortality" (1973, p. 170). Lancelot like the original lightning flash, fulfills an opening function. He himself will not journey on to become the master or the sage, but in his harrowing of hell he opens our imagination so that this can become a guiding possibility. Like Lancelot, I feel that in my practice, the sweetness of the Grail may be awakened, but not achieved. This bitterness of the sweet must also be incorporated into the practice and discipline of goalessness.

As Lancelot and Gawain begin the search for the abducted Guinevere, Lancelot has lost his horse and is on foot—signifying the loss of the supreme ego values: power, mastery, nobility. A dwarf driver comes to offer Lancelot guidance in this trial, but he must enter the dwarf's cart to receive it. "The cart" at that time was the public pillory where thieves and social deviants were exhibited and punished. Will this renowned hero, Lancelot, now on foot, suffer a further descent by entering and riding in this conveyance for all to see? His companion-in-arms, Gawain, refuses. To prepare for the coming blood sacrifice the knight hero must further relinquish his ego's glory, ride in the cart driven by the dwarf psychopomp, and approach the bridge in the psychological garb of the solitary pilgrim—in poverty, humility, and devotion. But, momentarily in the grip of humiliation, he hesitates a fraction before boarding. Guinevere will know of this defection of heart and will scorn him because of this wavering behavior. Elegant Guinevere is severe. Her way is narrow.

The dwarf driver brings Lancelot to the river he will cross, via the sword bridge, and Chretien de Troyes avows that

> if anyone asks me the truth, there never was such a bad bridge, nor one whose flooring was so bad. The bridge across the cold stream consisted of a polished gleaming sword, but the sword stood stout and stiff and was as long as two lances. At each end there was a tree trunk in which the sword was firmly fixed. (Zimmer 1973, p. 171)

The water beneath was "a wicked-looking stream, as swift and raging, as black and turgid, as fierce and terrible as if it were the devil's stream; and it is so dangerous and bottomless that anything falling into it would be as completely lost as if it fell into the salt sea'' (ibid.).

Appropriately, Lancelot's trial at the sword bridge takes place on the last day of the old and dying year. Readying himself for the dread passage, he divests himself of the armor that protects his hands and feet. Creeping and crawling like a very young child on all fours, he moves forward, slowly and painfully, tender flesh torn open. The blood sacrifice is willingly given. The "stone" is opened. A portion of the soul's red liquid sun must wash back into the abysmal black and churning waters below. The three worlds, air, earth and water, man's three components, are bound by the fourth, fire, his bright serpentine blood, shining and glistening, linking man to life. When the blood-fire is loosed and spilled into the abyss, the tie that binds us to the world dissolves. In the ebb, we and Lancelot gain anew a fresh and childlike vision of the life we live. But one must give life, blood, to the primordial waters of the unconscious to receive this boon. An exchange in kind develops. Only through the loss of blood, the essence, and the demand of the sword bridge passage can Lancelot cross to the land of the dead to restore his queen and with her, himself twice-born. The emphasis is on the birth of the soul to the physical life of the world, and within this new framework, another orientation to the life of the sword is achieved. The transmission of this knowledge comes through the feminine Guinevere who, like the ancient warrior goddesses, preserved and passed forward the knowledge of how to forge a sword with soul. To be alive to Guinevere is to live in deep relationship to the is-ness of things, to live from the heart with no hesitation.

The roots of the word *sacrifice*—*sacra*, meaning holy, and *facere*, meaning to make—indicate the potency and possibility of the sword bridge of sacrifice. When we voluntarily give what we value most—our "life blood," our self—that full renunciation leads us to the ground of sacredness: it is "holy-making," and paradoxically it lead to wholeness. In all the major religions, the gods renounce what they have created and what they hold as most dear—reflections of Self—Christ, Parusha (Hindu), Job. These mirrors of self are to be sacrificed in the name of new creativity and a more-complex consciousness. As the gods and their creations evolve through sacrifice, so do humans. Moreover, it is only through voluntary loss and renunciation that humans can touch the realm of the gods to make contact with the divine life force and the creative energy source. That which makes holy or whole is sacrifice: the *amriti*, the nectar of the gods, and the contents of the grail cup that confer immortality. Furthermore, it is by conscious sacrifice (in Hindu, *anicca* or impermanence) that humans enter into the shared play of the ever-moving cosmos to dance in rhythm with the Dancer. So while blood sacrifice satisfies the instinctive demands of the roiling abyss, it also is the ladder to the abode of the dancing gods. The vertical sword that sheds blood is an entry point which fixes a world axis that mediates consciousness of the lower, the middle, and the upper realms of being.

Lancelot has regenerated his life through the renunciations and death symbolized by the cart and the sword bridge. However, he wavered before entering the cart, so he accomplishes but the first leg of the journey, albeit a most significant developmental achievement. In sincere loving of Guinevere begins the polishing and perfecting of soul. Lancelot does not go on to achieve the Grail, the connection to spirit. It is his "son," his still-younger, reborn, and further-evolved self, Galahad, who does. The hero, Lancelot, must die to make way for "the heart of spiritual mastery (which) is this: the ego self dies to become the egoless self" (Ueshiba 1985, p. 8). Now a further reach of the blood sacrifice of the sword bridge must be traversed, as we shall see, to gain the unhesitant heart of lightning. Once again, something will have to disappear and die in this realm of the knight to reappear and be reborn in the next realm, that of the master.

Leading

The swordswoman who desires to be a swordmaster—because she comes to understand that there will always be another opponent to kill, or one bigger, younger, or stronger than herself—begins at this point to accomplish the second sword bridge. As the samurai master says to Toshiro Mifuni, again from the *Samurai* series: "You'll always remain just a rough man until your mind is relaxed." Here is the long and exhausting wilderness transverse from knight to master. The heroics of the outer world are to be slowly and gradually put aside, sacrificed. Spirit is brought to birth in this death of self on the next sword bridge crossing. This heart's beaconing light is a no less dangerous transit than the bridge to Guinevere: a sharpened edge of razor hard to transverse. A difficult path is this (to paraphrase a Upanishad).

The accomplishment of this spiritual adventure can be meditated forward in the image of the aikido master Ueshiba, who, through the vigorous and untiring discipline of body and mind, frees the expression of spirit to such a degree that a sword attack (steel; no wood here) by a young, big, and strong samurai warrior is handily parried by this small and fragile-looking old man whose weapon is but a paper fan. The internalized sword energy breaks apart yet another mode of existence. As we shift to a new paradigm, we begin to move easily in ways that seem miraculous from the vantage point of another who remains at the old level. The "miracles," such as a fan serving as a powerful sword, open new possibilities of wholeness.

In China, the fan is the reviver of souls. The warrior's steely sword of fire meets with Ueshiba's paper fan which cools the raging fire and then rekindles and animates spirit. In Greece the fan is associated with the goddess Demeter. With her fan, Demeter winnowed the corn, the selected fruits of her fertility, as the old warrior winnows the fruits of his fertile and concentrated practice.

Figure 5. *Ueshiba using folded fan. From:* The Spirit of Aikido, *Kisshomaru Ueshiba (New York: Kodansha International, 1985), p. 45.*

The sword and the fan, the masculine and the feminine, converge in a *heiros gamos*—a sacred marriage. This is a possible result of one-pointed training and practice when the husbanding of the inner self supersedes the killing of the antagonist or other. Here is Ueshiba, master of martial art, speaking in one of his lectures:

> Budo is not a means of felling an opponent by force or by lethal weapons. Neither is it intended to lead the world to destruction by arms and other illegitimate means. True budo calls for bringing the inner energy of the universe in order, protecting the peace of the world and molding, as well as preserving, everything in nature in its right form. Training in budo is tantamount to strengthening, within my body and soul, the love of "kami," the deity who begets, preserves, and nurtures everything in nature. (1985, p. 8)

Early in the 17th century, Japan began the conscious transformation of sword-cutting from that which kills to that which fans, revives, and winnows life. The goals of death, injury, combat, and power begin to reshape in the *athenor* of spirit so that the sword may emerge fresh, shining, freed from the blood lust, although still respected as an instrument of death. The sword now seeks to emerge as one of the paths of the Way (*Budo* or *Tao*), parallel to the then-developing ways of calligraphy, tea, or Buddha, providing a felt spiritual expression and sustenance in a time of great destruction, upheaval, and violence. Perhaps there is a parallel to the increasing sense of inescapable disorder that is being experienced in our current culture. To reconnect the sword energy to its cosmic root by the devotions of individual sacrifice is a path which provides an alternative response to the endemic personal helplessness that accompanies such pervasive disorder.

The quintessential warrior, Arjuna of the *Gita*, is told by Krishna that "what is night for all beings is the time of waking for the disciplined soul" (Schapper 1965, p. 99). For it is in the night, the empty wilderness of unknowing, where the warrior, weaponless, turns to the small inner voice to guide him onward. Sri Aurobindo, in commenting on the *Gita*, call this "*Arjunavisadyoga*—the yoga of dejection and the sorrow of Arjuna." Arjuna's "limbs quail, (his) mouth goes dry, (his) body shakes, and (his) hair stands on end . . . (The bow), Gandiva, slips from (his) hand and (his) skin too is burning all over. (He) is not able to stand steady. (His) mind is reeling" (ibid., p. 93). Arjuna the warrior prince is defenseless. For one at the pentagram point of Cuchulainn consciousness, this disempowered ego state would represent a trip to the Isles of the

Blessed—death. For Arjuna, however, whose warrior work has refined his consciousness, "It is a night and a negation, which however, is not a punishment of a fall but a condition of progress" (ibid.).

In this wilderness of unknowing, plagued by doubt, inertia, and depression, is the opportunity to struggle to listen to the often puny inner voice, which instructs the solitary in how to live in Krishna consciousness. After much turmoil, Arjuna finally surrenders to a will greater than his "own." This resistance to surrender is a basic problem of humankind. It is now being presented to us with greater and greater insistence. Can we, like Arjuna, surrender the illusory freedoms that we so dearly hold, to cross the sword bridge and be in relationship with an ever-changing inner ground of being, whether that ground be called Krishna, Tao, Self, God, or Christ?

Out of the wilderness, like Arjuna, we stumble to freedom. Open to sacrifice, we remain open to possibilities—infinite, and unexpected, and often beyond our comprehension. A warrior like Ueshiba lives joyfully—ready to fan and revivify all the corners of the life in which he finds himself. In this spirit, old Ueshiba told his youthful students that whomever could unbalance him at any time could take his place as master. Consequently, going up a set of stairs, or going to the market, at any moment in his daily life, when he was weaponless, a move could be made to unbalance the master. However, no one succeeded in this. He lived in the flow of the life force coupled with an inner reality that was not subject to his control. Paradoxically, he was unshakable. The *axis mundi*, the vertical sword, was his very breath.

The practice on my small level of achievement is simply to practice—and to fail endlessly—at entering, blending, and leading my partner, mindlessly and harmoniously with *ki*. Again, again, and again: imitate, practice, fail. Boredom, resentment, fear, rebelliousness, exhaustion are punctuated with the exultation and joy of scattered lightning flashes that illumine my night sky. Solitary, I practice on for my self. In this manner, aikido—the way (*do*) of harmony (*ai*) with *ki* (the universal and individual life energy and force), slowly, with the blood of conscious effort, begins to exinguish one by one the dark greedy eyes of the ten-thousand-armed hydra who would every minute draw me into the furious and boiling abysmal waters that course under every sword bridge. Wolfe Lowenthal paradoxically calls the joys of this practice, "investment in loss" (1991, p. 82). A very long and life-encompassing sword bridge is this!

The fruits of self-sacrifice are realized in the last trajectory of the calligraphy of lightning, a turn downward in the pentagram to the low ground point of the sage. The realized sword is *axis mundi*; the sage is sword; and *axis mundi* is sage: an inner mystical marriage of the human and the divine whose child is the true alchemical sword—the inner ever—purifying crystallized fire, which like the fecund primal source, endlessly destroys and revitalizes as penetrating spirit, the stick of awakening. Ueshiba, the enlightener, at the pentagram's point of the sage, kneels in prayer and receives the light.

The sword has cracked open the cosmic egg of matter to liberate the wellspring of spirit:

Figure 6. *"In an attitude of Shinto prayer,"* photograph by K. Chiba. *From:* Martial Arts: The Spiritual Dimension, *Peter Payne (New York: Crossroad Publishing Co., 1981), p. 50.

Man is a thinking reed but his great works are done when he is not calculating and thinking. "Childlikeness" has to be restored with long years of training in the art of self-forgetfulness. When this is attained, man thinks yet he does not think. He thinks like showers rolling down from the sky; he thinks like waves rolling on the ocean; he thinks like the stars illuminating the night heavens; he thinks like the green foliage shooting forth in the relaxing spring breeze. Indeed, he is the shower, the ocean, the stars, the foliage. (Watts 1986, p. 192)

To master the sword and to cross the sword bridge is to be a warrior practicing dying daily. Dying is thus not an enterprise saved for the end of a life, but a necessary part of the moment-to-moment play of life's journey. In the pattern considered here—from the initial flash of the light, to Celt, to knight, to master, and to sage and back to the source—death is omnipresent and consciously faced in all the seasons and stages of our sword work. Also conscious and considered as well is our ego's natural and omnipresent unwillingness to die. Life and death interplay—the powerful hunger for life, lived deeply and intensely, is sharpened by the ever-present terror of the necessity of the sword of death.

The circle completes, but for most of us it remains unfinished. John Blofeld, Eastern scholar and Buddhist, traveling on the path since his early years, in his autobiography looks back to

Figure 7. *Copper engraving by M. Merian the Elder (1593–1651 A.D.). ARAS/New York.*

share his very rich life which included many rare and accomplished teachers. This discipline and committed man, a teacher and sword master himself, wrote at the end of his life:

> It is virtually certain now that Enlightenment is not for me in this life, but this is not for want of kindly teachers or generous encouragement. The enemy is Dragon Sloth, who owes his stature to the gargantuan meals provided by my evil karma in this and many former lives. I do not despair . . . May all sentient beings be happy! May I—even though at very long last—be one to assist them in gaining liberation. (1988, p. 286)

I will not achieve a black belt in this lifetime. Like Blofeld, I do not despair. The riches have been so great, and the many teachers so generous. I have also provided sloth with a goodly share of my flesh. This particular opus remains unfinished. "Individuation, becoming a self, is not only a spiritual problem, it is the problem of all life" (Jung 1944, par. 163). However, I do continue on with the forged sword of courage and strength, embracing the pattern of a swordswoman, unlocked through the practice of aikido. As I journey on my way, the integrity of the sword art guides me along the narrow path to the quintessence of mind, "the ever-hoped for and never-to-be-discovered 'One'" (ibid.).

> *Cloud pregnant with a million bolts of lightning*
> *Love gives birth to the philosopher's stone.*
> *My soul is flooded by your sea of splendor*
> *Being and Cosmos drown there silently.*
>
> —*Rumi*

Figure 8. Kyosaku, the stick of awakening.

References

Blofeld, J. 1988. *The Wheel of Life*. Boston: Shambhala.

Campbell, J. 1968. *The Hero with a Thousand Faces*. Princeton, N.J.: Princeton University Press.

Cavendish, R., ed. 1970. *Man, Myth, and Magic: An Illustrated Encyclopedia of the Supernatural*. New York: Marshall Cavendish Corporation.

Durrell, L. 1990. *Caesar's Vast Ghost*. New York: Arcade Publishing, Inc.

Eliade, M. 1962. *The Forge and the Crucible*. New York: Harper.

Goodrich, N. 1991. *Guinevere*. New York: HarperCollins Publishers.

Jung, C. G. 1950. A study in the process of individuation. In *CW* 9i:290–354. Princeton, N.J.: Princeton University Press, 1959.

———. 1944. *Psychology and Alchemy. CW*, vol. 12. Princeton, N.J.: Princeton University Press, 1953.

Kinsella, T., trans. 1970. *The Tain*. Oxford: Oxford University Press.

Lowenthal, W. 1991. *There Are No Secrets*. Berkeley, Calif.: North Atlantic Books.

Nhat Hanh, T. 1990. *Our Appointment with Life*. Berkeley, Calif.: Parallex Press.

Nichols, S. 1984. *Jung and Tarot: An Archetypal Journey*. York Beach, Maine: Samuel Weiser, Inc.

Paxson, D. 1984. The sword of Yraine. In *The Sword and the Soceress*, M. Bradley, ed. New York: Daw Books, Inc.

Schapper, E. 1965. *The Inward Odyssey*. London: George Allen and Unwin Ltd.

Ueshiba, M. 1985. *The Spirit of Aikido*. New York: Kodansha International.

Watts, A. 1986. *A Zen Life: T. D. Suzuki Remembered*. New York: Weatherhill.

Zimmer, H. 1973. *The King and the Corpse*. Princeton, N.J.: Princeton University Press.

Elizabeth Retivov is a graduate of the C. G. Jung Institute and has a private practice in New York City.

Atalanta's Sisters

Joan Lamb Ullyot

The history of women's distance running is very short, dating back only to 1967, at least in the public eye. That is the year that a bold woman named Kathrine Switzer dared to run the 26.2-mile Boston Marathon, a feat previously considered physiologically impossible for members of "the weaker sex." In fact, a handful of women had run the distance previously, even in Boston, but they had been overlooked. This year was different. A feisty Scotsman named Jock Semple, director of the theretofore all-male race, was so shocked to see that the runner who had entered as K. Switzer was, in fact, quite unmistakably female, that he jumped off the press truck and tried to tear off the interloper's official number. Switzer's powerfully built boyfriend, running with her, threw a body block at Semple, and Switzer, although shaken, went on to finish the marathon. The photographers on the press truck recorded the entire contretemps. When the next day's papers appeared, many people realized for the first time that women, too, could run—and wanted to.

Over the next few years, more and more women took up running for relaxation, sport, and fitness. Although generally welcomed by male runners and local race promoters, they continued to encounter opposition from both officialdom (the AAU, Amateur Athletic Union, and the IOC, International Olympic Committee) and from conventional society, which was not yet comfortable with the idea of women as truly physical, often sweaty, athletic creatures. The AAU, faced with the spectacle of increasing numbers of women demanding equal rights in the sport, finally capitulated in 1972 and gave official permission for women to compete in events longer than a mile and to run in the same races as men (although not "against" men—women have their own separate division in all races).

Society, apart from the esoteric and private community of runners, was even slower to accept women as athletes. Even at present, many women runners receive subtle messages that their sport is somehow "unfeminine" or less appropriate than, say, ballet or tennis. Because of this adverse cultural climate, as I have written elsewhere, the hardest step for a woman is the first one out the door—because that step requires her to put aside her old ways of thinking and limiting self-concepts (Ullyot 1974, p. 5).

Perhaps this psychological adversity explains the strong attraction women runners have always felt toward the mythological figure of Atalanta. One of the earliest all-women races, in 1972, was the Atalanta 10K run in Fremont, California, which awarded coveted golden apple charms to the top three finishers. The Avon women's running circuit, which sponsored prestigious races around the world from 1978 to 1984, held its first International Marathon Championship in Atlanta, Georgia, and used the running figure of Atalanta on the gold and silver medals. (Coincidentally, perhaps, the director of the Avon running circuit was none other than the same K. Switzer who had integrated the Boston Marathon years earlier.) To this day, one of the most prestigious and successful women's running teams in the United States is New York's Atalanta Club.

What attributes of the mythological Atalanta enable her to act as such an important role model for modern women? Her story is an ancient one which has undergone many permutations at the hands of Ovid and others, but the common thread is the tale of a woman who was extraordinarily gifted athletically but never accepted in her totality by the society in which she lived, even though that age was replete with archetypal male heroes. Here is her story in its simplest form (adapted from Hamilton 1940, pp. 173–177; except as otherwise noted, all direct quotes are from this source).

Atalanta, a descendent of Prometheus, was born to a father who had wanted a son. Deeply disappointed at being given a daughter instead, this father rid himself of the unwanted infant in the customary manner of ancient Greece—he exposed her to the elements and wild beasts, on a mountainside. A she-bear (an animal sacred to Artemis) found the tiny infant, nursed her to health, and then entrusted her to kindly hunters for upbringing. Thus Atalanta grew up strong, active, and daring, at home in the wild woods and fiercely independent. She was fleet of foot and an accomplished hunter. It was said that once, pursued by two lustful Centaurs, whom she could not outrun as she could any human assailants, she stood her ground and shot them both dead with two arrows.

Clearly a formidable maiden, Atalanta was as beautiful as she was strong and swift. When she left her home in the wild to seek adventure, she turned heads and captured hearts. But like Artemis herself, this young girl was a true virgin, "one in herself" (Harding 1971, p. 103), and spurned romance in favor of heroic deeds. Soon Meleager, smitten by Atalanta's beauty and equally impressed by her athletic prowess, invited her (over the objections of his companions) to join the epic Calydonian boar hunt. Atalanta justified his faith by drawing first blood, wounding and weakening the boar with her arrows, after the others' spears had failed to penetrate. When the boar finally fell dead, Meleager awarded the boar's hide to Atalanta as a trophy. This well-deserved but romantic gesture eventually cost the young hero his life, as his men objected violently to having such a prize go to a mere girl, however stalwart she had proven herself to be.

Meleager was but the first of many men who would eventually die for the love of Atalanta, but it is not known whether she mourned for long the death of her hunting comrade. She continued her quest for adventure and glory, sailing with Jason on the *Argo* in search of the golden fleece and then participating in the funeral games for Jason's uncle. Here she again proved her mettle by winning a wrestling match against the great hero Peleus, who later became father to the even more renowned Achilles.

Having amply demonstrated that she could outrun and outshoot and outwrestle, too, the men of one of the two great ages of heroism, Atalanta finally sought out her own father. One suspects that she hoped to win his love and acceptance, that he might be "reconciled to having a daughter who really seemed almost if not quite as good as a son" (p. 175). But while Atalanta's parents gave her a home, they apparently did not approve of her wild and unconventional (i.e., "unfeminine") ways. She was being pressured to marry one of the many suitors who came flocking, drawn by her beauty and athletic prowess.

But Atalanta was not at all eager to marry, have a family, and settle down. She had never yet felt the pangs of love, she still loved to run free in the woods and hunt and climb, rejoicing in the movement of her body. Marriage would put an end to all her carefree days, and, in fact, says Ovid, an oracle had warned her that marriage was not for her: "No need for husband, Atalanta; flee husband stuff! Still, you won't escape, and still alive, you'll lose yourself" (*Metamorphoses*, p. 223). But her father was insistent, so Atalanta came up with what seemed to her a creative, perfect solution: she agreed to marry the man who could outrun her in a footrace. Of course, she knew full well that no such man existed anywhere in the ancient world.

Her father, not fully aware of his daughter's dazzling speed, agreed to the compromise, and Atalanta, who loved to compete, had a delightful time running many races and winning them all, even when she gave her suitors a handicap to make the race more interesting. Some writers have added even more interest to the tale by specifying that suitors who lost the race would also lose their lives. One account has Atalanta ruthlessly shooting them dead with her own arrows, as the hapless young men staggered exhausted across the finish line. We will return to this interesting embellishment later; it seems to overlap with Atalanta's self-defense against the Centaurs.

Finally one of the smarter suitors, a young man name Hippomenes, had the brilliant notion of asking Aphrodite herself for help in what seemed to be a hopeless pursuit. And Aphrodite, "always on the lookout to subdue wild young maidens who despised love" (p. 177) answered his prayer with a gift of three glorious golden apples from the Garden of the Hesperides. No one alive could resist their allure. And Atalanta would be totally unprepared for such distractions in her race. Ovid also hints that Atalanta was beginning to feel Aphrodite's power, for the first time in her young life, even before the start as she looked favorably on Hippomenes' form and bravery and found herself wishing briefly that he might be the one to outrun her.

But it was only a passing thought, and Atalanta, "a hundredfold more lovely disrobed than with her garments on . . . looked fiercely around her" (p. 177) at the start. Then they ran, Atalanta "flying swift as an arrow, her hair tossed back over her white shoulders, a rosy flush tinging her fair body" (p. 177). The wily Hippomenes, clutching his golden apples, soon found himself falling behind, so he rolled an apple ahead and to the side. Atalanta couldn't resist and knew that she could make up for the moment's delay. She stooped to pick up the golden prize, and Hippomenes, no mean runner himself shot ahead of her—but not for long. Soon Atalanta passed him back, and Hippomenes played the same distracting trick with the second apple. Once again Atalanta fell for it, and once again, as they neared the finish line, she caught up and pulled ahead. Her speed was all the more impressive in that Aphrodite added extra weight to the apples, to slow the defiant maiden further. Desperate, Hippomenes rolled the final apple way off in the grass to the side, and as Atalanta, still confident, turned aside for the third time, she lost the race—the first defeat in her life. Now she had to marry, and as Hamilton tellingly writes, "her free days alone in the forest and her athletic victories were over" (p. 177).

They married, no doubt to her parents' delight, and Atalanta settled into her new role at least long enough to bear a son. But it is said that the married lovers failed to offer proper homage to Aphrodite. Angered, the goddess caused them to be overcome by passion in the temple of Cybele, who then turned them into a lion and lioness yoked forever to her chariot. Thus was the prophecy fulfilled: "Still alive, you'll lose yourself."

This ancient tale is obviously a meaty one, with numerous resonances for physically active women, most of whom have at some time been considered as "wild and unconventional" as Atalanta herself. But beyond the superficial level of identification with an athletic heroine, women runners seem especially drawn to this myth. I think this is because it presents on a symbolic level certain core issues of identity and self-discovery for modern women. Reviewing Atalanta's story from a Jungian viewpoint can thus reveal more of its existential meaning.

The Psychology Behind the Myth

The infant Atalanta is rejected from the moment of her birth, exposed on the mountaintop because she is born female. She differs thus from Oedipus, who was also left to die, but only because he was seen as a threat to his father, not because of a perceived inadequacy rooted in his very being. Atalanta's plight reflects the low valuation of the feminine in ancient Greece and is closest, in its stark brutality, to Agamemnon's sacrifice of his own daughter, Iphigenia, to obtain favorable winds for the Greeks who sailed toward Troy. Agamemnon's wife, the formidable Clytemnestra, brooded unforgiving for ten years and exacted revenge on her husband's return. But Atalanta's rejection is condoned, however reluctantly, by her own mother, who thus accedes to the societal devaluation of women, and remains powerless.

Although the infant exposed to die has no conscious awareness of her unacceptability and its cause, Atalanta's totally unconventional life as a woman can be seen as a symbolic response to this original existential crisis. Despite being "dead" to her parents, psychologically and emotionally, she goes on not only to salvage a sense of self, but to do so on a heroic scale. My feeling is that Atalanta's psychic growth and epic successes result from her immediate and close identification with the Artemis archetype, which directs her life almost exclusively until the fateful race with Hippomenes.

It comes as no surprise, then, that the helpless infant is rescued and suckled by a she-bear, an animal sacred to Artemis. In Attica, young girls celebrating the rites of Artemis dressed up in tawny robes and were call "bears," giving a sacred role and outlet to their adolescent unruliness. In some versions of the story of Iphigenia, Artemis saves the young victim by substituting a bear for Agamemnon's sacrifice. So it is clear, in the story of Atalanta, that the virgin nature goddess herself comes to the rescue. Thus, the baby girl's first and only mother image, her source of nourishment and warmth, is the shaggy, kind bear. Bear and child alike are creatures of the wild, both under the protection of the most independent and athletic of goddesses.

If a bear is Atalanta's mother image, the hunters who eventually co-parent the child become her collective father image. There is a remarkable overlap here, since Artemis is also goddess of the hunt and patron of hunters. Mario Jacoby describes the hunting drive as archetypically goal-oriented, focused and competitive:

> The question arises of whether, and to what extent, the hunting drive ignores or even insults the god Eros, whose realm is that of love. People who are concentrating and expending a great deal of energy on achieving certain goals are, during such activity, often closed to the loving approach of others, which they may shrug off as a disruption. (1990, p. 18)

Certainly an exclusive focus on athletic prowess and achievement, instilled in Atalanta by her hunter father figures, is the element in her character which eventually provokes Aphrodite to undermine her.

So Atalanta grows up in the forest, in splendid isolation from the rest of humanity—an isolation which is as much psychological as physical. According to Apollodorus, "she remained a virgin, lived in the wilderness as a huntress" (Simpson 1976, p. 168). As in descriptions of her patroness, a moon goddess, the term *virgin* used here refers to a state of mind rather than simple lack of sexual experience or marriage. Esther Harding gives us a beautiful description of the psychological virgin who is "one-in-herself," who

> does what she does—not because of any desire to please, not to be liked, or to be approved, even by herself; not because of any desire to gain power over another, to catch his interest or love,

but because what she does is true. Her actions may, indeed, be unconventional. (1971, p. 125)

Atalanta fits this description perfectly and adds a certain element of power in the service of self-sufficiency. Apollodorus tells how, pursued by Centaurs, the young huntress stands her ground, shoots and kills them both. The Centaurs, half man and half horse, represent the dark, aggressive instinctual, and most threatening aspects of the masculine. In resisting rape by such creatures, Atalanta asserts her goddess-derived independence and mastery over the more brutal and primitive aspects of her own animus. This is a necessary stage in her maturation as a woman, helping her overcome the masculine roughness of her upbringing by hunters.

The next phase of Atalanta's life is her quest for adventure, and here she sets no limits for herself—perhaps, as a wild creature, she is simply unaware of the limits commonly imposed by society, which restrict women in their aspirations. Certainly she appears sublimely oblivious of convention when she applies to sail with Jason, hunt the Calydonian boar, or participate in athletic contests. Her quest, however unusual for a woman, is a response to a universal drive, youth's "intense need to seek and find identity" (Jacoby 1990, p. 26). Perhaps this need is especially important for Atalanta, who is not woman-identified, having grown up among men. She continues to pursue her boyish ways, apparently viewing the men she encounters as friends and companions rather than potential lovers.

Most of the men Atalanta encounters seem willing to accept her as a companion, with the notable exception of Meleager, who loves her. There is no suggestion in the myth that Atalanta returns his love, even though Meleager's passionate admiration eventually leads to his death. Much more decisive for Atalanta's future development is the renewed experience of rejection on the grounds of her sex, not her abilities. Some stories of Jason and the golden fleece say that Atalanta was barred from that adventure because the mariners feared a woman would bring bad luck. Certainly, when Meleager insists that she join the Calydonian boar hunt, there is a near mutiny, led by the older generation, Meleager's uncles. The suggestion that she is not "good enough" to participate, no matter how skilled, must shock the young girl, who has never (since birth) encountered what we would now call sex discrimination.

Atalanta, eager for adventure and a chance to show her mettle, persists in the hunt and eventually draws first blood with her arrows, when the spears of others have failed. But when Meleager awards her the boar's hide, which is her just due, she is again rejected. Apollodorus reports that Meleager's uncles, "insulted that a woman should receive the prize when there were men to get it," attack their nephew, who kills them in self-defense. Hearing the news, Meleager's mother burns the brand she has guarded until then to preserve her son's life, and Meleager dies in agony by his mother's will—another example of female ruthlessness in this myth.

And what of Atalanta, meanwhile, who only wished to find joy and athletic glory in the hunt? What has become of her own search for identity? One suspects that she is bewildered and self-doubting as never before. It is after this epic but fatal hunt that she apparently learns of her real parents and goes to find them. I see in this turn toward home, the same home from which she was coldly cast out at birth, Atalanta's desperate yearning for acceptance as the woman she truly is, with all of her talents and skills, unrestricted by society's notions of "proper" feminine deportment and limitations. But instead of acceptance, she experiences renewed pressures toward the more traditional woman's role, incorporating the values of Hera, Demeter, and Aphrodite. Her father would prefer her to be an obedient daughter, rather than a famous runner.

Atalanta here runs headlong into the conflict which lends ambivalence to the rest of her story: Does she remain more true to her own self by continuing in focused exploration of her Artemis nature or by undergoing a necessary, human expansion outside of this limited archetypal role? Is it self-betrayal or fulfillment to undertake the role of wife and mother, as her father urges her to do? She consults the oracle, whose message is as clear as such voices from the unconscious ever are: in marriage, although "still alive, you'll lose your self."

Thus we come to the races, in which Atalanta indeed seems most herself. She rejoices in the running, which for her is celebration and self-expression. When she runs, she seems transfigured, "running itself producing beauty" (*Metamorphoses*, p. 225). Jean Bolen (1992) has suggested that Atalanta, like the modern elite women runners who are her sisters, enters into *kairos* time during races, staying completely in the moment, losing track of "real time" during this period of intense focus. This state is wonderfully described by Leon Lewis in his review of the modern film, *Chariots of Fire*: running a race, for runners of this caliber, is "a moment of heightened reality, when time is distorted, the senses intensified, the psyche made vulnerable, and avenues of insight opened into the self" (1982, p. 65). The fact that Atalanta wins all her races, thus saving herself from her fate, time and again, is almost incidental. What matters in her running is the running itself, which seems essential to her nature.

There is another aspect of the myth, not found in the earliest accounts, which reflects the ruthlessness of Artemis: the young men who are beaten by Atalanta "die on the spot," as Apollodorus recounts with a certain relish. Sometimes it is Atalanta herself, seizing her bow and arrows, who dispatches the hapless suitors as soon as she crosses the finish line. Or else their lives are forfeit to the king, her father, while Atalanta looks on with (perhaps) a tear of regret for their fate. While the goddess Artemis indeed was often ruthless, especially when her dignity was affronted, this "outrun me or die" element in the story of Atalanta doesn't ring true. There are no other signs of cruelty in her past; rather, she shows a touching innocence in her eagerness to be accepted as a sporting comrade.

It seems more plausible to view the marriage-or-death option as a later embellishment reflecting male fears of physical prowess or mastery in women, a kind of castration anxiety. On a subtler level, this antagonism to physical achievement by women is manifest, even today, in negative valuations of women athletes, their competitive spirit, strong bodies, and discipline training, all of which are equated with "lack of femininity" by more traditional segments of society. Such depreciation where she seeks admiration and approval must be especially confusing to Atalanta, who has grown up apart from civilized men and their prejudices.

Atalanta's growing ambivalence is the real theme of her final race. Ovid indicates that Atalanta is strongly drawn to Hippomenes—for the first time in her life, she is vulnerable to Eros. So, in effect, she colludes in her own seduction by Aphrodite's golden apples. The truth is, if Atalanta stays in *kairos*, maintaining her athletic focus, she would never notice the apples, much less turn aside from her path for them. By falling back into "real time," she also ends up falling into real life, with all its complexities and competing demands.

Of course, these are no ordinary golden apples. Plucked from the Garden of the Hesperides, they are irresistible to both humans and goddesses—probably the same apples awarded to Aphrodite by Paris, in his famous judgment (and thus, ultimately, the cause of the Trojan War). And there are three of them. We know at once that Atalanta hasn't a chance—the third apple, like the third guess or the third door in fairy tales, is the magic one, and when Atalanta chases it, she loses the race. Edith Hamilton and Esther Harding, who admire Atalanta's independent nature, see her seduction by glittering baubles as betrayal, defeat, and finally loss of self. This interpretation is supported by Atalanta's final fate, her life-in-death as a lioness in the service of another moon goddess.

But these apples are also three golden spheres, and thus a triple symbol of the self. So Atalanta's swerve toward them can be seen also as a move toward wholeness and self-expansion. Jean Bolen takes this more positive view, that the apples remind Atalanta of other aspects of life and turn this perhaps too narrowly focused woman toward other feminine values. In her version of the myth, the three apples represent new awareness of time passing, of the importance of love, and of the (pro)creative instincts. Atalanta's choice to turn aside for the apples, then, reflects an inward turn toward relationships, intimacy, and motherhood (1984, pp. 72–74). Atalanta does embark on these new pathways, for a while; she gives birth to Parthenopaeus, one of the Seven against Thebes. But Bolen's account stops with the race and does not consider Atalanta's loss (or betrayal) of self.

Most of the women runners I spoke with about this myth lean toward the negative view of Atalanta's final race, ascribing her defeat to Hippomenes' trickery and her own loss of focus. But there is also much sympathy for Atalanta's capitulation to the lures of Aphrodite and Demeter. As Kathrine Switzer put it, "I also think that Atalanta could have just gotten a bit tired of it all, which is what I relate to as well. I mean, she proven her point and it was okay to relax a little, and the apples sweetened the pill a bit."

Atalanta's Modern Sisters

Switzer is unusual in her familiarity with the details of Atalanta's story. Most women runners, even those who wear medals bearing her image, know her only as a fleet-footed and independent maiden who defied tradition to run and compete alongside men. But all can identify strongly with this image, since they are truly trailblazers and pioneers in their own right. It is perhaps difficult for men, and for nonathletic women, to realize the extent of bias against women in sports, which was strongly apparent until very recently. Atalanta wins the sympathy of elite women runners because she follows her own path and excels despite similar bias.

But there are numerous other ways in which Atalanta's life has resonance and meaning for modern athletic women. In particular, her lifelong search for identity and the exploration of her physical nature are concerns of the present. For example, most women runners over age thirty were called tomboys in their childhood and adolescence. One suspects that they would have had happy hours as Artemis's "bears" in ancient Greece. But in mid-twentieth-century America, the love of sports and competition was considered somehow inappropriate for girls and somewhat suspicious after puberty. Some women had strong encouragement from their fathers to excel athletically, but many others, lacking such support, felt doubts about their own femininity, if not their sexuality.

Like Atalanta, modern women runners seek to define their individuality through physical activity and achievement. And in the process, many have encountered the same bias that Atalanta found in her quest for adventure. Arlene Blum, a runner, mountaineer, and leader of the first women's expedition to climb Annapurna, quotes a letter she received from the leader of a (male) expedition to which she applied several years earlier (1980, p. 1):

> Dear Miss Blum:
>
> Not too easy a letter to write as your prior work in Peru demonstrates your ability to go high, and a source I trust has furnished a glowing account of your pleasant nature in the mountains.
>
> But one woman and nine men would seem to me to be unpleasant high on the open ice, not only in excretory situations, but in the easy masculine companionship which is so vital a part of the joy of an expedition.
>
> Sorry as hell.

One suspects that Arlene's emotions on receiving this reply closely paralleled those of Atalanta when (in some versions) she was barred from sailing with Jason on the *Argo*.

Besides contending with societal attitudes, Atalanta had to face disapproval in her own home, an experience shared by many modern runners. One elite woman athlete recalls how her husband frowned when she first began to outrun men in races. "Why can't you get your exercise in a more feminine way, like golf or tennis?" he suggested. Rather than contend with such subtle disparagement, most women runners end up marrying men who share their love of the sport and support their competitive goals.

There are other, more positive ways in which elite women runners resemble Atalanta. The best competitors, at any age, share her total disregard for conventional, limiting beliefs. Sister Marion Irvine, a Dominican nun who took up running at age 49 and qualified for the Olympic marathon trials at age 54, never heard or believed that "older" women can't run fast. She just went out and did regular workouts with the younger women and men (Ullyot 1979, pp. 82–84). Now in her sixties, she holds the age-group world record for every distance she has run. Like Sister Marion, all top runners start with the unswerving belief that they can achieve their goals, however lofty. Without such belief in their own ability, they are sure to fall short.

Similarly, elite runners must be able to focus during races and stay in *kairos* time. This intense concentration is found in all top competitors and may be a natural gift. Studies of marathoners have shown a striking difference between mental strategies used by runners in the middle of the pack and those who finish near the top. The less competitive or recreational runners tend to "dissociate," thinking of anything but the race at hand, to help themselves through the pain and hard work of running the long miles. Elite women runners, like their male counterparts, "associate" for the entire race, focusing on their bodies, how their muscles feel, where they are tense and need to relax, holding a fast pace, keeping to a plan. Time seems to stand still, or to go very fast, or both at once. As one woman describes her mental state in a long race, "I don't notice anything around me. I'm just listening to my body, and in the moment, and then after a while I come out of the moment and the race is over. It doesn't seem to take long at all."

Perhaps the closest connection between Atalanta and her modern sisters is the pure joy they can experience in running. Not all runs are glorious, of course, and real women, unlike those in myth, get sore muscles and feel fatigue. But the satisfaction and pleasure derived from using and moving the body in a free and natural way are profound. Until this century, women were discouraged from being physical, both by custom and by the confining clothes they had to wear. The simple tunic worn by Atalanta, leaving her limbs free, would have been scandalously immodest before the modern era. In many parts of the world, women are still forbidden to show their limbs, much less use them. Unless women are recognized as physical creatures, with as much natural desire for movement and activity as men, they have no chance to find or express themselves through sports. Atalanta led the way in reclaiming the fields of play for women.

Finally we come to the question of Eros, the need for intimacy and relationship. Atalanta was so focused on her athletic goals that she had to be tricked into honoring Aphrodite—or perhaps she feared losing herself, as the oracle warned. In ancient times, marriage and family marked the end of childhood, play, and freedom for women—Atalanta's choice was a stark one, either/or. Modern women runners, fortunately, have more options. In effect, they can pick up the apples and run their own race, too. Many are married or in other long-term relationships, many have children. Motherhood may even turn out to be advantageous, since several top runners have come back after childbirth to achieve new personal and world records (Ullyot 1986, pp. 24–30). But that's another story.

References

Blum, A. 1980. *Annapurna: A Women's Place*. London: Granada.

Bolen, J. S. 1984. *Goddesses in Everywoman*. New York: Harper and Row.

_____. 1992. Personal communication.

Hamilton, E. 1940. *Mythology*. Boston: Little, Brown and Company.

Harding, E. 1971. *Women's Mysteries*. New York: Harper and Row.

Jacoby, M. 1990. *Individuation and Narcissism*. London: Routledge.

Lewis, L. 1982. Sprinting toward Jerusalem. *Running* 4:65.

Ovid. *Metamorphoses*, Charles Boer, trans. Dallas: Spring Publications, 1989.

Simpson, M. 1976. *Gods and Heroes of the Greeks: The Library of Apollodorus*. Amherst, Mass.: University of Massachusetts Press.

Ullyot, J. 1974. *Women's Running*. Mountain View, Calif.: World Publications.

_____. 1979. *Running Free*. New York: G. P. Putnam's Sons.

_____. 1986. Will motherhood improve your running? *Runner's World* 21:24–28.

Archetypology and Jungian Typology in Elite Women Runners

Joan Lamb Ullyot
Katharine Myers

As discussed in the previous paper in this volume, the myth of Atalanta has special resonance for modern women runners, who identify with her athleticism, directness, and joy in using the body (pp. 145). Atalanta, who was rescued and suckled by a she-bear, symbol of Artemis, is herself a human personification of this virgin goddess. Artemis, the huntress with her arrows, embodies qualities valuable and necessary for women who want to excel in competitive running—a "solitary" sport demanding self-discipline, inner directedness, self-confidence, and perseverance in the face of adversity. It is safe to assume that successful women runners share a strong unconscious identification with the Artemis archetype.

The present study explores to what degree this unconscious identification, as expressed in real-life running success, may correlate with both conscious identification with the archetype, and traditional Jungian personality types. We assessed the first variable, conscious identification (or sympathy) with Artemis qualities, by using a simple ranking questionnaire (fig. 1) based on attributes of the seven goddesses described by Jean Shinoda Bolen (1984, pp. 301–302). To explore personality type, we used Form J of the Myers-Briggs Type Indicator (MBTI). This enables us to utilize two scoring systems: the standard system and a new scoring system still in the research stage, the Type Differentiation Indicator or TDI (Saunders 1987). The standard scores on four scales (Extraversion-Introversion, Sensing-iNtuiting, Thinking-Feeling, Judging-Perceiving) yield sixteen basic personality types, e.g., INTP, ESTJ, etc. The TDI uses twenty-seven subscales to indicate differences within type (we will describe these subscales as well as the construction of the TDI later).

Figure 1. *Goddess Archetypes*

Artemis (Diana)	Sister, competitor, athletic, feminist. Independent, loves autonomy. Focused; sets and achieves goals for herself. Persevering, self-sufficient. Goddess of moon and hunt.
Athena (Minerva)	Father's daughter, strategist, thinker. Problem solver, intellectual. Works well with men and in "men's fields." Craftswoman. Goddess of wisdom and crafts.
Hestia (Vesta)	Maiden aunt, wise woman, keeper of the hearth. Lover of solitude and spirituality. Homemaker. Goddess of hearth and temple.
Hera (Juno)	Wife, commitment maker. Values marriage and fidelity. Goddess of marriage.
Demeter (Ceres)	Mother, nurturer. Generous, supportive, giver of love and food to family, children. "Earth mother." Goddess of grain.
Persephone (Proserpina)	Mother's daughter. Receptive, compliant, innocent, youthful. Open to imagination and the psychic. Maiden, queen of the underworld.
Aphrodite (Venus)	Lover. Sensual, sexual, passionate. Creative and procreative. Enjoys pleasure and beauty. Goddess of love and beauty.

(Adapted from Jean Shinoda Bolen, *Goddesses in Everywoman* (New York: Harper and Row, 1984).)

We were particularly fortunate to enlist as subjects in this study some of the most renowned and successful women runners in the world. Thirty-nine out of fifty elite runners contacted returned the MBTI questionnaire, while twenty-seven out of thirty also completed the goddess ranking form. A review of the MBTI literature did not reveal any prior studies of a comparable group of female athletes, but we were able to make a comparison with type distribution data from a group of elite male marathoners (Gontang, Clitsome and Kostrubala 1977, pp. 263–271).

In order to explore possible differences in typology within our total group of runners, we further divided the thirty-nine MBTI respondents into three equal subgroups, corresponding roughly to degree of athletic success. Group C included women who train and compete regularly and win local races or age-group awards, but consider running an avocation rather than a vocation; all these women have full-time jobs and/or families. Group B included

Table 1. *Ranking of Archetypes by Elite Women Runners*

Scale	1	2	3	4	5	6	7
Artemis	19	6	1	0	0	1	0
Athena	2	10	3	4	3	4	1
Hestia	0	2	3	3	5	6	8
Hera	2	2	3	8	7	4	1
Demeter	2	4	6	4	1	8	2
Persephone	0	2	1	2	5	4	13
Aphrodite	2	1	10	6	6	0	2

women who compete successfully in national events, Olympic Trials qualifiers, and several Olympians and age-group record holders. Several women in this group are professional runners who support themselves by their athletic skill. Group A, who might be called the "super-elite," are the top international racers, holders of national and world records, and Olympic contenders and medalists. Almost all of these women are full-time, professional athletes, although some also have families making other, important demands on their attention and energies.

Archetypal Identification

Participants were asked to rank the seven goddesses in order of preference, 1 through 7, "according to how much of each you feel is in you." They were also assured that "each of us is a mixture of many types." Thus, each runner had to decide with which archetypes she felt the least affinity (ranked 6 or 7) as well as the most (ranked 1 or 2). No description of the archetypes was given beyond the very brief capsule summary by each name. Only two of the respondents indicated that they were already familiar with Bolen's book, our source for the descriptions, or otherwise well acquainted with these classical female archetypes. The goddesses were listed in the order they are discussed by Bolen, with Artemis at the top of the page. We do not feel that this order had any particular influence on ranking, as high ranking was also given to goddesses further down the list, such as Aphrodite.

The responses were tabulated by hand and appear in table 1. The most obvious and striking finding was a powerful conscious identification with Artemis, who was ranked in the top two by 25 out of 27 respondents. Only one runner ranked Artemis lower than third in affinity. In view of Artemis's listed attributes (competitor, athletic, focused, independent . . .), it is hardly surprising that elite runners would recognize and value these traits in themselves. Interestingly, Artemis was ranked lowest by a former world-class runner who is currently more preoccupied with home and family than with competition—truly an Atalanta who has been lured from the fray by the golden apples! However, she was the exception in her lower valuation of attributes which served her well in the past.

No such clear pattern of preference emerged among the other six goddess archetypes, although Persephone was scored in the bottom two by 17 runners (63%). Since Persephone is described as "receptive, compliant . . ." and "Mother's daughter," she is in many ways the opposite of Artemis and thus did not strike a strong chord with most respondents. Conversely, the "Father's daughter," Athena, was first runner-up to Artemis. Twelve of the respondents ranked her in the top two, ten others in the middle. This high valuation of Athena presumably reflects the strong paternal support and encouragement of athletic endeavors, reported by so many women runners. Athena also tended to be ranked higher by respondents who have excelled in academics or in "thinking" endeavors such as writing.

Almost all the women felt some identification with both Aphrodite and Hera, the former being ranked in the middle (3, 4 and 5 on the scale) by 22 runners, the latter by 18. Demeter, archetype of the nurturer, was valued highest by the newer mothers among the respondents, but also garnered points from women without children, especially those who noted that they enjoy cooking and/or homemaking. Generally, the women who ranked the goddess archetypes in themselves felt that they were indeed "a mixture of many types." Apart from one or two strong preferences or aversions (i.e., for Artemis or to Persephone), there was evidence of much indecision around the middle rankings, in the form of erasures and two- or even three-way ties on some of the forms. For purposes of tabulation, such ties were eliminated by follow-up questioning, so that all respondents eventually chose a specific numerical rank for each archetype.

In view of the marked variety in responses to all but the Artemis archetype, we felt that there was a great psychological diversity among elite runners. Indeed, the only common threads seem to be athletic success and a conscious affinity for the goddess that Jean Bolen calls "a personification of an independent feminine spirit" (1984, p. 49). Perhaps it is the successful expression of this spirit, utilizing the essential Artemis qualities of "goal focus, intensity, competitiveness, and will," that frees up these women to honor other archetypes and play other roles in their non-running lives.

Personality Type

Is there any particular Jungian personality type which may correlate with athletic success? How does one measure such intangibles as determination, self-confidence, focus, and self-discipline?

To the extent that these traits define character rather than behavior preferences, they would seem to elude study by any scientific instrument, whether qualitative or quantitative. However, we hoped that by using the twenty-seven subscales of the TDI, in addition to the broader MBTI groupings, we might see a pattern emerging, reflecting traits useful for training and racing. For example, elite runners must inevitably spend long hours alone on the roads, training 100 miles or more per week. Top marathoners must stay intensely focused for two to three hours straight during competition. Also among our respondents were several ultra-marathoners, women who race for 24 hours or longer along rugged mountain trails. Knowing the solitary nature of such sports, we speculated that we might see a strong tendency toward introversion among our subjects.

Such was not the case. Almost two-thirds (64%) of our group scored as extraverts. Jung might regard this finding as evidence of unconscious compensation, in a social setting, for long introspective hours spent in training! If so, however, such unconscious compensation must be peculiar to women, since one of the most striking findings in the previously mentioned study of male marathoners was indeed a strong tendency to introversion (found in 68% of the men). This inversion of the introverted/extraverted ratio was the only significant difference we found in type distribution between our female runners and the men studied (Gontang, Clitsome and Kostrubala 1977, p. 270).

The actual number of each basic type, and the percentage of each type in our group compared to the female norm, are shown in table 2. Nine of the runners (23%) are ENFP types; this percentage

Table 2. *MBTI Results for Elite Women Runners*

	Sensing Thinking	Sensing Feeling	Intuiting Feeling	Intuiting Thinking
Introverted *Judging*	I S T J N = 3 % = 7.69 I = 1.58	I S F J N = 2 % = 5.13 I = 0.54	I N F J N = 0 % = 0.00 I = 0.00	I N T J N = 4 % = 10.26 I = 7.26[B]
Introverted *Perceiving*	I S T P N = 0 % = 0.00 I = 0.00	I S F P N = 1 % = 2.56 I = 0.45	I N F P N = 3 % = 7.69 I = 1.77	I N T P N = 1 % = 2.56 I = 1.20
Extraverted *Perceiving*	E S T P N = 0 % = 0.00 I = 0.00	E S F P N = 2 % = 5.13 I = 0.43	E N F P N = 9 % = 23.08 I = 2.45[A]	E N T P N = 2 % = 5.13 I = 1.61
Extraverted *Judging*	E S T J N = 3 % = 7.69 I = 0.61	E S F J N = 2 % = 5.13 I = 0.25[B]	E N F J N = 4 % = 10.26 I = 2.30	E N T J N = 3 % = 7.69 I = 3.28

[A]Implies significance at the .05 level, that is, chi-square > 3.8
[B]Implies significance at the .01 level, that is, chi-square > 6.6
N = 39
% = percent of total choosing this group who fall into this type
I = self-selection index: ratio of percent of type in group to percent in sample

is significantly higher than the norm (2.43 times). Of equal significance was our high number of INTJ's (4 out of 39, or 10.3%). We had no one with the types ISTP, ESTP, or INFJ, which are all less common generally. Of greatest statistical significance in our type distribution study was the predominance of the intuitive function (N) which was preferred by two-thirds of the runners. The percentages of NT, EN, and NJ combinations among these elite athletes were all equally high. The "self-selection index" of the women runners, in comparison to the base population of female students (representing a heterogeneity of types), is very high. It is intriguing that the elite women runners are simultaneously so different from the female norms and so close to the male marathoners, apart from the extraversion/introversion ratio.

Despite the highly significant tendency toward intuitive perceiving in our thirty-nine women runners, we cannot identify any particular preference type or types associated with success as a long-distance runner. We know from experience that top women runners have to be what we might call "strong-minded," but measurable correlates of this term remain elusive. And since 13 of the 16 basic types are represented in this one small group of strong-minded women, it seems that there is no special "athletic personality" category.

Type Differentiation Study

A limiting aspect of the usual MBTI typology is that it utilizes dichotomous scoring; that is, one is either extraverted or introverted, either sensing or intuiting, and so on. Individuals who are only slightly on one side or the other are grouped with those who may be quite extreme in their preference. For example, one of our runners, listed as our only ISFP type, scored very close to neutral in her S and F preferences; two or three different responses might have turned her into an INFP or ISTP type. It is for this reason that we expanded our analysis by using the TDI, which is designed to reveal differences within each type, using twenty-seven continuous scales (Saunders 1987). For example, the sensing-intuiting alternative is described by five subscales (8–12 on our graphs), on each of which a score of 0 to 10 is possible. These scales are described as concrete-abstract, realistic-imaginative, practical-intellectual, experiential-theoretical, and traditional-original. Thus, a runner who tends to be very abstract and intellectual generally, and who is an N in regular MBTI testing, might score as low as 0 or 1, i.e., S, on any single scale of the expanded analysis.

The TDI represents the continuing development of major unpublished work that Isabel Myers was in the process of validating at the time of her death in 1980. Her primary focus had been on meticulous crafting of the MBTI to achieve the maximum possible accuracy in determining an individual's Jungian preference type, as well as on research to assess the validity and reliability of both the instrument and the theory. However, from the beginning of her development of the type indicator, she was interested in patterns of individual differences within type. Each form of the indicator, with the exception of Form E, included unscored research items addressed to this issue.

David Saunders, who had worked closely with Myers in the early years of the indicator's development at Educational Testing

Services, developed the subscales and groupings in the TDI through an elaborate process of factor analysis in which each item is correlated with every other item. This analysis results in groupings of items which have a common core content. Saunders found twenty-seven groupings, called first-order factors, and these are the basis of the twenty-seven subscales of the TDI. A second factor analysis of the subscales was undertaken, producing five groupings of the subscales, or second-order factors. Four of the groupings correspond with the four MBTI scales (E-I, S-N, T-F, and J-P). The fifth factor includes seven subscales called the comfort-discomfort scales. These scales suggest the degree of ease individuals feel within themselves and display in their use of Jung's four basic functions—two of perceiving (S-N) and two of judging (T-F). Taken together, the twenty-seven subscales thus give a detailed view not just of one's preferred mode of functioning, but also of individual variations in the way this mode is used in daily life.

As an example of variability within type, and to help in understanding our graphs based on TDI reports, figure 2 shows the TDI data for one of the authors, Joan Ullyot. Although Joan is listed at the top of the page as an INFP type (introverted, intuiting, feeling and perceiving), her low preference for F, indicated by a score of 7 (where 0 = no preference, 60 = maximum preference), suggests that she might equally well by typed as INTP. The T-F subscale analysis (third from the top) on the TDI, using a continuous scale of 0–10, shows Joan to be way toward the left (T) side of the norms for scales 17 and 19, but more F than the norms on the remaining three subscales. Such out-of-pattern responses can be reflective of strong personality quirks which account for many of the fascinating differences among people of the same general type.

To explore whether there was any characteristic intra-type pattern among our group of runners, we calculated the mean score (0–10) on each of the twenty-seven continuous TDI scales, first for the entire group, then for each of our three subgroups, A, B, and C. These results were then plotted against the underlying norms (based on 7,157 adult females) used in the TDI reports.

Figure 3 is a comparison of our total group of thirty-nine athletes, the subgroup (A) of 13 super-elite runners, and the norms. The x-axis in this figure shows the scale numbers corresponding to the functional pairs listed in figure 2. Thus, the first five scales represent scores along the E-I continuum; the next five, numbered 8–12, are for the S-N preferences; the third set of five, numbered 14–20, show the T-F range; and the last five scales, numbered 20–25, show the J-P preferences. For greater clarity, we have

Figure 2. *MB Type Differentiation Indicator: Joan Ullyot Profile*

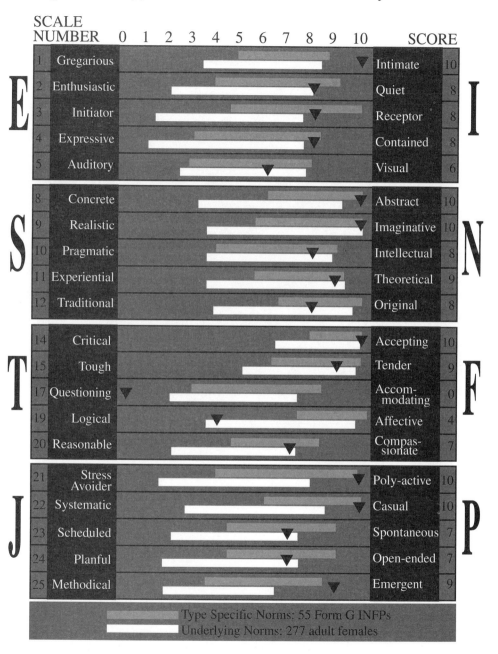

Figure 3. MB Type Differentiation Indicator: Elite Female Runners

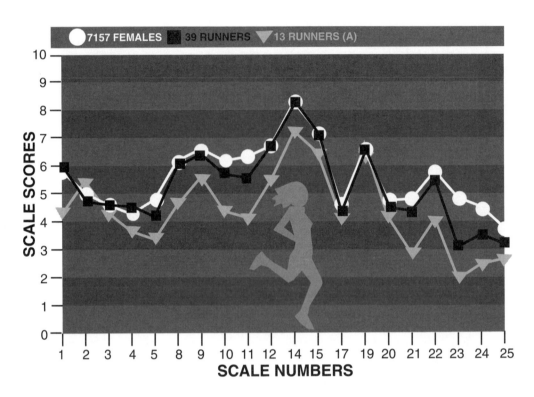

omitted from this graph the last seven subscales, the so-called comfort-discomfort indices. Although we have data on these scales, which are an integral part of the TDI, our group of runners did not show any significant deviation from the norms currently available for them, which are based on a much smaller population (277 women).

In all twenty scales illustrated in figure 3, low scores show a preference for the first function in each pair (E, S, T, and J), high scores a preference for the opposite function (I, N, F, and P). Scores for the 7,157 female norms average in the midrange, 4–7, for most subscales, indicating a balance of types in the general population. A leaning toward the feeling function, seen in women more than men, is shown by slightly higher scores on scales 14 and 15. One striking aspect of this graph is the degree to which the first two lines, those for the norms and for our total running group, can be superimposed. This similarity is all the more interesting in view of the small number of women in our study and the fairly large standard deviation for the population norms (Saunders 1987, p. 15). There is a suggestion of group divergence in the direction of judging (23–25), but this is barely noticeable in the general overlap of the thirty-nine runners' means and the normal means.

For the group, the TDI results appear to support our conclusion based on the MBTI typing alone, that no particular personality preferences are associated with the ability to excel in running. In fact, the differences in type distribution that were significant in the dichotomous scoring, reflecting a preference for intuiting rather than sensing perception among the runners, are not seen here in the expanded analysis (where scales 8–12 correspond to the S-N preferences). This difference may be related to the different ages of the base populations used in the MBTI and TDI analyses, since the adult female norms used in the latter are higher, more N, than the student scores currently available.

However, when we separated out the scores of our group A, comparing just this top third of the runners with the population norms (bottom line, fig. 3), we found a significant enhancement of the points of divergence only hinted at in the larger group results. The line for group A, while paralleling that of the population norm, appears to be consistently lower (more S) on the S-N scales and also lower (more J) on the J-P scales (number 21–25). Because there are only thirteen women in group A, and in view of the larger standard deviations in the norms noted above, not all of these trends can be called statistically significant at present. However, we did find significant variation from the norms on threes scales: 11, 23, and 25.[1] Referring back to figure 2, we can say that the top women runners we studied are measurably more "experiential," "scheduled," and "methodical" than the general population. David Saunders, who developed the TDI scales, defines these traits as follows:

> Experiential (contrasts with Theoretical): "Rely primarily on direct experience; particularly cautious not to overgeneralize;

---

[1]Significance was measured by performing a t-test on all the divergent scales. Probability of getting these results by chance was lowest on scales 11 ($p = .03$), 23 ($p < .05$), and 25 ($p = .0007$).

may be fussy and adamant about details, even at the expense of larger considerations."

Scheduled (contrasts with Spontaneous): "Comfortable with routine; regard tried methods and tested routines as the only reliable, efficient way to get things done; routine provides an important degree of comfort and security."

Methodical (contrasts with Emergent): "Develop plans in great detail; program themselves in advance in a very thorough and precise way; identify and order specific steps well before undertaking any project." (1989)

These descriptions will sound very apt to anyone familiar with the high level of long-term, focused training required of top-caliber runners. The strong goal orientation implied in the "methodical" attitude also correlates with the capsule description of Artemis in figure 1: "focused . . . sets and achieves goals for herself . . . persevering." This intense focus is essential for elite runners who, regardless of their particular personality type, need to plan for important races months and often years in advance and show enormous self-discipline in adhering to detailed daily running schedules. Their international success in racing shows that the statistically significant trait preferences identified by the TDI have very practical career benefits. But personality type is certainly not destiny: despite the preponderance of S and J traits among the top runners, one of this group scored strongly P (non-J) and another strongly N (non-S). No one in group A, however, was strongly both N and P, a combination found in four of the B group. We can postulate that it is very helpful, but not crucial, for elite runners to be experiential, scheduled, and methodical in their training—if not in other aspects of their lives.

Summary

We studied thirty-nine women who excel in competitive long-distance running, a sport demanding "Artemis" qualities of focus, self-sufficiency, discipline, and perseverance as well as joy in athleticism. All the women were tested for MBTI type, with further intra-type differentiation using the TDI subscales. Twenty-seven of the respondents also filled out a simple form ranking their preferences among the seven goddess archetypes described by Bolen (1984).

The most striking finding was a strong conscious identification with the Artemis archetype, which earned high ranking with all but one runner. The MBTI results showed significantly more intuiting (N) types among runners as compared to female norms; this difference disappeared when all thirty-nine elite women runners were compared to elite male marathoners, who were, however, much more introverted than the women runners. Thirteen of the sixteen basic MBTI types were represented among our thirty-nine runners, leading us to conclude that there is no particular personality type associated with success in running.

More detailed comparison of the total running group (all thirty-nine) against 7,137 female norms, using the TDI subscales, suggested that certain S and J qualities might be more prevalent among runners. Comparison of group A, the thirteen top competitors, against the norms showed that these internationally successful women were indeed significantly more experiential (S), scheduled, and methodical (J) than the general population. These traits, particularly the last, seem to correlate well with the Artemis qualities that almost all of our runners consciously admired and identified within themselves.

References

Bolen, J. S. 1984. *Goddesses in Everywoman*. New York: Harper and Row.

Gontang, A., T. Clitsome, and T. Kostrubala. 1977. A psychological study of 50 sub-3-hour marathoners. In *The Long Distance Runner*. New York: Urizen Books.

Saunders, D. 1987. *Type Differentiation Indicator Manual*. Palo Alto, Calif.: Consulting Psychologists Press, 1992.

_____. 1989. *MBTI Expanded Analysis Report Scales*. Palo Alto, Calif.: Consulting Psychologists Press.

Joan Lamb Ullyot, *M.D., is a master's distance runner and authority on sports medicine and psychology. She has a private practice in psychotherapy in Snowmass, Colorado, and is a candidate in the Interregional Society of Jungian Analysts.*

Katharine Myers, *M.A., is a consultant in the development and applications of the Myers-Briggs Type Indicator.*

Versus

Archetypal Images in Professional Wrestling

Eric Zengota

> Empirically, the self appears . . . in the form of
> a totality symbol, such as the circle, square,
> *quadratum circuli*, cross, etc. When it repre-
> sents a *complexio oppositorum*, a union of
> opposites, it can also appear as a united dual-
> ity, in the form, for instance, of *tao* as the inter-
> play between *yang* and *yin*, or of the hostile
> brothers, or of the hero and his adversary (arch-
> enemy, dragon) . . . as a play of light and
> shadow, although conceived as a totality and
> unity in which the opposites are united.
> —C. G. Jung, *Psychological Types*

Two nearly naked men grasp each other. They twist limbs, pound
backs, stomp stomachs, and chop throats. They wind around each
other's bodies in myriad positions. Finally, as one lies helpless on
his back, his opponent covers his body, hooks his leg, and presses
his shoulders to the mat. Sweaty, at times bloody, the victor exults
in either the cheers or the excoriation of the crowd.

This scene—part ancient *pankration*, part simulated
foreplay—is the stock in trade of professional wrestling or, as it is
also known, rasslin'. Matches on both network and cable television set viewing records. Matches by the hundreds are held across
the country, and successful subindustries—videotapes, T-shirts,
feature films, photographs, fan clubs and magazines, fantasy
match clubs—attest to its widespread popularity. One thing is

Reprinted with permission of *Quadrant: The Journal of Contemporary
Jungian Thought. Quadrant* is a publication of the C. G. Jung Foundation in
New York.

clear: professional wrestling has secured a hold over millions of American psyches.

Why does this sport exert such fascination for people of all ages? What makes otherwise placid people scream insults in frenzied abandon? Why do hundreds of hands stretch out to touch a wrestler as he walks to and from the ring?

The reasons are as diverse as the millions of fans, but a Jungian viewpoint reveals certain recurring archetypal images that pattern the phenomenon and are all the more powerful because they appeal to the fans' subliminal, instinctive needs and desires.

Opposites: Conflict and Conjunction

To paraphrase Heraclitus, "War is the father of all rasslin'." Call it battle, conflict, or contention, the clash of dualities is the heart of the sport. No matter how the industry has evolved into the gimmickry of glittering robes, shouted interviews, and prematch strutting around the ring, the struggle between two men remains its essence, just as the elemental combat between polarities is one of Jung's basic thematic concerns.

What happens when men clash in the ring? Basically, one defeats the other by a "pinfall" or "submission hold." Although any style is possible—from scientific moves leading to a pinfall all the way to an out-and-out brawl—defeat and triumph are the inextricably linked opposites toward which the entire drama is played out.

The choice between clever moves and all-out brutality has its corollary in ancient Greek wrestling, which featured both regular grappling and the vicious, often fatal *pankration*. Professional wrestlers today have also died in ring accidents, and they commonly suffer an array of broken bones, separated vertebrae, concussions, bruises, and cuts. The injuries are often debilitating, even career-ending. In this sense, the flavor, if not the fact, of death is present as the inevitable fate of the warrior. So it is no surprise that one wrestler is nicknamed The Modern Day Warrior, another is The Warlord, and The Ultimate Warrior has arrogated the mana of them all.

Like any phenomenon, even sadism—the sport's driving force—has two faces. An active, aggressive man often enters the profession exactly because he can enjoy rough-and-tumble encounter while getting fairly well paid for his trouble. Others sound more primitive. "I like to hurt people," states one rassler in a particularly blood-filled videotape which uses his statement as a title.

On the other hand, the passive sadist, multiplied by millions, attends the matches and watches the programs. The fevered delight of today's howling masses has its counterparts not only in Greek spectators watching men die in bloody pain and Roman mobs reveling in the slaughter of gladiators, but also in the psychological dynamic that underlies all these manifestations.

Simply put, this dynamic is the intrapsychic struggle between endless pairs of opposite tendencies. The more unintegrated and less conscious the struggle, the more it is projected onto the extrapsychic canvas. Both wrestler and fan externalize their potentially self-conquering energy so that it receives at least a temporary resolution via the heightened battle in the ring. The psychodrama is addictive; the wrestler craves the thrill of battle, and the spectacle plays to a packed house night after night.

The most common duality employed in professional wrestling illustrates how the strife of opposites fuels the spirit of the match. "Hero" and "villain" are sophisticated evolutions of victor and vanquished. The terms imply that the spectators have an interest beyond the outcome itself. Very often, opponents are of different physical types, enhancing their polarity: fair-haired/dark-haired; clean-shaven/bearded; lean and muscular/rounded and smooth. Often, the interaction employs all the symbols of Good versus Evil, as in a morality play.

But, as Jung said, "every psychological extreme secretly contains its own opposite or stands in some sort of intimate and essential relationship to it. Indeed it is from this tension that it derives it particular dynamism" (Jung 1952a, par. 581). He could have been describing the mutual dependency and volatile changeability of hero and villain roles. Hulk Hogan turned from vicious rulebreaker to beloved champion after his feud with a Russian. (Foreigners, the ultimate others, are particularly useful in effecting transformations.) In contrast, nice guys like Mike DiBiase flip into villainy, usually when betrayed by a tag team partner or offered a "lucrative contract" by a "manager." Such enantiodromic switches can be either instantaneous or the result of long-seething feuds.

Once the reversal is engineered, the public picks up the new cues at once. Fans switch loyalties as fast as wrestlers switch roles or, as Jung described the "uncritical eye" that perceives change in simplistic terms: "the good man succumbs to evil, the sinner is converted to good, and that . . . is the end of the matter." Looking more closely, however, "those endowed with a finer moral sense or deeper insight cannot deny that this seeming one-after-another is in reality a happening of events side-by-side" (Jung 1955–1956, par. 206).

When switches occur, even physical attributes lose their traditional connotation, indicating their secret interdependence. African-Americans and Native Americans are often swarthy heroes instead of archetypal "shadows." Blond beauties are mistrusted despite their "lightness." One transformation provided a triple whammy: a black good guy went bad, bleached his hair, and called himself The Natural.

Essentially, the changeability of hero and villain roles is rasslin's version of the problematic relationship between ego and shadow. The hero falling precipitously into public disfavor is like the ego losing integrity and strength as it is cut off from the approval of the larger arena, the betrayed collective. In contrast, the redeemed villain is like the shadow element that comes to light and is integrated within the larger sphere of the Self. This interplay never loses its dynamism. Energy travels between the two poles in a constant flurry of mutual tension. After all, Hulk and Mike can switch back at any time!

In one contest, a cogent symbol came to life. Each man—one dark, one fair—had gripped the head of his opponent between his own shins. It was up to the referee, the third man in the ring, to end the stalemate by prying apart this *coniunctio*, this living yin-yang.

Extrahuman Figures

The archetypes of the extrahuman are divided into "the demonically superhuman and . . . the bestially subhuman" (Jung 1948, par. 419). Adopting the look and manner of either elevated or degraded figures, some rasslers are abstracted from the merely human world and enter a timeless realm where they are granted different privileges and treated with expectations appropriate to their image. Chief among them is that they rarely if ever exhibit pain. They are indestructible, like comic book figures, and as such "are indications of the *transconscious character* of the pairs of opposites. They do not belong to the ego-personality but are supraordinate to it" (Jung 1955–1956, par. 4). In fact, some wrestlers were transformed into characters in a Saturday morning animated series, thereby losing another "dimension."

The Superhuman: Divinities, Kings, and Personae

The extrahuman rassler is often associated with divine mythical counterparts. The current pantheon includes, for example, Hercules, who favors the standing bear hug, recalling the legendary Hercules' defeat of Antaeus. From Adrian Adonis and Argentina Apollo to Zeus, the gods have descended.

Hyperbole also catapults a wrestler into the transhuman realm. The Million Dollar Man (Ted DiBiase gone bad), who stuffs dollar bills into the mouths of his defeated opponents, recalls both the fabled Croesus and the real Roman emperors. His arrogant image increases the distance between himself and the mere mortals who insult him by word and gesture. Bruno Sammartino has long been know as The Living Legend. His protégé, Larry Zybysko, attacked him with a chair and became an instant villain who immediately dubbed himself The New Living Legend. Such a scene is a clear if unwitting reference to the Old King and the New King as described by Frazer in *The Golden Bough*.

A less than subtle pandering to the psychological craving for royalty was apparent in the recent "dynastic" conflicts staged in one promotion. The King of Wrestling, a curly blond Midwesterner in crown and robes, was carried into the ring by his retinue (all villains, of course) and forced his vanquished foes to bow in homage before him. He was dethroned by a bulky Samoan with an allegedly real royal background, who in turn was replaced by a brown-haired astigmatic Southern redneck whose banner was the American flag and whose scepter was a two-by-four. Ironically, these kings never become champions, which is rasslin's version of the (parliamentary) distinction between head of state and head of government.

Often wrestlers' real names are suppressed. Assumed titles add to the men's mystery, even when they do not wear masks. As it is, looking right at the face of a nameless man means he is no longer really "there." A persona called Sting or The Brooklyn Bomber has supplanted his individuality. Such a wrestler often finds himself trapped in his character. Even outside the arena, the persona retains its mana for many fans: villains are frequently provoked into real fights and seriously assaulted.

Once again, there are analogies to ancient Greek wrestling.

When those athletes engaged in combat, they were living out the multileveled myths that informed that civilization. On a civic level, they competed for the glory of their polis; Olympic victors were often awarded a lifetime food ticket at the communal refectory. Wrestling also formed part of their training as members of the standing militia. Finally, since religious ritual underpinned athletic games, they were more or less consciously recreating their myths of constant strife: gods against titans, gods against gods, gods against men, men against men—and Hercules against everyone.

The Subhuman: Animal Powers

When a wrestler takes on theriomorphic form, he appears to be possessed by a totemistic animal. The qualities and power of that beast then become the man's trademark. As Jung points out, "the phase of the conflict of opposites is usually represented by fighting animals, such as the lion, dragon, wolf and dog" (Jung 1955–1956, p. 360n). Each of these and many others are in the rasslin' zoo.

True to the ambivalence of archetypes, some animals are friendly, others dangerous. Porky Pig, Leo "The Lion" Nomellini, and The Wolfman flourished in the past. Today, Manny "Raging Bull" Fernandez mows down the opposition. Moondogs Rex and Spot howl at the spotlights and gnaw at hug bones before clobbering opponents with them. Any of these "pets" can change in the fans' estimation without altering his style. Terry Taylor crowed after victory when he was the evil Red Rooster, right down to his dyed cockscomb, but a barnyard victory over his traitorous manager, Bobby "The Weasel" Heenan, established him as a nice guy. Jake "The Snake" Roberts, now heel, now hero, not only dresses in snake skin leotards but carries a boa constrictor named Lucifer, which he drapes over his fallen victim. George "The Animal" Steele is a slobbering fan favorite—at least this week. Only Ricky "The Dragon" Steamboat remains an uncontested hero; as a Polynesian, he is a "good" dragon.

Such ring characters mirror humanity's love-fear relationship with animals. Whether the beast is friendly or vicious, admired or laughed at, it is always given its due as a viable symbol of the man who adopts it.

Tricksters

There is very little outright comedy in professional wrestling. Laughter derives mostly from miscalculations and humiliation, although a special manic laughter is provided by wrestlers in the trickster guise of idiot outsiders. As in primitive cultures, they are accorded special privileges and are occasionally revered. New Zealand's Bushwhackers slaver, bulge their eyes, and strut grotesquely around the ring; their heavily accented speech adds to the caricature of drooling idiot. Until recently, they were hated as The Sheepherders, but they dropped the animal connection and metamorphosed into lovable fools. All the actions for which they were booed and hissed are now good-naturedly mimicked by ringside fans.

Other less infamous idiots routinely adopt the same vacant eyes, drooping jaw, and unintelligible speech. Far from being offended, fans respond positively to their rule-breaking zaniness. Chaos is part and parcel of the rasslin' cosmos.

As times, managers who have only villains under contract take on the part of the trickster. A disruptive third element, they taunt the fans, assault their man's opponent, distract the referee (the manager's complement, the good but naive third man), and generally pull focus from the battle proper. Often former wrestlers themselves, they add comic relief when hauled into the ring and given a much anticipated drubbing by the put-upon hero.

Phallos and Eros

Rasslin' underscores, paradoxically, the precariousness of masculinity. In every contest, the male principle is challenged to come out "on top." Phallic dominance, however, almost always involves erotic interplay. In a recent situation comedy, an interviewer asked professional wrestlers in a locker room, "So what is it with you guys, taking off your clothes and wrapping yourselves around each other?" Of course, he is hauled off to the showers for retribution. His line, however, sums up the ambiguity surrounding manliness and rasslin'.

Nicknames such as Megaforce and The Barbarian underscore the image of crude but effective masculinity, as do the "illegal" chains and other gladiatorlike implements. Interviews consist primarily of threats and of accusations that an opponent is a weakling. The powerful victor demonstrates his supremacy by showing off the raw strength of his near-naked body. A masked Mad Russian, taunted by the crowd, points confidently at his crotch.

In this respect, rasslin' can be seen as a legitimization of male-male eroticism, made acceptable precisely because, as a bonding element, it is overshadowed by the more culturally approved intermale aggression.

But as Jung pointed out, the brighter the light, the darker the shadow. The loser must be not only beaten but vanquished and humiliated. A victim of phallic dominance must be limp. The negation of his power is built into the very act of competition, and he is less a man for being laid out on his back, spread-eagled.

All this gives rise to degrading, sadomasochistic goings on. A wrestler pulls his opponent's trunks down to force a break or just a laugh. "Moon over Miami!" chortled one announcer as spectators leered and jeered. The trunks are quickly pulled back up—except in a recent case where the villain was stripped in front of thousands of fans and fled the ring wearing his boots and a grimace. His shame was recorded on a videotape that is now sold across the country.

More direct ploys include low blows with an arm or leg, dropping a man astride the ring ropes, reaching into the trunks for a "foreign object," and torturous holds that provoke a submission. When a loser is spread-eagled, one leg hooked to prevent his escape, he is in the passive posture known as "presenting," indicating subservience to a superior foe. A graphic combination of sex and violence occurs in a "chain match," where the men are literally chained together. At the end of one such match, a bloody Terry Funk lay face down, limbs bound askew. According to the caption, The American Dream Dusty Rhodes, howling in glee as he straddled Funk, was "riding" him.

Spectators fan the flames of the erotic subtext. A wrestler headlocking an opponent hears, "Kiss him now!" Cries of queer and fairy are meant to rile and distract a villain, except for those who feed on the insults by wearing the Gorgeous George variety of high-camp regalia. Children can also take part vicariously in reducing a rassler to passivity. Small flexible dolls enable youngsters to hold fantasy matches; the dolls are manipulated by sticking a finger up the plastic rectum.

Wrestler Nick Bockwinkel hinted at another factor in rasslin's appeal when he said that nowhere else could women, dominated and rendered sexually passive, see the men who oppress them appear in underwear and get beaten up. If he is right, then pure resentment of phallic power accounts at least in part for delight in its destruction in the ring.

Blood

Blood is life, and the gushing forth of life signals both its abundance and its fading away. Even in these days of AIDS, when athletes have voiced concern about potential infection from teammates or opponents, blood in the ring is a familiar, galvanizing image.

Some wrestlers glory in blood; when cut, their rage increases and they make the final push to victory. Winners wear their gore as a triumphal badge, while losers are carried off on stretchers or stagger away to the dressing room. Fans are thrilled by the sight, despite occasional complaints that this or that "cage match" was just too bloody. Two young men came to the matches with their girlfriends (and sat in the middle, separating the women); when a bleached blonde was flung into a corner and red spurted forth to stain his hair, the men turned to each other, eyes gleaming: "Blood? Is it? Yeah, it's blood! Awright!"

Even cannibalism has its place: many are the meanies who gnaw at a foe's forehead. Another chomped away for several minutes at his victim's shoulder, drawing streams of blood amid cries for help. In this update of the Pelops myth, the white shoulder was again the sacrificed "portion."

Not even the brightest hero is immune to the call of blood. Bob Backlund, with an impressive amateur career, was everyone's professional golden boy. But when Stan Hansen pushed him too far, Bob took to rampaging, smashing and mauling Hansen, to the fans' delight. Fanzines dubbed it "The Blood Lust of the All-American Boy."

The mingled disgust and fascination induced by blood stems from the long-standing debate about its reality. In spite of claims that capsules are always used, others maintain that certain wrestlers' skin, after years of pounding and scratching, will tear at the slightest provocation. These "bleeders" serve as players in rasslin' dramas which need just that much more excitement. Their deeply scarified skin is as much a badge of honor as it was for African warriors and nineteenth-century German student duelists.

The question of the authenticity of the blood has a curious parallel in Jung's alchemical writings, where he mentions Gerhard Dorn's *homo putissimus*, a figure who sweats blood just as Christ, *homo purissimus*, did in Gethsemane. Wrestlers also routinely get their arms tied up in the ropes, crucifixion-style, and are pounded unmercifully until the blood flows. That their sweat mingles with blood is enough to consider at least a subconscious parallel to the alchemical figures whose blood, Dorn made clear, "is 'rose-colored'; not natural or ordinary blood, but symbolic blood" (Jung 1954a, par. 390).

That blood still fascinates is evidence of its deep, instinctual power. The veritable ritual bloodletting that paints a ring scarlet provides a sustained thrill to those seeking concrete images of throbbing life.

Puer and Senex

Matches between old and young wrestlers are common. Instead of taking this for granted, it is important to remember that no other sport pits boys just out of high school against men approaching or even past sixty. Even in sports where the age range spans twenty years, there is no similar, sustained skin-to-skin contact.

The young-old dynamic is described in forthright terms, such as "that hot new sensation" facing the "raw-boned grizzled veteran." Often the newcomer is defeated by the wily seasoned combatant. One fanzine covering a match between young Tommy Rich and the old Sheik compared Rich to a South Seas virgin sacrificed to the vengeful god of war. If a newcomer is to have a successful career, the article continued, he has to bear up under any horrible experience. Only by ghastly lessons can he integrate his own power. This, then, is a rite of initiation in which a virile boy-becoming-man has to endure ritual castration for the duration of the trial.

In the reverse case, the younger wrestler demolishes the older. "Preliminary" wrestlers, men who never made it to the big time, play fall guy to the new stars year after year. The newcomers are climbing the ladder to fame and public approval, while the veterans submit to the power dynamic and the passage of time.

One interesting variation involves the large number of wrestling "families," literally father and son(s) who team up together. Fritz von Erich has had four sons at once in the sport (three of whom committed suicide), and Jacques Rougeau and Bob Armstrong three each. At the beginning of his career, the son benefits from his father's name and experience. The father's eventual retirement is often described in poignant terms as the crown being passed to his heir. In between, there are piquant clashes when two father-son tag teams face off in the ring, each defending a partner who is much more than just another wrestler.

No matter who wins, the puer/senex archetype is at work. Youth is freshness, possibility, and the future; the boy's career, full of wins and losses, lies ahead. Age is experience, limitations, and loss; a man may beat the new hope but is bound by necessity to be defeated by time. That either can be the victor demonstrates again the secret intimacy of the two sides of every archetype.

Love Slaves and Amazons

As one promotion bills them, the Gorgeous Ladies of Wrestling certainly lend a GLOW to the sport. Trapped in a blend of eroticism and violence, however, the feminine principle as embodied in professional wrestling is little more than a projection of the anima at the biological, instinctual level or a glorification of antinurturing physical prowess.

GLOW is, in fact, a cable television program designed in part to satisfy those fans who find very few female wrestlers on either broadcast shows or the live circuit. This relative scarcity reflects other fans' ambivalent attitude toward women mauling one another as well as the knowledge—or at least suspicion—that female combat is a staple of the pornography industry. To get on the air at all, even the most blatant "wrestlerette" has to tone down pornography's string bikini look, mud and Jello matches, and humiliating cat fights in which the women strip off each other's clothes.

"Like the 'supraordinate personality,' the anima is bipolar and can therefore appear positive one moment and negative the next . . ." wrote Jung (1951, par. 356). From this perspective, it is not unusual that, like their male counterparts, females face off in obvious heroine-villainess antagonisms. Women further draw from the same storehouse of instantly identifiable signs in a wide range of styles. Pretty cheerleaders and down-to-earth cowgirls face off against slinky leopard women and ratty-haired biker molls. Even goddesses such as Black Venus and Madusa [sic] Micelli incarnate in the ring, while the Terrible Mother is found in Big Bad Momma. Obese, wildly red-haired, and wearing a calico dress and bloomers, she paints her face half white and half black in a startling evocation of the maternal imago's light and dark aspects. Such a spectrum of styles, combined with some fans' delight in women warriors, adds a new dimension to Jung's insight into anima psychopathology. "The splitting of the anima into many figures is equivalent to dissolution into an indefinite state, i.e., into the unconscious, from which we may conjecture that a relative dissolution of the conscious mind is running parallel with the historical regression (a process to be observed in its extreme form in schizophrenia)" (Jung 1952b, par. 116).

One feature of pornography that has made some headway on the professional circuit is matches between men and women. Still few and far between, mixed matches has been banned in some states. Generally they are relegated to county fair or carnival settings and treated as comic interludes. Such matches could be read as the questing hero battling a vicious or bewitching female opponent. They could also reflect the deeper contrasexual relationship which, positive or negative, Jung finds is always filled with "animosity": "it is emotional, and hence collective. Affects lower the level of the relationship and bring it closer to the common instinctual basis, which no longer has anything individual about it" (Jung 1954b, par. 31). To defuse the uneasiness that may be engendered, rasslers play up outrageous behavior. Routinely breaking the same-sex-only opponent rule, they treat fans to women stomping men, men pulling women's hair, and each embarrassing the other no matter who is "on top." Their tangled limbs are a bizarre *coniunctio* fashioned by Mars rather than Aphrodite. To distance the unseemliness of sexual brawling even further, promoters frequently heighten the ludicrous aspect by teaming women with male midgets. Introducing the dwarf/cabiric motif adds a "childish" and thus less threatening tone to the slapping and spanking.

Women are also present as valets, the female equivalent of managers. They are most often depicted as clinging love slaves of muscled villains, pouting seductively at the camera, stripping the man of his outer garments before the match and interfering during it to save "their men," who are occasionally their real-life husbands. Valets exhibit little more than the dominated aspect of the feminine principle, as indicated by their names, such as Precious, Baby Doll, and Miss Blossom, with Woman being the most archetypal of all. In contrast was the cool, executively attired Ms. Alexandra York. As her men—appropriately, The Million Dollar Man and Irwin R. Shyster (IRS)—destroyed their opponents, she stood at ringside calculating their moves and predicting the time of their victories on a laptop computer. That her "Foundation" quickly foundered is a reflection not only of economic hard times but also of the short-term appeal of anima as market analyst.

Circulus Quadratus

One of the most potent images described by Jung is the "squared circle"—the same phrase used in professional wrestling to designate the ring. For Jung, squaring the circle meant foursquare solidity, wholeness, and integrity, and the resulting mandala is a symbol of the Self, the central coordinating archetype. In rasslin', it is the arena in which the physical drama is played out and onto which the inner drama of each spectator is projected in high relief.

Combat sports are the only ones in which action takes place in a square rather than on a rectangular court or playing field. Thus the primal action between warring dualities finds its home in a "perfect" geometrical area. There seem to be no limits to heightening the drama of the squared circle. In a grudge match held in Puerto Rico, oil was placed in receptacles on the ropes. When the oil was set ablaze, the ring flared with smoke and flame as the combatants pushed each other's bodies—and faces—into the fire. The thrill experienced by the crowd was evident from the cheers picked up by the ringside microphones.

As in any sport, boundaries define the field of engagement, bestowing on it the special qualities of a ritual space. Wrestlers provide a give-and-take, back-and-forth quality to the field by their use of the sides and corners. At times they crisscross, propelling themselves into the opposite ropes until one careens into the other. Such antics match Jung's observation that "often the polarity is arranged as a *quaternio* (quaternity), with the two opposites crossing one another . . . thus producing the cross as an emblem of the four elements and symbol of the sublunary field" (Jung 1955–1956, par. 1). "Posting" an opponent, throwing him into a corner with its hard turnbuckle, usually devastates him; more agile rasslers end upside-down in the corner, doubling the destruction motif. Perhaps the most potent use of the square occurs at the end of a chain match, when a man must drag his victim to all four corners before being declared the winner.

Two-man tag team matches by definition form a quaternity, pitting two light and two dark elements against one another. These matches are always chaotic, set up expressly to flout the rules. When all four are in action—strictly illegal, which is the point—partners pair up and fling their foes into each other from opposite corners, thus using the longest interior line to gather the most force.

When the edges of a ritual space are violated, the rules go out the window. Being "on the ropes," a common expression for being in trouble, prompts the referee's order to break the hold. Throwing an opponent over the ropes can result in disqualification. Landing past the borderline on the often unpadded floor immediately surrounding the ring can signal the end of the match if the victim cannot return to combat and is counted out.

This perimeter, however, is another acting space where the fans have the drama brought to their level and can interact with the players to the greatest extent possible. Here, before a match, heroes work the crowd, running around all four sides to collect the hugs and kisses of their supporters. During a match, villains and managers dish out their most dastardly punishment here. As in any play, however, in which the proscenium convention has been violated, new "no touching" rules go into effect. Fans, who have been warned before the start of the program to stay behind the ropes because of flying furniture and bodies, stand literally nose-to-nose with baddies and managers, trading insults and rude gestures. All this takes place usually without any physical contact, and even the most vicious-sounding fan may sink back to his seat with a self-conscious grin once he has made his point.

Ringside fans who literally get splashed with the sweat of combatants serve as the front-line representatives for all the others in attendance. The audience actually forms the larger, all-encompassing *quaternio* that determines the very character of the dramas played out in its center. In fact, the crowd's presence underscores the source of rasslin' in theater more than in competition, because unlike a collegiate or amateur program that is held no matter what happens, a professional wrestling card will be canceled if not enough tickets are sold. Performers require feedback;

wrestler and spectator share the "intimate and essential relationship" that Jung observed in all interdependent dualities.

Fans tend to act like theater patrons, expressing emotions appropriate to a willing suspension of disbelief. In one instance, as the crowd pressed against the doors of an auditorium past the hour when they should have been let in, someone called out, "Aren't you finished rehearsing yet?" His remark elicited good-natured, knowing laughs from everyone in earshot, but everyone poured in anyway. Perhaps the simple words of another young man, stalwart and athletic-looking himself, summed up the fans' need for catharsis. "Ah, it's fun," he said with a shrug. "I like to shout at the guys."

When rasslin' hit its media stride in the early 1980's, pundits predicted a saturation of the market. At that time, the latest trends soon broke on the shores of boredom. But as professional wrestling continues to make its profitable way into the homes and hearts of millions of fans, it is evident that its fascination is still potent. Large segments of the collective American psyche continue to be enthralled by men in combat—not simply because the wrestling culture is a heady mixture of violence and legalism, but because wrestlers embody mythical figures and act out archetypal motifs that, being timeless, will always appeal to our deepest, unconscious needs.

References

Jung, C. G. 1948. Phenomenology of the spirit in fairytales. *CW* 9i:207–254. Princeton, N.J.: Princeton University Press, 1968.

―――. 1951. The psychological aspects of the kore. *CW* 9i:182–204. Princeton, N.J.: Princeton University Press, 1968.

―――. 1952a. *Symbols of Transformation. CW*, vol. 5. Princeton, N.J.: Princeton University Press, 1956.

―――. 1952b. *Psychology and Alchemy. CW*, vol. 12. Princeton, N.J.: Princeton University Press, 1968.

―――. 1954a. The philosophical tree. In *CW* 13:251–350. Princeton, N.J.: Princeton University Press, 1967.

―――. 1954b. Archetypes of the collective unconscious. In *CW* 9i:3–41. Princeton, N.J.: Princeton University Press, 1968.

―――. 1955–1956. *Mysterium Coniunctionis. CW*, vol. 14. Princeton, N.J.: Princeton University Press, 1970.

Eric Zengota, M.A., is executive director of the Florida
Assisted Living Association and has lectured on various Jungian topics at universities and workshops.

Hephaestus and the Modeler

J. L. Campbell

A niggling, recurrent question in the minds of people curious about the interplay between consciously chosen recreational activities and unconscious motivations for them is this one: "Why do people 'play' what they play?" From a Jungian perspective, the activity one chooses to fill leisure time often completes in the conscious world an area of the personality prompted to closure in the unconscious domain. In other words, the pursuit of an avocation— a "hobby"—helps some people achieve wholeness. Throughout the country, people involve themselves in bowling leagues, tennis leagues, softball leagues, and the like. But few of them ever ask themselves why a certain sport appeals to them, why "their" sport (particularly if it is an activity acquired during one's adolescent years) comes to be an integral part of their lives or why the sport (for some) dominates their lives.

Anyone familiar with Carl Jung's work appreciates the importance of archetypal "stories," for they are germane to specific aspects of personality manifestation. Indeed, archetypal patterns reveal a great deal about the siren call that motivates people's participation in specific competitive or sporting activities and about the obsessive quality they often assume.

I recognize the danger of sweeping generalizations. Even so, I do not feel uncomfortable suggesting that if a random sampling were taken from people at a shopping mall about their notion of sport, more than three-quarters of the respondents would exhibit a myopic view of activities that they consider to be sporting events. For the most part, the idea of sports is equated in the popular imagination with major adolescent participation/spectator games like football, baseball, basketball, and so on. Both direct and vicarious participation in such activities are available on weekends at sports arenas across the country and daily on both network and sports television.[1] During any given week, viewers are likely to see a variety of competitions, from the Stihl Lumberjack Championship to the NCAA Lacrosse Championship to the Hawaiian Tropic Professional Beach Volleyball Championship to the National Pocket Billiards Championship. But despite television's success in raising viewer awareness regarding the variety of competitive activity, few sports fans have ever heard of the National Model Airplane Championships (all phases of aircraft model competition), the Top Gun Championship (exclusively for radio-controlled scale models) or the Circus Circus Tournament of Champions (exclusively for radio-controlled acrobatic models).

Of those who do recognize these competitions, few are inclined to regard these events as serious, competitive sporting endeavors with legitimate fans and participants. The typical reaction to model aviation as a sport reveals a condescending "big boys and their toys" attitude. This suggests that flying model airplanes in competition is hardly a basis for serious, competitive sport. But the people who engage in model tournaments are intensely serious. Every weekend of the year, people travel to flying sites with their models and compete with each other in myriad ways amid a flurry of frenzied activity with a passion equal to the intensity displayed by those who race automobiles or motorcycles, sail in regattas, play golf, or engage themselves in other familiar sports.

Model aviation is currently dominated by enthusiasts whose interests lie in radio-controlled models. In fact, the pages of most general hobby magazines (*Flying Models, Model Builder*, and *Model Airplane News*) are largely given over to material which touts this segment of the sport. Although what I have to say here is applicable to every segment of the modeling community, my primary concern is with the people who comprise one of the more highly specialized groups within the aeromodeling community— the modelers who fly control-line precision acrobatics or, as they call themselves in the hobby, the stunt flyers.

People built and flew model aircraft competitively before World War II, but soon after that, Jim Walker popularized a system for piloting model aircraft which he called "U-control." Walker's device consisted of two wires (fifty to seventy feet in length) attached inside the model to a bell crank and outside to a U-shaped

---

[1]Interestingly, television is gradually correcting sports myopia. While sports television networks (like ESPN) predominantly air the standard competitive activities, they also air newer, more esoteric ones.

PSYCHE AND SPORTS
179

handle held by the pilot. By moving the handle, the pilot (via the bell crank and a push rod to activate the elevator) provided up and down control. The system enabled the flyer to maneuver the airplane through climbs, dives, loops, etc. After a while, a proscription for competitive maneuvers developed. Within a short time, a stunt event evolved. By the 1950s it attracted participants from every part of the country and became a part of the National Model Airplane Championships.

Throughout the 1950s and 1960s participation in the event increased, but with the boom in radio-controlled models during the 1970s and early 1980s, interest in stunt events waned. A persistent, dedicated few enthusiasts maintained the sport, and their enthusiasm was sufficient to sustain competitions at the local, national, and international levels. Today, the event's popularity is increasing, making a comeback largely because modelers who flew the event in its heyday seem to be inexorably and enigmatically drawn back to it. For these people—and indeed for those who never left the sport—stunt flying assumes an obsessive significance in their lives. This significance can be better understood by exploring the Hephaestus archetype.

What is observed here about stunt fliers has generic application for all modelers, but those who have had a long-term involvement with stunt flying or those who have enthusiastically returned to this phase of model aircraft competition after a lengthy hiatus tend to exemplify Jean Shinoda Bolen's description of people (predominantly men) caught up in the process of searching for (and finding) their own myths—that is, "re-membering" themselves. Bolen, specifically addressing this element of mid-life depression, writes

> There is an alternative [to depression]—which often doesn't present itself until mid-life—on which men I see in my practice embark out of necessity when life becomes painful and empty, or arid and flat. They seek to find what is true for them, to uncover their feelings and find meaning in their lives . . . . For each man, the process is a gradual descent to find buried feelings, to discover his inner world, where he can pick up the threads of his personal story. The story always begins in childhood. (1989, pp. 284–285)

Appreciating the single-mindedness stunt modelers have for their activity lies in understanding the archetypal pattern "personalized" by Hephaestus, who is the god of the forge and armorer to the gods. A consummate craftsman, Hephaestus is an inventor and innovator. His happiest moments come while he is at work at his forge—alone—under the earth.[2] He is a perfectionist whose creations, representing a unique blend of form and function, are never quite "finished."

The basic approach the stunt flyer takes toward both the event and the implements used to pursue it are Hephaestian. A primary Hephaestus drive is the creation of artifacts which are exceptional blends of form and function. For Hephaestus a beautiful object is incomplete—inferior—unless it also exhibits a demonstrable utilitarian function. Following this reasoning, a finely crafted model (from the standpoint of workmanship and finish and airworthiness) put to use as a competitive tool is ultimately beautiful. The importance of this relationship is underscored in the rules governing stunt competition: although the majority of points competitors earn is garnered from flying ability, they are also scored on the appearance of their models. For the person who is strongly influenced by the Hephaestus archetype, this situation creates a dilemma: having the model judged for "beauty" (which for such a person is an integrated wholeness rather than mere appearance) becomes the real competition. One becomes one's own rival.

A person with whom I competed years ago provides an excellent example. An average flyer, he consistently finished in the middle of the pack at competitions (only rarely was he in the top five when scores were posted). But he was a master craftsman. His airplanes were stunning pieces of work, and each one of his models was the result of long hours of agonizing deliberation over its visual impact. When he unveiled his creations at contests, they always drew exclamations of envy from every other contestant. For my friend—given that his airplanes flew respectably (which they always did)—the flight score and placing in the competition was *not* the contest. Instead, the core of the event for him was earning his fellow competitors' accolades and having his craftsmanship publicly acknowledge with high appearance scores from the judges. Constructing models which performed well (better than he was able to fly them) and which were esthetically wonderful was the heart of the competition for him. Thus, he did not

[2]For readers who wish to refresh their understanding of the Hephaestus archetype, two excellent sources exist: chapter 9 of Jean Shinoda Bolen's *Gods in Everyman* (1989), "Hephaestus, God of the Forge—Craftsman, Inventor, Loner" (her treatment of the complexities of the archetype are precise and illuminating); and chapter 4, "Hephaestus: A Pattern of Introversion" by Murray Stein (whose treatment of Hephaestus's polar nature is precise and equally exacting) in James Hillman, *Facing the Gods* (1980).

compete so much against his peers as he did against his own unattainable standard. My friend was, in true Hephaestian fashion, a man caught in the frustrating loop of continually trying to best himself and never being able to reach closure in his subconscious world.

Even if the Hephaestus influence is less strong (that is, if the participant tends to be more of a flyer than a builder), the competitive format emphasizes the Hephaestian notion of pitting the participants against perfection more than against each other. The pattern (that is, the mandatory program of maneuvers through which contestants have to pilot their aircraft) is an idealized goal. "By the book," a phrase used by contestants to describe the perfect maneuver, acknowledges this fact. Each competitor goes in knowing that no one will fly a perfect pattern, but each one is obligated to try. This results in a competition structured such that individuals compete less with each other and more against an ideal—an ideal set by the contestant, not the rules. Hence, the competition is a matter of ascertaining which flyer on a given day comes closest to being perfect.

Golf provides a rough analogy in a well-known sport because golfers (aside from television spectacles like the "Skins Game") basically compete against the course. Competition against each other is secondary, although the popular spectator view reverses the sequence. Bolen observes that "through his work, Hephaestus and men like him . . . see themselves reflected intact and functioning; through this reflection flows self-esteem and self-respect as well as the respect and esteem of others" (1989, p. 224). Consequently, stunt flyers yearn to compete—not so much against their fellows (in the normal sporting sense of one competitor dominating the others) as with them. They derive fulfillment by acting as a part of a group of comrades unified and resolved to try and be perfect in the same way—to build a model to fly the perfect pattern.

Ironically, the Hephaestian is entirely self-sustaining even though the sense of community realized through competition is rewarding. Murray Stein, considering P. E. Slater's observations about Hephaestus in *The Glory of Hera*, gets to this point. Stein writes:

> The pattern of meaning and movement within the Hephaestian configuration itself . . . reflects a fundamental failure of the imagination. Instead of looking at and "explaining" myths through the concepts of an ego-building psychology (a psy-

chology governed, it seems to me, by Zeus and Apollo), we are trying to let myth instruct our psychology, to broaden and deepen its visions, and to move us out of our narrow preconceptions of "what it means to be a man." (in Hillman 1980, p. 82)

There emerges from time to time a need for the Hephaestian to be with others like himself. Their gathering is an ironic blend of individual and group dynamic because Hephaestians do not *need* competition to justify themselves. In that respect, they are unique among other sports competitors. With others (baseball players, for example) the game provides a rationale for the existence of those who play it. With stunt flyers, the situation is reversed. They do not exist for the game; the game exists for them. It is a stamp of affirmation that work of the highest order has been done—an artifact has been created wherein the material has metamorphosed into the spiritual. Consider Bolen's observation:

> When the Hephaestus archetype is present, beauty and expressiveness that otherwise would remain buried inside a man (or a woman) can be liberated through work that gives tangible form to these aspects of himself. The way of becoming conscious is the opposite of insight in which experience is translated into meaning inside. Instead something inwardly present becomes literally visible, after which awareness of what it means can follow. (1989, p. 222)

Among stunt flyers, the phrase "dedicated modeler" is used to recognize and pay tribute to a modeler's creative persistence and tenacity—i.e., the degree to which he is committed to his modeling activity (read "work"). And what could be higher praise for Hephaestus? Typically stoic, Hephaestus is consistently reluctant to share his feelings. Indeed, he is satisfied at those junctures when his creations are complete. Even so, he appreciates the mirror of his work by having others who are able to recognize his driving force—his commitment to task—appreciate it. Bolen asserts that Hephaestians are not fraternity brother types (1989, p. 234). Although they are not joiners, they welcome the company of those who share or who appreciate the focus of their inner struggle (as Dionysus archetypes are often able to do).

This mirroring is realized when stunt flyers attend contests or when their activities are written up in construction articles for magazines. Somewhere in every such article there is implied the idea that the creation of the model described is the result of a long and arduous program (a birthing process). In a recent issue of *Flying Models*, I read an article which began this way:

> This particular sojourn begins in Atlanta in the summer of 1986 when I met a friend and fellow competitor, Bill Rich of Florida. He had recently moved from the New Jersey area and was setting up his flying program for the Nats at Lake Charles like I was. (Brickhaus 1992, p. 48)

What caught my interest in these opening sentences was that, even though the writer described what transpired during a temporary visit in Atlanta, the implication is that the incident marked a "beginning" for him. The sojourn in Atlanta was not an "idyll" but a kind of genesis for a new "program." At a deep level, one gleans that the writer's commentary is intended to communicate to his audience his desire that they appreciate the pain and suffering (i.e., work) implicit in the birth of the model he has created and about which he is writing the article. In another piece published several months earlier, the country's top stunt flyer, Paul Walker, chronicles the development period for his model—a period which lasted over a decade (1991, pp. 46–51). The commentary of these writers emphasizes the Hephaestus trait of attempting to reinvent the wheel, for in each case the story line is that the model described brings the builder's endeavors closer to his idea of perfection (liberal use of words like *perfection*, *ultimate*, and *final* help make the point, as do statistics about the number of flights a plane has logged). Such sentiment is not wasted on Hephaestus readers who appreciate the effort described.

A current controversy in the world of stunt flyers also points to the prevalence of the Hephaestus archetype among people who devote their leisure time to stunt competition. The controversy arises from a conflict created by the presence of two archetypes: Hephaestus and Dionysus. Hephaestians often associate themselves with Dionysians. And while they get on well together for the most part, they do clash over basic issues. In the stunt world today, the clash concerns whether or not a competitor has to build his own model to compete or suffer a penalty of some sort to compensate for the pain and suffering he, as a nonbuilder, does not have to endure.[3] To an outsider—a nonstunt type—such concerns

---

[3]Every issue in 1991 of the national newsletter of the Precision Acrobatics Model Pilots Association, *Stunt News*, had lengthy, passionate commentaries on the question.

may seem petty. But for those who are involved, the question is a crucial one. Battle lines are drawn according to dominant archetype. The more sensual Dionysians, for whom the flight is the important element of the event, do not see the necessity of building one's own model as an entree to competition. The Hephaestians, on the contrary, resolutely plant their heels and opine that not having a BOM (builder of the model) requirement in the structure of the competition is unthinkable. The Hephaestian is not able to abrogate the creative responsibility. The spiritual union of form and function requires time at the forge. As pointed out previously, the work, far from being a prerequisite, is an organic part of the creation process and is perceived as ritual birthing. A staunch defender of the BOM rule expressed this sentiment in *Stunt News*, the national stunt flyers' newsletter:

> I have never been involved in an avocation less "exclusive" nor more egalitarian than stunt. Name me one other highly competitive event [in model competition—or perhaps anywhere at all] where wealthy doctors and airline captains can get their collective butts kicked by guys who don't make a fraction of their [doctors and airline captains] income but who simply have more talent and dedication . . . . All compete on a level playing field *because* of BOM and appearance points . . . not in spite of it. (Fancher 1991, p. 7)

A willingness to work and work and work and work and work—dedication—is what the Hephaestus modeler prizes. True to the archetype, he affirms himself through his work.

Having a shop is also an important Hephaestus trait. The literature of modeling is replete with references to modelers' work areas and photographs frequently appear to show them off. Modelers' workshops are like artists' studios or basement workshops—places where men go to be alone with their Hephaestus archetype and where they spend pleasant hours translating or transforming what they feel deeply into something outside themselves (Bolen 1989, p. 223).

Indeed, "when a Hephaestus man finds work he loves, the problem arises of becoming so absorbed in work that he does not develop any other facets of himself or make space for others to exist" (Bolen 1989, p. 249). A persistent criticism leveled at stunt flyers by their nonmodeling spouses and by nonmodeler acquaintances is that the stunt flyers are antisocial. Superficially, they are right, for introversion is a dominant character trait. Persons in whom the Hephaestus archetype is dominant *enjoy* their own company, even though it appears to others illogical to do so. Such a personality is comfortable alone but does not, however, make a deliberate effort to avoid people; they are not misanthropes. They are simply oblivious both to those who do not readily appreciate and share their preoccupation and to those who somehow are not directly involved in their projects.

Years ago, when building and flying my models were my single most important leisure activities and I was active in competition, it was not unusual for me to spend an entire spring holiday either working on an airplane or practicing the pattern. Although my friends invited me to accompany them on trips, I refused, opting to stay at home with my work. During that time, hours passed for me most pleasantly. When I emerged—usually with some major phase of construction on the airplane completed—I felt good. My creative work was done, I was recharged, I felt more ready to tackle the problems and challenges of my vocation.

The aforementioned quality certainly emerges as a factor in marital relationships. The archetype's creation process sooner or later causes misunderstandings. When they occur, the Hephaestian is quick to make peace in the marriage just as Hephaestus was quick to keep the bickering Olympians at peace. In addition, Hephaestians perceive their spouses as mother images, and they often seek feminine "approval" of the end result of the toil of the creative process. As Stein (1980) suggests:

> Through Hephaestus, the great forms of nature image themselves forth in art [in this case airplanes, man's mimicry of birds] . . . . The springs of creativity, which are rooted in the depths of the Great Mother, take a turn in Hephaestus from the concrete childbearing and body-centered sexuality toward the realization of the cosmos as imagination and symbol . . . . Hephaestus always remains in the service of the feminine. And the Hephaestian passion for creative work is deeply of the Mother. (In Hillman 1980, p. 73)

This observation provides some insight into the odd (and often awkward) formal acknowledgments modelers give to their spouses. The acknowledgments, published in articles written for magazines, are at once petitions for permission to continue work in the future, overtures for approval, and timorous attempts to assert a facade of male dominance. This paragraph selected from a recently published construction article provides a case in point:

> My wife Kathy allows me to build in the house and I am not relegated to the basement, garage, or other isolated area. We

enjoy talking about daily affairs and events while I am building or she is sewing or working at the word processor. Kathy is also my main supporter, co-driver and absolute main launcher at local contests and at the Nationals. Men, please don't be upset if I prefer that Kathy launch me for officials at contests. If she is not there due to job or educational reasons, ask as I will be glad to have your assistance. (Brickhaus 1992, p. 51)

The author writes what he believes to be a sincere, appreciative acknowledgment. And, of course, it is. Yet his choice of words points to his Hephaestus nature. *Allows* and *relegated* are words which suggest that the author suffers himself to be placed—or perhaps tolerated—in a specific area. And the appeal to "men"— his peers—in the last couple of sentences further acknowledges the dominance of the feminine. It is also ironic that the specific task mentioned—that of launcher—is both menial and patronizing. There is an inference, however, that it is the release on which the activity depends.

And so it goes. In many modelers—and most especially in stunt modelers—the Hephaestus archetype is a strong influence. For persons in whom Hephaestus is a dominant force, a better understanding of its influence will certainly aid in dealing with frustration and stress that often arise in their efforts to, as the Reebok gym shoe commercial dictates, "play hard."

References

Bolen, Jean Shinoda. 1989. *Gods in Everyman: A New Psychology of Men's Lives and Loves.* New York: Harper & Row.

Brickhaus, Allen. 1992. Arcturus. *Flying Models* (March), pp. 48–51.

Fancher, Ted. 1991. President's message. *Stunt News* (November–December), pp. 6–7.

Hillman, James, ed. 1980. *Facing the Gods.* Dallas: Spring Publications.

Walker, Paul. 1991. Impact. *Flying Models* (May), pp. 44–51.

J. L. Campbell is currently a professor of English and humanities at Abraham Baldwin Agricultural College and interested in men's studies, the literature of the Vietnam War, and archetypal analysis of popular culture.

The Hero Archetype and High-Risk Sports Participants

Steven R. Heyman

When humans recognized their earthbound limitations as their consciousness developed, gods and demigods were endowed with the ability to transcend the limitations of human existence (Neumann 1954). If, in reality, heroes could show great courage or strength, as they took on mythic proportions they, too, like Daedalus or Perseus could fly or engage in other superhuman activities normally reserved for the gods. The cosmic themes of speed, motion, and the heroic defiance of nature's laws, such as gravity, in dreams are clear indication in Jungian thinking of archetypal activations (Jung 1943, p. 250).

Science, particularly in the last half century, has taken the possibility of engaging in many of these activities from the world of dreams, daydreams, and myths and made them available to any who so desire. Yet only some are attracted to these activities, and superstar status, a godlike quality, is given to those who achieve particular excellence. It does seem that participation in such activities may reflect archetypal activations not only in those who participate, but in the fascination of the general public with these people and their actions.

For Jung, "the hero is always the embodiment of man's highest and most powerful aspiration, or of what this aspiration ought ideally to be and what he would most gladly realize. It is therefore of importance what kind of fantasy constitutes the hero-motif" (1918, par. 100).

Heroic pursuits are not without risks. Icarus, like Bellerophon, flies too close to the sun. Both are fascinated by their wonderful experience, and tragedy results.

If we can assume that high-risk sports have heroic and mythic qualities, then an understanding of archetypal patterns may help us to understand the participants and the general public's fascination (a fascination that has a quality of ambivalence).

At the same time, archetypal patterns may tell us of the dangers participants face and how the encountering and transcendence of these dangers may lead the participant to self-discovery and self-growth.

It first is necessary to come to some definition of high-risk sports. For the purposes of this paper, it is taken to be an activity that can be accomplished only because science has given humans the ability to participate in what would otherwise defy nature's physical laws. More specifically, the activities involve exceptional speed, flight, or being underwater. Clearly, we now take travel in an automobile, boat, or jet for granted, where our recent ancestors would have seen this as miraculous. Earlier in the century, when the pace of life was slower, there were those who could elect to avoid these "threatening contraptions." But for our purposes here, the activity must be beyond the participation of most. While many of us take flying in a jet plane for granted, only a relatively small and select group seek to be jet pilots.

Furthermore, contact sports, although risky, are not included in our definition. Boxing, karate, and football, while certainly of considerable risk and with certain warriorlike and heroic qualities, do not achieve the godlike, magical quality of the other high-risk sports to be considered here.

As a general group, the activities considered high-risk in this paper would include those involving flying (piloting an aircraft; hot-air ballooning, hang gliding); moving at great speeds (in powerboats, motorcycles, race cars); and existing underwater (scuba diving), as only gods or mermaids could have done, although other activities could be named as well.

Before considering deeper issues within the human psyche that relate to the participants in these activities, it might help to look at some of the more basic research done within sport and personality psychology. Relative to participation in high-risk sports, perhaps the most studied construct has been "sensation seeking." Zuckerman (1979) postulates that humans have different levels of need for sensory input and stimulation and that those individuals who require higher levels of sensory stimulation will seek out any of a variety of activities. Zuckerman developed a scale called the sensation seeking scale (SSS), which has been used fairly widely in research. A series of studies indicates that sensation seekers will take part to a greater extent than non-sensation seekers in high-risk sports (Connolly 1981, Hymbaugh and Garrett 1974). Those who work in occupations with physical danger (e.g., fire fighters) are also likely to be higher in sensation seeking (Kusyszyn, Steinberg and Elliott 1974). As might be expected, however, this is only one component of sensation seeking. Sensation seekers are also more likely to use drugs and to seek sexual activities at a higher frequency. There is also a modest relationship between sensation seeking and delinquent behavior. While this research points to a general pattern and suggests a confirmation of Zuckerman's theories, it is typical of psychological research in that it uses large groups, which obscures individual differences.

Several years ago I was lucky enough to be able to collect data on college students who enrolled in scuba training classes (Heyman and Rose 1980, 1981). The research involved the administration of questionnaires and the observation and rating of students on various skills, including their checkout and free dives which were required for certification. There are clearly people drawn to this activity who likely have a biologically based need for stimulation. There are also those who are drawn to it for what it represents at both conscious and unconscious levels. Perhaps more important than having selected this activity is why individuals complete training successfully. Such training is often physically and psychologically demanding and has some danger connected with it. Beyond completing training, we can ask why some individuals continue while others lose interest. Although firm data does not exist, it has been estimated that only 10 percent of those who became certified scuba divers continued to dive after certification (Strykowski 1976). Heyman and Rose (1981) found an attrition rate between 10 and 30 percent during different semesters.

Previously, it was suggested that society has an ambivalent attitude toward those who participate in high-risk sports. While, on the one hand, such individuals may be admired for their actions and bravery, on the other, it is said "they must be nuts." This is reflected in the literature, the most famous paper being Fenichel's in which he conceptualized the "counter-phobic attitude" (1939). Murray (1955) also discusses an "Icarus complex," which involves a pattern of seeking to overcome human constraints with a craving for admiration and attention. Both draw primarily from case studies of individuals considered to have problems as opposed to groups. Murray notes that with a "relatively stronger ego structure supported by tested abilities, which serves to constrain the reckless aspirations of youth within the bounds of realizable achievements," a more positive pattern can be achieved (1955, p. 639). The impulsive individual, who might be counter-phobic with an impaired sense of intentionality and deliberateness

(Shapiro 1965), is likely to be a far different person from the high-risk sports participant able to undergo the long, intensive periods of instruction and practice that characterize these sports. Similarly, the ability to take part in these sports on a long-term basis and survive would not suggest a reckless or dangerously impulsive individual.

Relative to military parachuting, Bernstein (1950), Neel (1951a and b), and Kepecs (1944) discuss the conflicts that led to failure or refusal to jump but not the mechanisms that allowed most to succeed. In terms of more contemporary work on high-risk sports participants, neither Huberman (1986), Hoover (1978), nor Heyman and Rose (1980, 1981) found pathological features within these individuals. Huberman did note that parents of participants tended to reward risk-taking beginning in early life and fathers "tended to have a courageous attitude toward life" (1968, p. 98). When he states that "risky, as well as non-risky sports will have their share of morbid and disturbed participants," he indicates his findings suggest that, as a group, high-risk sports participants have very positive psychological characteristics (ibid., p. 121). Similar findings of adaptive personality patterns in high-risk sports participants were reported by Johnsgard, Ogilvie, and Merritt (1975). Torrence (1974), examining wartime fighter pilot aces, found these high-risk participants to have similarly positive, highly effective personality patterns. In his discussion of research on personal soundness, MacKinnon (1960) described personality components similar to those found in high-risk sports participants. The highly effective individuals were found to be more robust and vigorous, more physically courageous, and to have greater stamina than less effective individuals.

Is it possible to reconcile the psychoanalytic conceptualizations and the research findings? It should be noted that, while the hero is described in positive terms by Jung, he states: "In men, sexuality, if not acted out directly, is frequently converted into a feverish professional activity or a passion for dangerous sports" (1907, par. 105). In contrast, Zuckerman (1979) reported that high sensation seekers were not only more likely to engage in dangerous sports, but were more likely to be sexually expressive. We would have to know the individual to determine if the sexual and risk-taking activities were syntonic or if one displaced the other.

First, it is important to view a broad cross-section of those involved in high-risk sports. Second, judgments based on a biased sample, such as individuals in psychotherapy for problems in functioning, cannot be generalized to all individuals. Third, it is important to note the many different motivations that draw a variety of individuals to the same activity. With these in mind, the discussion will proceed.

For Jung, it was not surprising that America developed a passion for sports and that this attraction to sports was related to a hero archetype unique to America.

> The hero is always the embodiment of man's highest and most powerful aspiration, or of what this aspiration ought ideally to be and what he would most gladly realize. It is therefore of importance what kind of fantasy constitutes the hero-motif. In American hero-fantasy the Indian's character plays a leading role. . . . only the Indian rites of initiation can compare with the ruthlessness and savagery of a rigorous American training. The performance of American athletes is therefore admirable. In everything on which the American has really set his heart we catch a glimpse of the Indian. His extraordinary concentration on a particular goal, his tenacity of purpose, his unflinching endurance of the greatest hardships—in all this the legendary virtues of the Indian find full expression. (1918, par. 100)

Later, Jung describes American sport along the same archetypally based lines as "the toughest, the most reckless, and the most efficient in the world" (1930, par. 977).

Although Jung was likely thinking of more conventional American sports, the popularity of high-risk sports has dramatically increased in the past few decades, and although popular throughout the world, they have a distinct American character (e.g., scuba diving, surfing, even the childhood pursuit of skateboarding). Although many sports have many well-known participants and dare devils, for much of the 1960s and 1970s one American's name was almost synonymous with risk-taking: Evel Knievel. A research project done during that time period found that of 157 children age 3–5 a very high percentage (80–90 percent) saw Knievel as a brave and good man (Settles and Klinzing 1975). Almost three-quarters of that group, however, also knew that he could get hurt, that he was not a fantasy hero imbued with invulnerability. One can only wonder what their imaginations and dreams would have to say.

A brief summary at this point would suggest that we know some people will seek to move at great speeds, to fly, or to live underwater, at least briefly, acting out the dreams and myths long held by humankind. We know that these individuals reflect a select sample of the general population. While some may enter these activities as a reflection of deficiencies they are seeking to correct or as part of an impulsive or self-destructive style, most participants have more positive motivations. The next section of the paper will examine the more positive motivations involved and what we can learn from examining the archetypal implications of high-risk sports for the participants.

Archetypal Implications for High-Risk Sports

For the mythical hero, the act of becoming a hero involves not only physical challenge, but confronting incredibly threatening circumstances which must be overcome, and successfully returning from the conquest with knowledge, "the embodiment of man's highest and most powerful aspiration" (Jung 1918, par. 100). Can participation in high-risk sports be a model for this, as opposed to a simple, transitory, if enjoyable, experience?

Perhaps the best place to begin is with the concluding paragraph of Campbell's classic work, *The Hero with a Thousand Faces*:

> The modern hero, the modern individual who dares to heed the call and seek the mansion of that presence with whom it is our destiny to be atoned, cannot, indeed must not, wait for his community to cast off its slough of pride, fear, rationalized avarice, and sanctified misunderstanding. "Live," Nietzsche says, "as though the day were here." It is not society to guide the creative hero, but precisely the reverse. And so everyone shares the supreme ordeal—carries the cross of the redeemer—not in the bright moments of the tribe's great victories, but in the silences of his personal despair. (1974, p. 391)

One could note that many of the activities in which we take part, including driving our cars or flying in planes, have depended on those who were willing to try them, not as well-defined sports but as new activities. Yet, we must go beyond these. Astronauts and their equivalents in every generation are truly unique, and important similar patterns may be operating in many high-risk sports participants.

Campbell, in his conversations with Bill Moyers, reminds us that the hero must have courage, knowledge, and the capacity to serve (Campbell and Moyers 1988, p. 126). He also reminds us that Prometheus suffered for his heroic adventure (ibid., p. 127).

> All these different mythologies give us the same essential quest. You leave the world that you're in and go into a depth or into a . . . distance or up a height. There you come to what was missing in your consciousness in the world you formerly inhabited. Then comes the problem, either of staying with that, and letting the world drop off, or returning with that boon and trying to hold on to it as you move back into your social world again. That's not an easy thing to do. (Ibid., p. 129)

Providing us with other clues to be utilized in understanding the hero, Campbell notes that the hero must be able to follow an inner sense of trust and to follow personal feelings (ibid., p. 144). The hero leaves "the realm of the familiar over which he has some measure of control and comes to a threshold, let us say the edge of a lake or sea, where a monster of the abyss comes to meet him . . . learning how to come to terms with this power of the dark . . . and emerge, at last, to a new way of life" (ibid., p. 146). He reminds us that "the first requirements for a heroic career are the knightly virtues of loyalty, temperance, and courage" (ibid., p. 145).

There are two other important elements, more applicable to us in our everyday lives and to participants in high-risk sports. He suggests that Blake was correct—for the hero, there is a cleansing of the doors of perception, and the infinite is understood (ibid., p. 162). Finally, the "adventure of the hero" is "the adventure of being alive" (ibid., p. 163).

No doubt many individuals, in their own way, become heroes by confronting a personal abyss and come back from it with a personal knowledge and awareness that can be used to help others and to help the individual live more fully. Leonard (1989) reminds us of how like the hero's journey is the situation of the person struggling to recover from addiction.

A person who marvels at the possibilities of high-risk sports must clearly confront physical danger. Although Huberman (1968) noted that participants often see these sports as less dangerous than nonparticipants, there are clear physical dangers. Survival depends on mastering oneself and the anxieties and fears that one has. It also involves an ability to become comfortable over a long period of participation. A series of research projects (Heyman and Rose 1980, 1981; Morgan 1987; Morgan, Lanphier, Raglin and O'Connor 1989) has shown that the more anxious are less likely to succeed. Long-term participants have to become comfortable and in tune with their actions—the qualities of one-ness with the activity and the physical medium that Campbell described. Someone constantly fighting to do well is more likely to slip and more likely to find the experience so difficult that it would soon be abandoned. If these sports were easy to take part in, they would have more participants. If the ability to transform this par-ticipation into a heroic adventure were more common, more of the participants would do so. Both Satinover (1986) and Eideger (1976) remind us of how often mythic tales of the hero end in tragedy.

Moreover, and regrettably this hasn't been researched, the heroic participant is likely to come back with a personal experi-ence of the infinite because all of these activities have numinous qualities. How wonderful it is to participate and to be successful, and yet how humbling are such experiences! When one gradually descends to earth after jumping from incredible heights, or ascends from the depths of the oceans, one cannot but feel a part of and awed by nature. It would be expected that individuals in these sports who are in tune with their heroic qualities would report these actualizing and self-actualizing experiences. Although again this has not been studied, such knowledge and appreciation may be channeled into important social and political activities. Based on personal observation, many of those involved in high-risk sports become very environmentally and ecologically aware.

The qualities of oneness, of transcendence, and of Campbell's hero are possible through high-risk sports. However, there may be even deeper meaning, as well as deeper threat.

> The hero is a hero just because he sees resistance to the forbid-den goal in all life's difficulties and yet fights that resistance with the wholehearted yearning that strives towards the trea-sure hard to attain, and perhaps unattainable—a yearning that paralyses and kills the ordinary man. (Jung 1952, par. 510)

Speaking of Hiawatha, the heroic, archetypal Indian, Jung reminds us:

> He can only turn to his human side after he has fulfilled his heroic destiny: firstly the transformation of the daemon from the uncontrolled force of nature into a power that is his to command; secondly the final deliverance of ego-consciousness from the deadly threat of the unconscious in the form of the negative parents. The first task signifies the creation of will-power, the second the free use of it. (1952, par. 548)

In this transformation, there is also likely to be a syzygy, the union of the male and female. One of the important elements, therefore, of the successful and heroic participation in high-risk sports would be a union of the male and female within an individual at conscious and unconscious levels. This involves more than the physical mastery, which would involve a masculine stance. The ability to become one with the infinite, to pass through the potential abyss many times and to be comfortable with it, to develop a sense of oneness and an ability to go with one's feelings, not in a controlling or wantonly wild way but in a natural way, would suggest an ability to become more passive. Therefore, in order for the experience to be heroic and transforming, a man must be able to integrate the masculine and the feminine, not only within the performance, but within himself. Walker, in writing about the Olympic Games, notes that they "were concerned with knowledge and transformation of wild masculine instinctuality . . . into a force which can be fruitful in life, serve life, and therefore be truly humane" (1980, p. 37).

For women, there may be an added challenge. Within the high-risk sports, the statistics suggest that women are considerably underrepresented (Heyman and Rose 1981; Metropolitan Life 1974). Most physical activities within our society, but particularly risky activities, are encouraged for men but discouraged for women, beginning in early childhood. Often these activities are thought to require physical endurance and psychological coping skills that women are perceived as not having. Women who do gravitate to these activities will first have to develop physical and cognitive styles traditionally considered to be masculine. If they are successful, they will then have to regain the feminine parts of their conscious and unconscious in order to achieve heroic oneness and transformation. For some, this might be easier in that the feminine may be more accessible and familiar. For others, it may be more difficult in that the achievement of the "masculine" components may have occurred by disowning or repressing the "feminine," the rediscovery of which may require an even greater heroic pursuit. For many, however, the activities may be enjoyable, pleasurable, even exciting, but this heroic expression and integration may not occur.

Analytic psychology also suggests that, for some, participation may entail additional risks either because of characteristics they bring to the sport or because of the way they participate. Eideger, writing about the tragic hero, discusses a Shakespearean sense of the tragic hero "in terms of a fatal flaw . . . (which) would correspond to what Jungian psychology knows as the problem of the inferior function" (1976).

If the masculine component of the person does not come to terms with the hidden, mysterious, feminine unconscious, there may be an exaggerated sense of masculine control and, perhaps as part of that, an undue fascination with the sport. This process is generally know as inflation of the ego. In such a condition, the archetype "seizes hold of the psyche" with a tremendous force (Jung 1943, par. 110). The person experiences a strong feeling of personal exaggeration, a loss of free will, and perhaps even delusions. Of particular concern for high-risk sports, the inflated ego "is hypnotized by itself and therefore cannot be argued with. It inevitably dooms itself to calamities that must strike it dead" (Jung 1944, par. 563). Leonard, discussing physical addictions, states "inflation occurs when one takes what belongs to the gods—when one sees oneself as 'godlike' and loses touch with one's mortality" (1989, p. 256). Not unlike the person addicted physically to alcohol or drugs, some individuals seek out high-risk sports to express their personal needs for power or control.

It is also possible that by becoming involved in high-risk sports, individuals experience ecstasy but not union. This ecstasy, along with the nature of the sport, can create a godlike sense of ego at both conscious and unconscious levels, which may cause the person to become overwhelmed by the activity. The myth of Icarus, who ultimately flies too close to the sun, is one such reminder. Similarly, while Evel Knievel was for some time a great heroic figure, he kept escalating the level of danger in his activities until, ultimately, he failed very publicly in his attempt to jump the Snake River and nearly died.

A person with strong needs for dominance and control drawn to high-risk sports, but who cannot allow union and transformation, may experience psychological and physical risks beyond those of the sport. Unlike the person who approaches these activities with anxieties or fears and may "freeze up," these individuals face other risks. It is here that we see patterns closer to what Fenichel described as counterphobic or Murray saw as involved in the Icarus complex. The quality of the participation may be compulsive, even seeming addicted, as Leonard (1988) describes: compulsive, risky, and in and of itself, joyless.

Unfortunately, the addiction to risk or the sense of inflation often requires continual escalation of the level of risk-taking. The person, like Icarus or Evel Knievel, may "fly too close to the sun" within whatever means possible in the activity. Death, survival with injury, or survival without injury are all possible results.

Concluding Thoughts

In a world lacking in heroes of mythic proportions, science and technology have placed within our means the opportunity to engage in high-risk sports which reflect dreams and myths across cultures and time. Most of us do not participate, either because they do not hold an attraction for us or because we perceive them as being too risky. Some do take the opportunity, however, and many of the rest of us watch with mixed admiration, perhaps wishing we could join in while considering those who do either heroic or crazy, or perhaps a bit of both.

For the participants, there are brief moments of achieving speed or flight or underwater existence which humans have only dreamed about for most of history. Some are adventurers, but not heroes, and the activities will be interesting and enjoyable, infrequent or regular, but they will not hold great meaning beyond the transitory experience. Sensation seekers, in particular, are likely to try a number of such activities.

There are others, however, who confront the very real dangers of these sports not only because of the thrills involved but for the deeper meaning. In participating they must master the physical challenge and confront the very real possibility of death. However, they learn to feel and to be one with themselves and with the infinite they confront, at least briefly. If the person is able to take this awareness back to everyday life, subtly or overtly, gradually or quickly, the experience leads to transformation in the person's life. There is a greater union, at conscious and unconscious levels, of the masculine and feminine, which may translate itself into changes in the individual's personal relationships or in social or political arenas. This process is part of the hero's journey, as well as the person's individuation and actualization.

There are, however, risks. Participation in high-risk sports may be propelled by personal needs to seek godlike experiences, which can activate an inflation of the ego. Given the risky nature of these sports, there are, as in myth, tragic possibilities for flawed, would-be heroes.

Hopefully, a greater awareness of the possibilities will allow a greater number of individuals to see these activities as possible mediums for personal growth and for actualizing, in positive and heroic ways, the dreams of humankind. It is also to be hoped that the dangers involved will help those who might be at risk to recognize the risks involved and to seek alternatives to dangerous involvement. Those who do participate and who can constructively actualize elements of the hero archetype may find, as Campbell says, the "adventure of the hero . . . the adventure of being alive."

References

Bernstein, R. 1950. Mental reactions of the airborne soldier. *U.S. Armed Forces Journal* 1:1301–1306.

Campbell, J. 1947. *The Hero with a Thousand Faces*. Princeton, N.J.: Princeton University Press, 1972

Campbell, J., and B. Moyers. 1988. *The Power of Myth*. New York: Doubleday.

Connolly, P. M. 1981. An exploratory study of adults engaging in the high risk sport of skiing. New Brunwick, N.J.: Rutgers State University. Master's thesis.

Fenichel, O. 1939. The counter-phobic attitude. *International Journal of Psychoanalysis* 20:263–274.

Heyman, S. R., and K. G. Rose. 1981. The relationship of personality and behavioral characteristics to the SCUBA performances of novices. Paper presented at the annual meeting of the North American Society for the Psychology of Sport and Physical Activity, Asilomar, Calif.

_____. 1980. Psychological variables affecting SCUBA performance. In *Psychology of Motor Behavior and Sport—1979*, C. H. Nadeau, W. R. Halliwell, K. H. Newell, and G. C. Roberts, eds. Champaign, Ill.: Human Kinetics Press.

Hoover, T. O. 1978. Skydivers: speculations on psychodynamics. *Perceptual and Motor Skills* 47:629–630.

Huberman, J. 1968. A psychological study of participants in high risk sports. Vancouver, British Columbia: University of British Columbia. Doctoral dissertation.

Hymbaugh, K., and J. Garrett. 1974. Sensation seeking among skydivers. In *Perceptual and Motor Skills* 38:118.

Johnsgard, K., B. Ogilvie, and K. Merritt. 1975. The stress seekers: A psychological study of sport parachutists, racing drivers, and football players. *Journal of Sports Medicine* 15:158–169.

Jung, C. G. 1907. The psychology of dementia praecox. In *CW* 3:1–150. Princeton, N.J.: Princeton University Press, 1960

———. 1918. The role of the unconscious. In *CW* 10:3–28. Princeton, N.J.: Princeton University Press, 1964.

———. 1930. The complications of American psychology. In *CW* 10:502–514. Princeton, N.J.: Princeton University Press, 1964.

———. 1943. On the psychology of the unconscious. In *CW* 7:3–121. Princeton, N.J.: Princeton University Press, 1953.

———. 1944. *Psychology and Alchemy. CW*, vol. 12, Princeton, N.J.: Princeton University Press, 1953.

———. 1952. *Symbols of Transformation. CW*, vol. 5. Princeton, N.J.: Princeton University Press, 1956.

Kepecs, J. G. 1944. Neurotic reactions in parachutists. *Psychoanalytic Quarterly* 13:273–299.

Kusyszyn, T., P. Steinberg, and B. Elliott. 1974. Arousal seeking, physical risk taking, and personality. Paper presented at the 18th International Congress of Applied Psychology, Montreal, Canada.

Leonard, L. 1989. *Witness to the Fire: Creativity and the Veil of Addiction*. Boston: Shambhala.

MacKinnon, D. W. 1960. The highly effective individual. *Teachers College Record* 61:367–368.

Metropolitan Life Insurance Company. 1974. Hazardous occupations and avocations. *Statistical Bulletin* 55 (March):3–5.

Murray, H. A. 1955. American Icarus. In *Clinical Studies in Personality*, vol. 2, A. Burton and R. E. Harris, eds. New York: Harper.

Neel, S. H. 1951a. Medical aspects of military parachuting. *Military Surgeon* 108:91–105.

———. 1951b. The airborne soldier. *Military Surgeon* 109:599–605.

Neuman, E. 1954. *The Origins and History of Consciousness*. New York: Pantheon, 1964.

Satinover, J. 1986. The myth of the death of the hero: A Jungian view of masculine psychology. *Psychoanalytic Review* 73:553–565.

Settles, B. H., and D. G. Kinzing. 1975. Young children's perceptions of a public figure: Evel Knievel. *Young Children* 30:184–188.

Shapiro, D. 1965. *Neurotic Styles*. New York: Basic Books.

Strykowski, J. 1976. Keynote address. Southeastern Region YMCA SCUBA Instructor's Association Meeting, Dallas, Tex.

Torrence, E. P. 1974. A psychological study of American jet aces. Paper presented at the Western Psychological Association Meeting, Long Beach, Calif.

Walker, R. C. 1980. The athletic motif. New York: C. G. Jung Institute. Candidate thesis.

Zuckerman, M. 1979. *Sensation Seeking: Beyond the Optimal Level of Arousal.* Hillsdale, N.J.: L. Erlbaum.

Steven R. Heyman, *Ph.D., was a licensed clinical psychologist and a professor of clinical psychology at the University of Wyoming. He was the author of several works on sport psychology and psychotherapy, a Fellow of the American Psychological Association, and was actively involved in organizing psychological support for athletes participating in the 1994 Gay Games. He died in November 1993.*

The Psychological Meaning of Excellence in Competitive Performance

Cathaleene J. Macias
Ronald F. Kinney

Psychological research on competitive sports has increased substantially over the past two decades, with a growing number of studies investigating such topics as the viability of mental practice for improving performance (Feltz and Landers 1983), the role of psychological stress in sports competition (Scanlan, Lewthwaite and Jackson 1984), and the beneficial effects of regular exercise in promoting mental and physical health (Leith and Taylor 1990). However, the bulk of psychological research on sports has concentrated on the attribution of responsibility for particular outcomes, including fault for poor performance and credit for good performance (LeUnes et al. 1990). The accuracy of perception of responsibility has been linked to bias in spectator observation as well as to athletes' increased or decreased self-confidence (see McAuley and Gross 1983; Rejeski and Brawley 1983; Weinberg, Yukelson and Jackson 1980). The latter focus on athletes' perceptions of their own performance has become known as "self-efficacy" research (Bandura 1977, 1989), and the results of these studies clearly show the importance of believing in one's own ability to win or succeed in sports.

While extensive research has been conducted on beliefs about causality and agency, little attention has been paid to determining the impact of emotional and physical sensations that accompany very good and very poor sports performance. Surely the ecstasy of winning and the humiliation of defeat play a primary role in influencing an athlete's subsequent sports performance. Excellent performance may increase an athlete's self-confidence and lead to even greater achievements, while inferior performance may detract from a sense of efficacy and lead to a deterioration in achievement. On the other hand, there are obviously times when success makes an athlete too complacent and when failure spurs an athlete on to try harder. In order to determine more precisely the emotional impact of experiencing either a very good or a very poor performance, it is necessary to look at the actual experience in the context of an athlete's level of expertise and motivation to succeed. To our knowledge, no previous study has addressed the emotional aspects of excellent sports performance and its relationship to an athlete's continued striving toward success.

The research project described in this chapter was designed to study master's level swimmers' perceptions of particular swim strokes. More specifically, we were interested in the emotional experiences that these swimmers associate with their best and worst swim strokes. In this way, we sought to gain a better understanding of what it is about very good performance that could encourage and strengthen future performance and promote the attainment of excellence. Since this particular sample of swimmers performed even their worst swim stroke proficiently, we did not expect to learn as much about low levels of achievement.

Placing the investigation into a Jungian context, our focus was on the degree to which a feeling of movement and accomplishment is part of an active experience of sports excellence. We framed our research question as follows:

> To what extent is the experience of excellence associated with a numinous and transcendent state that blends the "Doing" aspects of performance with the "Being" aspects of goal attainment?

Swimming was selected as the sport of interest because we believe it offers athletes an optimal opportunity for the transcendent experience of excellence. Our theoretical explanation for swimming's facilitation of transcendence begins with a discussion of the most essential prerequisite for the sport: water.

The Symbolism of Water: Cultural and Religious Significance

Water cleanses, comforts, and sustains life. Water cults have been identified from water symbols engraved on ancient figurines and other artifacts found in all parts of the world. Anthropologists, archaeologists, and historians present ample evidence for a universal veneration of water that perseveres in spite of increased technology and the destruction of many primitive religions. Even in the Western world, water worship has continued up to the present day, especially in the British Isles. Sacred wells, rivers, and waterfalls are scattered throughout Ireland and England. Many of these water sources have been designated shrines; each has its own associated water spirit, nymph, or "water woman," and most are renowned for healing or curative properties (Bord and Bord 1985; Harding 1971). In the United States, hot springs and mineral waters were first frequented by native peoples and then by European settlers and their contemporary descendants. Water worship and reverence is still in conscious existence within Western culture and undoubtedly gives momentum to current environmentalist efforts to recover polluted rivers and lakes and to preserve underground water.

In alchemical texts, water is most clearly associated with the transformative process of *solutio*, wherein a substance is dissolved in water. The experience of *solutio* is a return to the *prima materia*, to the maternal womb, to the "friendly water" (Edinger 1985). In Christian theology, *solutio* is the rite of baptism, in which the individual symbolically risks drowning in order to resurface to a new life. Psychologically, *solutio* refers to a dissolution of the ego when confronted by the collective unconscious—an encounter of human consciousness with overwhelming unconscious forces that usually presents a crisis for the individual.

The *solutio* presents a danger, but it also symbolically presents a heroic challenge and an opportunity for transformation and rebirth. The danger presented by *solutio* for the individual psyche is what Neumann (1954) refers to as "uroboric incest," the loss of consciousness in final dissolution and death experienced as a return to the Mother. Paradoxically, only by risking total dissolution, only by descending into the realm of the collective unconscious can an individual ascend to a higher level of consciousness. To experience this death and to reemerge from the waters of the collective unconscious, reborn to a new conscious identity and a new awareness of self, is to experience the alchemical process in its fullness.

The Swimmer's Experience of Water

Insofar as he or she shares the cultural and psychological meanings associated with water, the competitive swimmer must repeatedly experience a personal *solutio*, a psychological encounter with the collective unconscious, when swimming. The competitive swimmer's relationship to water appears to be paradoxical in nature: the swimmer must depend upon water to reach a clearly defined goal, yet water is also an obstacle offering resistance which must be overcome by a powerful rhythmic motion of body and limbs. Water supports with its buoyancy but also resists with its mass. For this reason, we consider swimming to be the sport in which athletes are most likely to experience the *solutio*. Consequently, we would expect swimmer associations to particular strokes to be highly archetypal. We also predict that a swimmer will have a stronger experience of *solutio* when performing well. This enhanced archetypal experience should, in turn, make it possible for a swimmer to continue to perform at his or her best. We suggest that the experience of *solutio* results in a circular, spiral increase toward excellence. While it may be difficult to tease out the cause-effect sequence inherent in this interplay between psychological experience and performance excellence, it is possible to determine whether accomplished swimmers have a generally archetypal, numinous experience while performing their best strokes.

The present study was designed to test the hypothesis that a swimmer's reflection on the performance of his or her best stroke is highly archetypal and numinous in quality. More specifically, we hypothesize that when asked to describe his or her best stroke, a swimmer will select words with strongly archetypal associations. To link this hypothesis to the more elusive premise that swimmers experience the *solutio* while swimming their best strokes, we must assume that an expression of strong archetypal association is evidence of memory for a numinous experience. That is, a reflection on a previous experience must be accepted as a substitute for actual experience, since it would be extremely difficult to solicit a swimmer's free associations while swimming, and to do so would most likely disrupt the experience. However, to strengthen the link between reflected and actual experience, we asked swimmers to imagine that they were swimming a particular stroke for a few moments before deciding on the archetypal ratings for that stroke.

Instrumentation

Swimmers rated their associations to each of four strokes (backstroke, butterfly, breaststroke, and freestyle) on a variety of abstract concepts demonstrated by previous research to be representative or interpretative of symbols having archetypal meaning. They then indicated which stroke was their best or worst, fastest or slowest, and favorite or least favorite.

To measure the archetypal strength of these associations in a systematic and standardized manner, we designed the Archetypal Association Scale (AAS). The AAS consists of fifteen abstract concepts, each followed by a seven-point scale on which respondents indicate the degree to which a given concept is "descriptive" or "not descriptive" of a particular experience, such as performing a swim stroke (see figure 1). The AAS was derived from the Archetypal Symbol Inventory (ASI), developed by David Rosen and his colleagues (Rosen et al. 1991) in collaboration with Harry Prochaska and Katharine von Fischer of the Archive for Research in Archetypal Symbolism (ARAS) in San Francisco. The ASI consists of forty symbols and their interpretative meanings. The archetypal nature of the majority of these symbols has been substantiated through experimental learning tasks: the inventory symbols

Figure 1. *Archetypal Association Scale for Rating Swim Strokes and Academic Course Work*

NOT DESCRIPTIVE						VERY DESCRIPTIVE
Beauty	1	2	3	4	5	6	7
Birth	1	2	3	4	5	6	7
Intellect	1	2	3	4	5	6	7
Eternity	1	2	3	4	5	6	7
Feminine	1	2	3	4	5	6	7
Harmony	1	2	3	4	5	6	7
Masculine	1	2	3	4	5	6	7
Paradox	1	2	3	4	5	6	7
Perfection	1	2	3	4	5	6	7
Powerful	1	2	3	4	5	6	7
Progress	1	2	3	4	5	6	7
Quest	1	2	3	4	5	6	7
Rest	1	2	3	4	5	6	7
Synthesis	1	2	3	4	5	6	7
Spirit	1	2	3	4	5	6	7

were recalled significantly more frequently when paired with their assumed meanings than when paired with random meanings, even though subject knowledge of these meanings was demonstrated to be unconscious. Moreover, when asked to pair symbols with associative meanings, the match for inventory items was higher than what would be expected by chance alone (ibid.). While our study does not utilize the visual symbols of the ASI, it does rely on the interpretative meaning of fifteen of these symbols, deemed (by the present authors) to be appropriate for use with sports-related performances. These fifteen archetypal concepts compose the AAS, described in detail below.

At this point, it is important to caution against assuming that any of these conceptual categories (e.g., beauty) or dimensions (e.g., being) is synonymous with a particular archetype. According to Jungian theory, an archetype is essentially elusive and undefinable, manifesting multiple meanings and perceptible in diverse ways. The presence of an archetype is revealed not by the content of its manifestation, but by its emotional impact. This impact may have a generic component (e.g., the Great Mother), but an archetypal experience is always highly personalized (Jung 1926). To attempt to reduce any archetypal symbol to a single meaning would be absurd. Therefore, the intent of the AAS is not to present archetypes per se, but to elicit archetypal associations suggested by particular abstract concepts. These associative elements are not directly measurable but rather are evidenced by a high rating on the concepts that elicit strong archetypal responses.

The Associative Dimensions of the AAS

The Archetypal Association Scale is composed of three four-item subscales or dimensions—doing, being, and thinking—designed to reflect two categories of Jungian typology: feeling and thinking. The feeling category consists of the dimensions doing and being, reflecting active and static components, respectively. The unidimensional thinking category is a blend of active and static concepts that have cognitive connotations.

The Doing Dimension

The doing, or active feeling, dimension of the AAS was designed to reflect a dynamic quality of movement, incorporating the following concepts: "birth," "powerful," "progress," and "quest." The single item "masculine" was also included to assess the gender-specificity of the doing dimension. The inclusion of the "birth" concept on this assumed-masculine dimension provided a stringent test of the proposed gender association. It was hypothesized that because competitive swimmers exert extensive effort when performing any swim stroke, swimmers' best and worst strokes would both be perceived as high on the doing dimension.

The Being Dimension

The being, or static feeling, dimension of the AAS was designed to reflect a stable quality of positive being, encompassing the concepts "beauty," "perfection," "harmony," and "spirit." This dimension was intended to measure the degree to which an experience is perceived as numinous in quality, high in emotional associations, and representative of a state of timeless existence. It was hypothesized that the strokes in which swimmers excelled would be perceived as highly archetypal along the being dimension, because it is through excellent performance that a swimmer is able to realize the static state of accomplishment.

The single scale item selected to assess the gender-specificity the being dimension was "feminine." We hypothesized that it is a fusion of this feminine dimension being with the masculine dimension doing that ushers in the emotional "high" experienced during an excellent performance. In Jungian terms, the essential ingredient for a numinous experience is a sense of finality in the midst of change, a fusion of opposite feelings reflective of the *mysterium coniunctionis* (Jung 1955). The psychological association of the concept "feminine" with a static state of positive being and "masculine" with a dynamic, evolving state of doing has been explicated by several Jungian theorists (e.g., de Castillejo 1973, Greenfield 1983, Sullivan 1989, Ulanov 1981). Whether the source of these gender associations is innately psychological or cultural has been extensively debated (Goldenberg 1977, Lauter and Rupprecht 1985, Wehr 1987). The Archetypal Association Scale offers an opportunity to determine whether such gender-based distinctions are common among the fifty participants in our study. While the small study sample does not represent a true cross section of the American public, it does provide a beginning for exploring the prevalence of gender-specific archetypal categories.

The Thinking Dimension

The thinking subscale of the AAS was designed to reflect an intellectual, relatively nonfeeling, analytical evaluation of experience, comprising the concepts, "eternity," "paradox," "rest," and "synthesis." The single scale item selected to typify this dimension of cognitive assessment was "intellect." Because cognitive approaches to improving sports performance have become popular over the last decade, it was hypothesized that the thinking dimension would also characterize best swim strokes. However, thinking was expected to be lower in associative value for any swim stroke than either of the two feeling dimensions, being or doing.

Scale Directionality

The direction of affect or valence for all fifteen scale concepts was, by definition, positive, although the words used to denote the thinking concepts were somewhat more neutral in connotation. The exclusion of negative archetypal meanings from the Archetypal Association Scale was intentional. Because archetypal concepts are by nature multidimensional and multifaceted, many (e.g., death) elicit both positive and negative feelings. To limit the range of individual variation in emotional response, we restricted each dimension to concepts from the Archetypal Symbol Inventory whose valence was positive and relatively unambiguous.

Associative Dimensions versus Personality Traits

The dimensions chosen for the present study have their origin in Jungian typology (Jung 1921). This conceptual schema for classifying psychological attitudes (introversion-extraversion) with specific perceptual (sensation-intuition) and judgmental (feeling-thinking) functions has received a great deal of attention from contemporary Jungian theorists (e.g., Franz and Hillman 1972, Quenk and Quenk 1982). Within this tradition, at least three instruments have been designed to assess Jungian typologies as personality traits: the Jungian Type Survey (Wheelwright, Wheelwright and Buehler 1942), the Myers-Briggs Type Indicator (Myers 1962), and the Singer-Loomis Inventory (Singer and Loomis 1984). The use of the second two instruments has become widespread in organizational settings for climate and personality assessment (Hollwitz 1992).

It is important to distinguish the Archetypal Association Scale from typological instruments that focus on personality traits and individual differences. In using the feeling-thinking dimensions, we limited our interpretations of associative tendencies to the objects of perception (i.e., swim strokes). No attempt was made to infer the underlying personality traits of the participants. The AAS was designed to measure individuals' attributions, but not their attributional styles. Of primary interest were the kinds of experience that elicit particular typological associations, rather than the types of personalities that underlie certain response patterns. It is important to keep this distinction between associations and traits in mind when interpreting the results of the present study.

Psychometric Properties of the AAS

Dimensional Validity

The three individual scale items chosen to typify the conceptual meaning of the three AAS dimensions correlated highest with the scale that each was intended to represent. Averaging across "best" and "worst" swim strokes, the correlations were $r = .60$ for "feminine" with the being dimension; $r = .72$ for "masculine" with the doing dimension; and $r = .65$ for "intellect" with the thinking dimension. These correlations were statistically significant at less than the .01 level of probability. Item correlations with dimensions other than those they were designed to represent were lower, and either attained lower levels of statistical significance or did not reach significance ($p > .05$). Although our study sample was too small to permit a factor analytic examination of the AAS conceptual components, these correlational results provide preliminary evidence of the scale's dimensional clarity.

These psychometric qualities suggest that there are gender-specific cultural associations to the static being and the active doing dimensions. For our sample of community swimmers, "feminine" clearly connotes a sense of being and "masculine" a sense of doing. It is interesting, however, that the concept "masculine" had a relatively low correlation (r = .34) with the thinking dimension, negating the cultural stereotyping of academic and intellectual work as a male domain. Yet, considering that our sample was composed of accomplished athletes who were also predominately community professionals, this negation of gender associations with the thinking dimension may not be representative of the culture of the United States as a whole.

Scale Reliability

The Archetypal Association Scale demonstrated both high test-retest reliability and internal consistency. Fifteen of the study subjects were asked to rate their associations to the freestyle swim stroke twice during a three-week interval and high intrasubject reliability was obtained (r = .94, p < .01). There was also minimal variability within the separate subscales of the instrument between measurement periods and a high overall inter-item correlation (a = .84). Moreover, the low error of measurement and abundance of statistically significant findings produced using the AAS attest to the instrument's strong reliability and sensitivity to group differences.

Description of the Subject Sample

The sample consisted of 25 men and 25 women swimmers on the masters-level swim team at the Steiner Aquatic Center in Salt Lake City, Utah. All participants were Caucasian and between the ages of 20 and 47 years (M = 32). Only 10% of the sample were students at the University of Utah; 90% worked in the local community. Approximately the same percentage of men and women were students (12 percent of the men, 8 percent of the women) and community employed (88 percent of the men, 92 percent of the women). The occupations of the swimmers were quite diverse. The sample consisted of medical doctors, attorneys, professors, engineers, teachers, and swim coaches, as well as an airline pilot, a botanist, an architect, a chemist, an investment broker, a production manager, an advertising agent, an insurance broker, a store manager, a military officer, an accountant, a biomedical researcher, a restaurant manager, a nurse, and a physical therapist. This rich diversity in occupations and comparability between genders increases the generalizability of the research findings and the clarity of gender differences.

Most members of the swim team began swimming in childhood and swim often as adults. A majority of the swimmers learned to swim before age 8, began competitive swimming before age 12, and currently practice at least three times a week. There were significant differences between men and women swimmers in current age and in the age at which they began competitive swimming. Men swimmers were somewhat older than women swimmers (M = 35 and 28, respectively; $F(1,48) = 15.0$, $p < .01$) and began competitive swimming at a later age (M = 17 and 9, respectively; $F(1,44) = 7.31$, $p < .01$). However, none of the demographic or experience-based variables were significantly related to ratings of "best" and "worst" strokes on the Archetypal Association Scale. There was also no difference between genders in need for achievement in swimming, as measured by a ten-point scale on which subjects rated how important success in swimming was for them (with the endpoints of the scale labeled "success is not important" and "it's essential to succeed"). In fact, there were no gender differences in participant responses to any of the "need for achievement" scales, which covered such diverse areas as university grades, friendship, parenting, and career aspirations.

Results

The present study utilized a multivariate factorial research design with levels of "best" versus "worst" swim performance, being versus doing versus thinking archetypal dimensions, and gender comparisons. Analyses were also conducted separately for swimmers reporting high versus low levels of need to succeed in swimming. The primary statistical procedure employed was multivariate analysis of variance along with post hoc univariate tests.

Table 1. *Mean Scores for the Archetypal Dimensions: Swim Strokes*

Dimension	Best Swim Stroke	Worst Swim Stroke
Being	5.14[a]	3.88[b]
Doing	4.62[a]	4.01[c]
Thinking	3.92[a]	3.45[bc]
Total Score	4.56	3.78

[abc]Mean scores with the matching superscripts are significantly different at p < .05.

Swimmer Associations to Best and Worst Swim Strokes

Our hypothesis predicting stronger archetypal associations to better sports performance was supported by the research results. Swim strokes which were designated "best" were given significantly higher overall archetypal ratings when compared to swim strokes designated "worst" $(F(1,49) = 5.81, p < .001)$. This higher archetypal score for "best" stroke held true for each of the three dimensions of the Archetypal Association Scale (see table 1). "Best" stroke was rated by swimmers as more reflective of being $(F(1,49) = 5.90, p < .001)$, doing $(F(1,49) = 3.46, p < .01)$, and thinking $(F(1,49) = 2.82, p < .01)$ than was "worst" stroke. A comparison of mean scores on the separate dimensions revealed that the difference between "best" and "worst" strokes was strongest for the being dimension. These results indicate that accomplished swimmers experience a strong sense of emotional well-being while swimming their best stroke. In terms of sports achievement, this sense of well-being could be interpreted as an acknowledgment of personal accomplishment, of a goal achieved, or as the transcendence to a higher status as swimmer.

Best Swim Strokes

Fifty-six percent of the sample identified the freestyle as their "best" swim stroke; in contrast, only 6 percent designated the butterfly as their "best." The "best" swim stroke was also likely to be identified as a swimmer's "fastest" and "favorite." The ranking of the three archetypal dimensions with respect to the strength of their association to "best" stroke was as predicted: (1) being, (2) doing, and (3) thinking. The difference between each dimensional mean score was significant at the $p < .01$ level. Regardless of the specific stroke identified as "best," the primary concepts associated with "best" stroke were, in descending order, "powerful," "beauty," "harmony," "perfection," "progress," and "spirit." Both men and women gave these six archetypal concepts the highest associative ratings (i.e., a mean rating higher than 5.00) for their "best" stroke. These six concepts represent a blend of items from the doing dimension ("powerful," "progress") with the more dominant being dimension ("beauty," "harmony," "perfection," and "spirit"), suggesting that excellence in sports performance elicits both "masculine" and "feminine" associations. In Jungian terms, swimmers' associations to their best stroke appear to represent a reconciliation of opposites, reflecting a transcendent experience, a static state of ecstasy in the midst of movement.

Worst Swim Strokes

Two strokes predominated as "worst" stroke: 48 percent of the sample identified the butterfly as their "worst" swim stroke; 30 percent designated the breaststroke as their "worst." (Interestingly, the breaststroke was identified as the "best" stroke by another fourth of the sample.) Parallel to "best" stroke, the "worst" stroke was also likely to be a swimmer's "slowest" and "least favorite."

As table 1 shows, swimmers' archetypal ratings of their "worst" stroke followed a pattern of dimensional ranking different from that for "best" stroke. There was less emphasis on the being dimension, with a resulting nonsignificant difference between being and doing scores. However, means for both the being and doing dimensions were significantly higher than the mean score for the thinking dimension. Therefore, it is a low score on the thinking dimension that most clearly characterizes "worst" stroke, whereas enhanced being scores are most characteristic of "best" stroke.

The individual archetypal concepts for "worst" swim stroke which received the highest ratings (i.e., above a 4.00 mean score) were, in descending order, "powerful," "masculine," "progress," "perfection," and "beauty." Three of these five concepts are items on the doing archetypal dimension, and two are on the being

Table 2. Mean Archetypal Scores for Swimmers with High and Low Need for Achievement: Swim Strokes

Dimension	Swim Stroke	High Need for Achievement	Low Need for Achievement
Doing	Best	4.93[a]	4.38
	Worst	3.87[a]	4.11
Thinking	Best	3.95	3.89[b]
	Worst	3.48	3.42[b]

[ab]Mean scores with the same superscript are significantly different at $p < .05$.

dimension. Thus, for worst stroke, there was a reduction in the dominance of the being dimension so prominent in associations to best stroke.

Our analyses also revealed an interesting gender difference in swimmer associations to "worst" stroke. While female swimmers gave only the five items listed above a mean rating greater than 4.00, male swimmers also utilized "spirit" and "quest" to describe their "worst" stroke, giving these additional items comparably high ratings. It appears that men consider the performance of a difficult stroke to be a "spiritual quest," a description with mythological connotations of the hero figure.

The Role of Motivation

Although our results strongly support the hypothesis that the experience of excellence in sports performance elicits associations characteristic of the feminine being archetypal dimension, motivation to succeed at a sport appears to play a strong supplemental role in determining archetypal associations. While there were no significant correlations between need for swim success and any other demographic or experience-related factor (including age at which a swimmer began competitive swimming), there was a significant relationship between need to succeed in swimming and archetypal associations to "best" and "worst" strokes. Swimmers who rated themselves as high in need to succeed in swimming utilized the doing dimension in addition to the being dimension to differentiate between "best" and "worst" swim strokes (F(1,21) = 4.10, p < .01). However, the high-achievement swimmers did not give "best" and "worst" strokes significantly different ratings on the thinking dimension (see table 2). In contrast, swimmers who rated themselves low in need to succeed in swimming did not utilize the doing dimension but relied upon the thinking dimension along with the being dimension to differentiate "best" and "worst" strokes ($F(1,27) = 2.36$, $p < .05$). Therefore, the significant overall differences for best and worst strokes on the doing and thinking dimensions are attributable to different subgroups of swimmers: high-achievement swimmers were responsible for the overall difference between best and worst strokes on the doing dimension, while low-achievement swimmers were responsible for the overall thinking difference.

Thus, for low-achievement swimmers, the evaluation of best and worst performances was apparently less emotional, more objective, and more psychologically distant (i.e., intellectual) than for high-achievement swimmers. The fact that only highly motivated swimmers clearly combined the being and doing dimensions when describing their best performance suggests that only these athletes experienced the strong blend of masculine and feminine characteristics of a transcendent experience. It can be inferred from this finding that motivation to succeed accentuates the transcendent experience of excellence in sports performance.

A Replication: Academic Associations

In order to extend our theoretical base, we also asked swim team members to rate their associations to their "best" and "worst" academic courses using the same Archetypal Association Scale. "Best" course was defined as "the easiest for you and in which you feel you did well on tests"; "worst" course was defined as "the most difficult for you and in which you dreaded being tested the most." Course work referred to any high school or college course the participants had taken at any time. The results of the auxiliary academic analysis replicated the findings for swim stroke performance: "best" academic courses were given a higher overall archetypal rating than "worst" academic courses ($F(1,45) = 9.53$, $p < .001$). The archetypal superiority of "best" over "worst" course was statistically significant for all three dimensions: being ($F(1,47) = 14.01$, $p < .001$); doing ($F(1,47) = 7.47$, $p < .001$); and thinking ($F(1,47) = 3.12$, $p < .01$).

Table 3. *Mean Scores for the Archetypal Dimensions: Academic Course Work*

Dimension	Best Course	Worst Course
Being	4.88[a]	2.53[c]
Doing	4.83[b]	3.16[c]
Thinking	4.38[ab]	3.74[c]
Total Score	4.67	3.15

[abc]Means with the same superscript are significantly different at $p < .05$.

Best Course Work

The ranking of AAS dimensions for "best" academic courses followed the archetypal pattern noted for "best" swim strokes: the being dimension was rated highest, followed by the doing dimension, and finally the thinking dimension (see table 3). The mean scores for the being and doing dimensions were both significantly different from the mean for the thinking dimension, but were not significantly different from each other. Therefore, the emphasis on the being dimension characteristic of best swim strokes was not obtained for best academic courses.

The primary archetypal concepts characteristic of "best" academic course work were "intellect," "powerful," "progress," "beauty," "quest," and "spirit," all of which received a mean rating above 5.00 from both men and women. The primacy of the "intellect" concept is expected for the academic domain of performance, and the dominance of masculine concepts is consistent with the lack of emphasis on being in the dimensional rankings.

In summary, although the best course received higher archetypal scores than the worst course on all three AAS dimensions, replicating the swim stroke results, swimmers' imagery of their best academic course did not produce the strong association to the being dimension characteristic of best swim stroke. Since the majority of the participant sample were not students, but all were exceptional swimmers, these results are not too surprising. It may well be that because swimming is probably the only performance salient for all individuals in the sample, excellence in swimming is the sole activity that can consistently produce the high being scores considered reflective of a numinous archetypal experience. Because only the stronger overall archetypal associations to best performance were generalizable across performance domains, the AAS appears to be domain sensitive.

Worst Course Work

Interestingly, the mean ratings for swimmers' "worst" academic courses did not mirror the being-doing-thinking pattern of ranking obtained for "best" academic courses and for both "best and "worst" swim strokes. In fact, the ranking for "worst" course was exactly the opposite, with thinking receiving the highest mean score, doing the second highest, and being the lowest (see table 3). Each of these mean scores was significantly different from the others at the p < .01 level. In addition, "worst" course work elicited only three archetypal concepts with mean scores above 4.00 for both men and women: "intellect," "eternity," and "paradox." These three concepts are all from the thinking dimension, making "worst" academic course work the only performance that elicited no strong being or doing concepts. The lack of feeling associations to worst course work suggests that this category of poor performance was of little emotional consequence to the research participants, perhaps because the majority of swimmers in the study were former university students for whom academic performance was no longer salient.

The opposite findings for "worst" performance in swimming versus academics (i.e., swimmers gave their "worst" academic course high thinking scores but lower feeling scores, while giving their "worst" swim stroke high feeling and lower thinking scores) support our conjecture that the Archetypal Association Scale is domain sensitive. Our results also suggest that archetypal perceptions are strongly dependent on the nature of the challenge and its importance to the performer. For our sample of competitive swimmers, it appears that even performing one's worst stroke is laden with strong positive feelings (i.e., being and doing dimensions), since the ability to swim any stroke reasonably well is considered indicative of overall swimming competence. However, the level of performance achieved in one's worst academic subject cannot necessarily be considered indicative of a general level of academic performance, since a particular worst subject often has little or no connection to a student's area of academic strength or set of interests. For the masters-level swimmers in our sample, it may be that performing a worst swim stroke elicits the anticipation of a *solutio* experience (i.e., the possibility of achieving a higher level of competence through practice and perseverance), while taking an academic worst course may be perceived as simply an intellectual exercise. It would be interesting to examine whether excellent university students differentiate between best and worst courses within their specialized areas of study in the same way that accomplished swimmers assign higher being scores to their best swim strokes. An experience of *solutio* is probably common for excellent students who are capable of blending cognitive acuity with skilled performance (e.g., in essay composition).

The Role of Motivation and Gender in Associations to Academic Excellence

The converse results on the doing and thinking dimensions for swimmers with low and high motivation to succeed in swimming (i.e., highly motivated swimmers rated their "best" strokes as higher in doing, while swimmers with lower motivation rated their "best" strokes as higher in thinking) were not duplicated for academic course work. Motivation to succeed academically does not appear to influence archetypal attributes to either "best" or "worst" course work. However, a comparison of the same individual's level of motivation across performance domains is beset with difficulties. In particular, the intrinsic importance of academic course work to this sample of swimmers (most of whom were no longer students) was most likely not of the same order of magnitude as achievement in swimming. With respect to gender, there were no differences in mean dimensional ratings for either "best" or "worst" academic course, paralleling the lack of gender differences in swim associations.

Conclusion

The research results offer strong support for the hypothesis that the experience of excellence in sports performance is associated with a numinous and transcendent state which blends the "being" aspects of accomplishment with the "doing" aspects of performing. This numinous experience appears to be characteristic of competition-level swimming but not academic excellence, at least for athletes who have been active in both domains. Moreover, it appears that the cultural association of "feminine' with being and "masculine" with doing plays a vital role in the attribution of archetypal meaning to sports performance. Only when these two gender-based dimensions are fused do we find the experience of excellence.

The study findings also show a strong positive relationship between achievement motivation and the archetypal experience of excellence. Only those athletes who were highly motivated to succeed in swimming saw their best swim stroke as a fusion of being and doing. This finding suggests that motivation to succeed enhances the numinous experience of excellent performance and, in turn, is itself enhanced by such a numinous experience. Apparently, accomplished swimmers are motivated to excel in order to repeat the ecstatic archetypal feeling characteristic of excellent performance. This potential importance of the numinous experience for sustaining superior sports performance should be recognized by both athletes and trainers, and should be distinguished from a motivation to win or to excel for recognition alone. In the context of a highly competitive sport, focusing an athlete's attention on the pleasure inherent in a very good performance may increase the intrinsic motivation for excellence, thereby reducing stress and maximizing performance.

In future studies, we will explore the generalization of these research findings, questioning whether the numinous experience is evident in sports that are more team-based or that rely more heavily on cognitive skills than does swimming. It is our hope that the delineation of essential prerequisites for the numinous experience of excellence will contribute not only to the discipline of sport training but, most importantly, to the pleasure of sport performance.

Acknowledgments

The authors would like to thank the staff of the Steiner Aquatic Center in Salt Lake City, Utah, for their active support of this project; we are especially indebted to Robynn Masters, Dennis Tesch, and Doug Fadel.

References

Bandura, A. 1977. Self-efficacy: Toward a unifying theory of behavioral change. *Psychological Review* 84:191–215.

———. 1989. Human agency in social cognitive theory. *American Psychologist* 44(9):1175–1184.

Bord, J., and Bord, C. 1985. *Sacred Waters*. London: Granada.

de Castillejo, C. 1973. *Knowing Woman: A Feminine Psychology*. New York: Harper and Row.

Edinger, E. F. 1985. *Anatomy of the Psyche: Alchemical Symbolism in Psychotherapy*. LaSalle, Ill.: Open Court.

Feltz, D. L., and Lander, D. M. 1983. The effects of mental practice on motor skill learning and performance: A meta-analysis. *Journal of Sport Psychology* 5:25–57.

Goldenberg, N. 1977. Feminism and Jungian theory. *Anima* 3(2):14–18.

Greenfield, B. 1983. The archetypal masculine: Its manifestation in myth and its significance for women. *Journal of Analytic Psychology.* 28:33–50.

Harding, M. E. 1971. *Woman's Mysteries: Ancient and Modern*. New York: Harper and Row.

Hollwitz, J. 1992. Individuation at work: Considerations for prediction and evaluation. In *Psyche at Work: Workplace Applications of Jungian Analytical Psychology*, M. Stein and J. Hollwitz, eds. Wilmette, Ill.: Chiron Publications.

Jung, C. G. 1921. *Psychological Types*. CW, vol. 6 Princeton, N.J.: Princeton University Press, 1971.

———. 1955. *Mysterium Coniunctionis*. CW, vol. 14. Princeton, N.J.: Princeton University Press, 1963.

———. 1926. Spirit and life. In *CW* 8:319–337. Princeton, N.J.: Princeton University Press, 1969.

Lauter, E., and Rupprecht, C. S. 1985. *Feminist Archetypal Theory: Interdisciplinary Re-visions of Jungian Thought*. Knoxville: University of Tennessee Press.

Leith, L. M., and Taylor, A. H. 1990. Psychological aspects of exercise: A decade literature review. *Journal of Sport Behavior* 13(4):219–239.

LeUnes, A., Wolf, P., Ripper, N., and Anding, L. 1990. Classic references in *Journal of Sport Psychology*, 1979–1987. *Journal of Sport and Exercise Psychology* 12:74–81.

McAuley, E., and Gross, J. 1983. Perceptions of causality in sport: An application of the Causal Dimension Scale. *Journal of Sport Psychology* 5:72–76.

Myers, I. 1962. *The Myers-Briggs Type Indicator*. Palo Alto, Calif.: Consulting Psychologists Press.

Neumann, E. 1954. *The Origins and History of Consciousness.* New York: Pantheon.

Quenk, A. T., and Quenk, N. L. 1982. The use of psychological typology in analysis. In *Jungian Analysis,* M. Stein, ed. Boston: Shambhala.

Rejeski, W. J., and Brawley, L. R. 1983. Attribution theory in sport: Current status and new perspectives. *Journal of Sport Psychology* 5:77–99.

Rosen, D. H., Smith, S. M., Huston, H. L., and Gonzalez, G. 1991. Empirical study of associations between symbols and their meanings: Evidence of collective unconscious (archetypal) memory. *Journal of Analytical Psychology* 36:211–228.

Scanlan, T. K., Lewthwaite, R., and Jackson, B. L. 1984. Social psychological aspects of competition for male youth sport participants. II. Predictors of performance outcomes. *Journal of Sport Psychology* 6:422–429.

Singer, J., and Loomis, M. 1984. The Singer-Loomis Inventory of Personality. Palo Alto, Calif.: Consulting Psychologists Press.

Sullivan, B. S. 1989. *Psychotherapy Grounded in the Feminine Principle.* Wilmette, Ill.: Chiron Publications.

Ulanov, A. 1981. *Receiving Woman: Studies in the Psychology and Theology of the Feminine.* Philadelphia: Westminster Press.

von Franz, M.-L., and Hillman, J. 1971. *Lectures on Jung's Typology.* New York: Spring Publications.

Wehr, D. S. 1987. *Jung and Feminism: Liberating Archetypes.* Boston: Beacon Press.

Weinberg, R. S., Yukelson, D., and Jackson, A. 1980. Effects of public and private efficacy expectations on competitive performance. *Journal of Sport Psychology* 2:340–349.

Wheelwright, J. B., Wheelwright, J. H., and Buehler, J. 1942. *Jungian Type Survey.* San Francisco: Society of Jungian Analysts of Northern California.

Cathaleene J. Macias, *Ph.D., is research director of the International Center for Clubhouse Development, Fountain House, Inc., in New York City, and a project research director at the University of Medicine and Dentistry of New Jersey.*

Ronald F. Kinney, *M.S., is a research associate at the University of Utah in Salt Lake City.*

Tennis in the Second Half of Life as Related to Individuation

Margaret P. Johnson
Jeanine Auger Roose

The game of tennis involves two players who perform a delicately balanced dance with one another. The object is to catch the opponent off balance or to place the ball on the court in such a way that it is impossible for the other to return it in play. As a game, tennis requires concentration on the ball, focused aggression. The ball, a center for meditation, is in continuous movement, as are the two individuals; thus, the point of view of the player changes constantly. The game is analogous to a dynamic interplay between the ego and the Self, or "other," the latter providing an unpredictable response to the conscious intent of the ego.

Huizinga defines the formal characteristics of play as a "free activity standing quite consciously outside 'ordinary life,' as being 'not serious,' but at the same time absorbing the player intensely and utterly." It is a nonprofit activity which proceeds within "proper boundaries of time and space according to fixed rules and in an orderly manner." Last, it promotes social groupings (Huizinga 1955, p. 13). We suggest that tennis meets each of these characteristics of play in its own unique way. We will be discussing some of these in depth.

Both authors began to play tennis in the second half of life, following many years of serious study and work in the discipline of Jungian psychology. It was our individual experience that resulted in this material, namely the awareness that playing tennis has produced or been related to profound changes in the psyche. Changes occurred on two primary levels: increased consciousness of the body, and development of the inferior function, which for both authors was the sensation function.

It is crucial for the development of the individual to connect with the unconscious wherever the mercurial element lies, and perhaps for some it lies on the tennis court. Realizing that this is an unusual place to encounter Mercurius, from the traditional Jungian perspective, we looked more deeply into this question. We interviewed a sample of seven individuals on the subject of tennis, six women and one man. Our criteria for selecting them as subjects for our study was that they are presently playing tennis with some degree of enthusiasm and that they began to play tennis at some point in the second half of life. We wanted to know who our subjects were and why they had chosen to play tennis at a time when the majority of tennis players who take up tennis in the first half of life are retiring from the game.

Our subjects began to play tennis at an age ranging from 34 to 49, the average age being 42. They presently play tennis from one to ten hours per week, the average number of hours per week being 5.14. Although half of them had been physically active as children, the majority of them had become inactive prior to taking up tennis. They made a similar comment about themselves, that they had become serious and nonplayful. Tennis for them has become their major form of play. All of the subjects talk about still being in the process of improving their game, and the majority have taken or are presently taking lessons. Some have joined tennis clubs and participate on tennis teams and in local tennis tournaments. For our subjects there is a considerable commitment to the game of tennis, over a period of at least five years.

When we asked why they chose to take up tennis at this time in their lives, the subjects responded that, generally speaking, they did not clearly or consciously choose to play tennis. Rather, it felt to them as if tennis chose them, as if they fell into it, and then discovered that tennis met a need they did not know they had. More than half of the subjects were initially drawn into playing tennis by a spouse or significant other, or as a way to develop friendships or participate in an activity with friends who did play tennis. "I just thought it would be a sort of fun thing to do. There are a lot of people who play, so maybe I could play. . . ."

Once drawn into the game, however, the subjects experienced something new, something that fascinated, as only Mercurius can. One subject said, "It (tennis) was the coming into life. Sometimes I think it is life. When I first started playing, I was really addicted. I was playing twelve to fourteen hours a week." This subject adds that the reason she now plays tennis is "to live . . . it's like air and food and water. And I never thought in my entire life I would say that about a game."

We asked our subjects what adjectives they would use to

describe the way they presently feel about tennis, and the adjectives most frequently chosen fell into five categories. First, despite the difficulties and frustrations that learning to play tennis can present, the subjects were drawn to continue to play because it was "fun." They all spoke about a lot of laughter and good humor on the tennis court. Second, they spoke about gaining a new connection with their bodies that made them feel good, more alive, or about the discovery of a rhythm in body movement that was very pleasant. Third, they used adjectives that suggested the experience of a new kind of mastery, a new way of being creative with the body or a new way of being forceful and assertive. In the fourth category, the subjects used adjectives such as "playful competition," "sportsmanship," and "friendships," which suggest that the relationship with the tennis partner is an important variable. In the fifth category were adjectives that suggest more directly that the game of tennis has connected the subjects with a numinous or a mercurial place. The subjects used such expressions as "very important," "very exhilarating," "very spirited feeling," "if I don't get to play, I am very grumpy," "life giving," "fascinating," and "I love it." The also talked about frustration, "maddening," or an experience of their own limitations, suggesting an encounter with a powerful and unpredictable "other" on the tennis court.

From the point of view of psychological types, the most common pattern among our subjects was introverted with intuition as a first or a second function. No subjects claimed the sensation function as either a first or a second function. There were four intuitives, two of these extraverted and two of them introverted; two feeling types, both introverted; and one thinking type, also introverted. From this perspective it would follow that the subjects' involvement with tennis could parallel the development of their inferior function, the sensation function in the majority of cases. Marie-Louise von Franz has described the inferior function as behaving "after the manner of a fool hero, the divine fool, or idiot hero. He represents the despised part of the personality, the ridiculous and unadapted part, but also that part which builds the connection with the unconscious and therefore holds the secret key to the unconscious totality of the person" (1971, p. 6). Many of our subjects experienced the "fool" in themselves when they started playing tennis, asking the body to do something more than "carry the head around," as one of them said. On the other hand, they experienced something special, numinous, as well. "An ecstatic state is usually initiated by an experience of the inferior function" (von Franz 1971, p. 36).

We asked our subjects if they had any thoughts about playing tennis in the second half of life as opposed to playing in the first half, and they indicated that tennis may provide a different function. One subject, who had a busy first half of life raising children and developing a career, said, "I am not sure it is a first half of life thing at all. In fact, I think that there is definitely a place for tennis in the second half, for me an even better one." For her, playing tennis is a good balance and compensation for her professional work. "It is a complete change from what I do all day—sitting, thinking, analyzing, dealing with people. It uses the opposite gear . . . I leave the tennis court feeling very relaxed . . . it is very good for your health . . . good for relaxing." Another subject felt that tennis was good for her in the second half of life because it gave her "an important feeling of self-esteem." Almost all of the subjects have said that playing tennis makes them feel better about themselves and their bodies.

Other subjects indicated that psychologically, as well, tennis is different in the second half of life. In the first half of life one takes up tennis with the hopes and expectations of perhaps being number one in some significant league. In the second half of life, when one takes up tennis with the divine fool, those kinds of expectations are not so present. One subject said, "It is a different game in the second half of life. I think it is more psychological. It comes more from the psyche. In the first half winning the game is more important, whereas in the second half playing the game is more important than winning. It is more integrated in the second half of life. It has more attributes to it."

For some, the tennis court seems to provide a container in which they can observe themselves moving and reacting in a game that requires them to be as present as possible, and yet not be overly identified with the outcome. After all, one does not expect the divine fool to behave like a champion. One subject saw the task of the second half of life as becoming less identified with all of the manifestations of the Self, and yet remaining involved: "Tennis is really a wonderful model for that because you have to be there, be really engaged and take it seriously, but it would be stupid to be completely identified with it." The subjects were aware that more psychological dramas were being played out on the tennis court than simply the game of tennis. They were learning other things about themselves.

One subject described Hermes as "the Net God," in his trickster aspect. "One never knows whose side he will be on!" Hermes, the god of borderlines, of the ins and outs of the tennis ball, can sometimes be on your side, and then the points are easily won. Then the player feels supported by forces beyond the ego, which can feel numinous. But Hermes can change and support the other player unexpectedly. The player has to learn to deal with this change. At this point, the subjects speak of having to deal with their own inner critic coming up in a distracting and discouraging way. "It's been very helpful for learning to just let it go, because if you hang on to a bad shot, you will get distracted from the next shot . . . you can't hang on to the good shot either and get all puffed up." Another subject said, "Everything in my psyche is brought and has been brought to the tennis court. My lack of being able to be assertive is clearly on the tennis courts . . . even my anxiety about the net . . . when I back off instead of going towards it."

A number of subjects emphasized that tennis has been important for them to learn to stay focused in the present. This means watching the tennis ball with no other thoughts or images in the mind. For some of our subjects, many who are introverted intuitive types, this has been not only refreshing but also instructive. It has been a way to distinguish between fantasy and reality in an embodied way. One subject turned to tennis as a way to deal with addictions to smoking and alcohol, both of which pulled her into fantasy and repressed the expression of action or feeling. "I think tennis puts you in the world. It makes you act. I was paralyzed as a child, emotionally paralyzed. I always had to take care of my mother . . . or the other person."

Another subject felt that playing tennis was useful for "working through that mother problem." "That mother problem" was experienced primarily in two ways: in the way the subjects felt about or related to their bodies; and in their relationship to other people, in this case, the tennis player on the other side of the net. More than half of our subjects felt that relating to the tennis partner was an important aspect of the game, although three subjects did not. One subject felt that the social aspect of tennis gave her an opportunity to "work on my feeling function . . . it nidges my inferior function. It comes in relating to my partners, forgetting to give a compliment when it is due. It requires me to see these things, and then express them."

A number of our subjects expressed the idea that it is important to have a friendship or a relationship with the tennis partner and spoke of the difficulty they have in viewing the partner simply as "the competition." One subject said, I don't like competitive sports. I prefer the connection with a person who is a friend, one I'm not competing against, but who I'm playing against to improve my own skills." Another subject said, "For me the primary motive for playing tennis is a relationship. I don't really enjoy playing with strangers. I like the sense of camaraderie . . . it's the sharing, participating together. That's the positive side."

However, it seems to be in the competitive situation that our subjects have learned some important things about their patterns of relating to the other. Some subjects became aware of their tendency to mirror the other in terms of their playing style and to hit the ball back to, rather than away from, their opponent. This would fit into a pattern of mirroring or taking care of the other. The subjects with these kinds of relationship or mother problems had great difficulty learning to win or to beat their opponents. One subject said, "When I play in competition, I'm too aware of the other on a feeling level. If I get ahead of her, I feel sorry for her. I've lost more matches that way!" Another subject felt that tennis gave her an opportunity to have a kind of relationship with another person that was not mirroring, not mothering, and which thus felt like freedom. She said, "It is freeing to have a relationship with another person and not have to take care of them!" Another subject said, "Tennis has given me a life. It has released me from the complex of being an echoing wife."

Playing tennis has had the greatest impact for all our subjects on their relationship to or consciousness of their bodies. In this area in particular, there have been life-changing events and consequences. This can be looked at as another aspect of the "mother problem," or as a development of the inferior function, or, from the alchemical tradition, as the reunion of the soul and the body. Marie-Louise von Franz describes this as corresponding to the psychological goal of "conscious spontaneity," or "participating in the flow of life consciously yet without analyzing everything" (von Franz 1980, p. 232).

Tennis can bring about a new consciousness of the body, an awareness of how it moves and feels. One subject said, "Playing tennis, I felt my legs, I felt my feet, I felt my arms. I feel more of myself. I feel a sense of self." As a child she was skinny, sickly, and tall, had physical problems, and was "cut off from my body." Another subject talked about going through life "pretty much ignoring my body, considering it unimportant, irrelevant, pushing it around." She says that tennis has made her more aware of her body's feelings, and she has come to know and to value the pleasure she experiences from the body. She has made important changes in order to have room in her life for these new parts of herself. A third subject described how amazed she was to hear her tennis teacher talking about how swinging a tennis racket actually feels as it goes through. She said to herself, "You are taking about an experience that I don't have!" For her, prior to tennis, she had had no connection to the body. "The first 47 years of my life I had virtually no developed conscious relationship to my body. It's awful to say. I was an intellectual, successful in the academic world, in the thinking world, and I had developed a sort of snobbery about the body." Growing up, she had always felt "horrible" about her body. She carried a distorted image in her mind that she was fat and awkward. Looking at photographs of herself before and after tennis, she sees a different person. "Generally what I see before is a sort of dour, depressed, unhappy, slouching person. And now I see somebody who looks like they're out there and active, much more expressive." She has changed the way she dresses and wears her hair and feels about herself. "A lot has happened in seven years . . . a time of death and a time of new beginnings."

Another subject spoke about tennis being like a dance. "It can be very exciting when it works. The fascination is in the body, a feeling of mastery and connecting to the ball, and I had not had that in my life, so it is sort of a miracle . . . mind and body together." To learn that she could take lessons and get better, and then feel better about herself, was important information for her. She has learned that by bringing loving attention to her body and how it moves, the body will respond positively and support her in an activity that she loves. It is as if she has found a new companion in her life that she did not know that she had before.

Important changes in consciousness about their bodies were paralleled by changes in the way the subjects related to their outer worlds as well. One subject commented on how her discovery of the creativity within her body in terms of how she "places" her shots in tennis has affected her work as a psychotherapist. "I feel myself. I feel a Self inside that I didn't feel before. I feel that Self in therapy, and I feel that I can assert myself more. In tennis, you come out with it, you hit the ball, you place it. I think that has helped me with my practice." Another subject described herself as emerging from a quiet, hidden stance in life, never taking a controversial point of view, to a place where she can take a point of view publicly without allowing the fear of some potential criticism to shut her down. She has begun to travel in the world and to take some risks. She says that "the outer journey is important as a parallel or a reflection of the inner one, neither is complete without the other."

In general, there has been a development of some extraverted functions. The subjects have become more extraverted, conscious of the outer world and reality, and more conscious in their relationships with others. One subject said that through tennis she began to feel confident about herself, which broke some kind of dependency and allowed her to begin to see herself as separate from her husband. Her journey has led her to a divorce and beyond. "I'm happy, fulfilled, divorced. It (tennis) has given me a life."

We were curious about how the unconscious would express itself on the subject of tennis. It appears, in general, that the inferior sensation function may be felt in the body more than dreamed about. For subjects who are regular tennis players, there are fewer dreams directly about tennis. Three of our subjects had had no dreams with a tennis theme as opposed to four who had had dreams about tennis. One of our subjects had had a powerful archetypal dream about tennis eight years before she began to play. At the time of the dream she was considering symbolic interpretations, and it did not occur to her actually to take up the game. This was the dream:

> "I am at a convention. A man has a chart that is a demonstration of the masculine and feminine archetypes. There were two large rectangles with a shiny appearance and imbedded in one were two tall pillars that looked like two stones and imbedded in the other were six stones that formed a jagged peak. It formed a circle. I tell the man that the first two looked like two chromosomes and he explains to me that these two pillars represent man, or the masculine, while the second is called the Decker formation and that represents the feminine. And when I look down on the Decker formation, in the center it plunges down . . . and at the very center of the depths was a tennis ball. It represented the core or the center."

Commenting on the dream she says, "I think that's what it is for me. It really has been the centering principle of my development. It brought me into a relationship, the ego into a relationship with the Self, that is totally different. But I was scared of it. It took a long time."

Several of our subjects spoke about the mystery and the fantasy of tennis as being related to an experience with their bodies, a new kind of body awareness, a feeling in the body. One subject, who is also a painter, said, "I think the imagination is in the body in tennis. It serves as a place for me to paint my brushes with the ball."

As an example of how the unconscious may work through body feelings, one subject reported the sensation that she had been a very good player at some time in the past. "I have been trying to remember how to play. I have the sensation that maybe it was a prior life, or maybe it was an inheritance. But I feel that I am picking up on memories, some prior memories, quite intact memories, because I remember how to hit forehands and backhands. I have the feeling that I had been a great tennis player, and now I am drawing on prior knowledge that I did not get in this life. The drive to play came from a prior experience, too. I don't consider this a fantasy. It is a reality. I know it is real."

The realness and importance of these feelings must be directly related to an experience of the Self in the body. The Self within her is experienced as a champion tennis player who is her teacher. The medium of communication between them is the realm of body feelings, the body in motion.

Discussion

All seven people who participated in the interviews have been successful, serious, high-achieving individuals for whom work has been a dominant source of pleasure in their lives. "All work and no play" not only leads to dullness, but to one-sided development as well. Tennis has provided a means for creating a more-balanced life-style which permits the expression of energy in a physical as well as mental form. Playing matches is only a limited part of the whole experience—additional changes included development of exercise regimens, walking, dietary changes, weight loss, and the motivation to change long-standing addictive behaviors such as alcohol abuse, smoking, and overeating. The game and all of the secondary rewards of playing provided a focus for life that compensated excessive mental activity.

When playing tennis, one experiences moments when everything comes together, smoothly and without thought. Professional players call this being "in the groove." Psychologically, it is analogous to the experience of the *aesthetic moment*. Christopher Bollas described the aesthetic moment as an

> experience of "rapt, intransitive attention," a spell which holds self and other in symmetry and solitude. Time seems suspended. As the aesthetic moment constitutes a deep rapport between subject and object, it provides the person with a generative illusion of fitting with an object. (Bollas 1987, p. 32)

He suggests that the original experience of these moments of harmony with others, where time and space are transcended, represent the original experience of the infant mediated by the maternal presence. Further, it is just such moments that the individual searches for in life, which Jungians define as an experience of wholeness, of the Self. Tennis, in this context, becomes a transcendent function which mediates this experience of aesthetic wholeness.

We have suggested that one primary benefit of playing tennis is that it has a facilitative effect on the development of the inferior function. Von Franz suggests that the inferior function is always directed towards the unconscious and the symbolic world. The location of the unconscious will vary according to the individual's natural superior function. Thus, for those who are introverted in type, which was true for the majority of our participants, the unconscious moves toward outer objects and other people. These outer objects and other people are carriers of the symbolic world and must be experienced for genuine development of the inferior function to take place.

> It must not be said that the inferior function is always directed inwards. It is directed toward the unconscious, whether it appears on the inside or the outside, and it is always the carrier of symbolic experience which may come from within or without. (von Franz 1971, p. 8)

Later, von Franz proposes that the only way to deal with the fourth function is through active imagination: "One can get on not by living the fourth function in a concrete outer or inner way, but by giving it the possibility of a phantasy expression, whether in writing or painting or dancing or in any other form of active imagination" (ibid., p. 62). The danger, it seems, is in the failure to experience the outer phenomenon as a "symbolic" process, which for the introvert needs to be experienced in the world outside. Part of the reason that tennis has been so effective in developing the inferior function for these individuals is that they have not literalized the process but rather have maintained a consciousness of the symbolic function of the game simultaneous to its actual function. Consequently, it would seem that tennis represents a form of active imagination that permits development of the inferior function through engagement with outer objects and people. As analysts, it is important that the psychological value of such activities be acknowledged. The bias of analysis reinforces introspection, reception, and intuitive thinking, all of which support the natural superior function of most analysands. Inclusion of the symbolic world of outer objects and people is an essential experience for the development of consciousness for the introverted type, and tennis is one example, of many possibilities, of an activity that can serve this process.

In an article on psychoanalysis and sports, Descamps suggests that it is necessary to consider both the imaginative and unconscious elements of the sport. He noted that studies of professional athletes' personalities have been relatively rare because "the athlete could not express unconscious themes in words" (1989, p. 168). It is of interest that some of our respondents noted that when they are playing tennis intensively, many hours a week, they have fewer dreams. Perhaps the shift of libido from imagination to physical expression is the source of the diminished dream activity. It would suggest that expressions of the psyche, physical as well as imaginative, share a common pool of libido, and that a shift in dominance of one form of expression over the other may result in a change of focus of material. In an analytical process, when an individual begins to participate in a physical activity, the expression of the unconscious may be experienced through the activity, which can then be analyzed in the same way a dream or active imagination would be analyzed.

The fact that tennis is a shared experience is of psychological significance. The game requires participation of two players, subject and object, in a shared process. Narcissism, in which there is limited recognition of the other as a separate, independent object, can interfere with the play. Alternatively, narcissism that has its expression in the form of echoing also interferes with the game. In the first situation, the narcissist plays with himself. In tennis he must come to terms with the reality of an outer tennis ball that cannot be controlled by fantasy or wish. In the second situation, the player echoes the other and has no independent style of play.

Some of the participants suggested that playing the game of tennis had enabled them to experience, in a direct way, their unconscious tendencies to mirror or echo their opponent. These tendencies ranged from "automatically" returning the ball to the location of their opponent to empathic identification with feelings of envy in the event of winning the match. Playing the game requires confrontation with the opponent as a real, separate, independent, unpredictable person, as well as confronting internal feelings of aggression, envy, power, and the desire to win through the defeat of the other. The safety of the sacred space of the tennis court allows the individual to experience these feelings and become more conscious of their relationship to the "Other." Such experiences can assist in the healing of early woundings that have resulted in poor or faulty development of relationships.

In conclusion, tennis as a form of psychological development in the second half of life would seem to support the individuation process by providing an external, symbolic process for relationship with oneself as well as with the other. The conscious development of the inferior function, through relationship with outer object/person has been a common experience among those who were interviewed. Their relationship to the body was enhanced and became more conscious as well.

Perhaps the image of being born into the world is a useful frame of reference—the world as a reality becomes a place of playful activity, not simply one of work and achievement. Martina Navratilova commented, "You must challenge your own psyche" (1984, p. 7). That challenge has provided a broad range of experiences for those of us who have begun to play in the second half of life.

References

Bollas, C. 1987. *The Shadow of the Object*. New York: Columbia University Press.

Descamps, M.-A. 1989. For a psychoanalysis of sport. *Etudes Psychotherapiques* 20:168–174.

Huizinga, J. 1955. *Homo Ludens*. Boston: Beacon Press.

Navratilova, M. 1984. *Tennis My Way*. New York: Penguin Books.

von Franz, M.-L. 1971. *Jung's Typology*. Dallas: Spring.

_____. 1980. *Alchemy*. Toronto: Inner City Books.

Jeanine Auger Roose, Ph.D., is a psychologist in private practice in Sherman Oaks, California, and a graduate of the C. G. Jung Institute of Los Angeles.

Margaret P. Johnson, Ph.D., has a private practice in Los Angeles and Ventura, California, and is a graduate of the C. G. Jung Institute of Los Angeles.

Sports and the Archetypal Hero

Carol F. Odell

On the tied scoreboard, three seconds loom in the digital display. The final hike sets the players in motion and brings the anxious crowd to their feet. Behind the clashing helmets and the line of scrimmage, the quaterback pauses, arm cocked. Quickly he snaps, and the ball spirals through uncharted territory. In the stands no one breathes for an eternity of seconds as all search for the intended receiver. There he is, sprinting deep amidst jerseys that are the other color, the ball arcing now in a loss of altitude. But wait, with an extended reach of athletic excellence, the new rookie makes the improbable catch, and the stadium unleashes an explosive victory yell. The football is paraded high above dancing feet, well beyond the goal posts.

Every culture since the beginning of time has had their version of sporting events. The Olympic trials of the ancient Greeks, the ball games of the Aztecs, the lacrosse games of the Iroquois. What is it about this age-old obsession we call sports?

Sports provide a manageable and accessible slice of life, and act as a catalyst for the transformational possibilities of the athlete as well as the fan. How an athlete addresses the inherent trials and challenges of the sports world parallels how he or she addresses life. Once lessons are learned on the court, field, or track, they can then be effectively applied within life's greater arena.

Sporting events parade as contests between individuals and between teams of players, but this is only one part of the story. For, just as with life, the real challenge is always with oneself. An athlete, searching for that extra spurt of energy, suppressing tired, aching muscles, and confronting all forms of self-doubt, knows that the real contest is within.

The conscious quest for any athlete is to discipline the body and focus the mind. However, sports can also kindle unconscious parts of the psyche as well. It is through physical trials that the primal instincts, as well as the hero archetype, can be activated.

When these aspects of an athlete's psyche are set in motion, energy is released and athletic excellence is achieved. These are the moments when a player makes a winning shot, catches a spectacular pass, or sets a new world record.

For the fan, sports offer a microscopic view of life's larger parallel dynamics. On a conscious level, the avid observer can vicariously identify with the athlete. On an unconscious level, the heroic proportions given to these players create modern-day myths that, in turn, penetrate the fan's psyche in deeper ways.

We all have an inner drive to reach for greater spiritual awareness. Consciously or unconsciously, we contain an urge to know our divine nature or that which is symbolized by Jung's concept of the archetypal Self. The participation in sports, whether as fan or athlete, can provide a means of amplifying the beginning steps of this individuation process.

This is not to say that one can become self-actualized through sports alone, but rather that sports awaken the athlete's psyche in its drive towards conscious wholeness, and, in turn, these heroic athletes provide their fans with all the elements of a modern-day fairy tale.

Athletes Become Heroes

Joe DiMaggio's unbeatable record of ninety-one hits in fifty-six consecutive baseball games earned him the tag "hero symbol" back in 1941. In 1930, Bobby Jones won all four golf titles comprising the Grand Slam, a record that can only be matched, never improved upon. In 1973, O. J. Simpson was the first to top the record of two thousand yards rushing in one season.

What is it about a game of baseball, football, basketball, or soccer that drives men and women to excel, to attempt to outdo their own records, to devote so much of who they are to this pursuit? Sporting events enhance the transformative possibilities within an athlete by tapping into both the psyche's instinctual nature and the inner archetypal patterns. When these dual aspects of the psyche are set in motion, energy is released and peak experiences occur. This merging of instinct and archetype results in those moments when an athlete "feels his individuality to be exalted, as though he were transported for an instant to a higher dimension of being" (Progoff 1973, p. 83). The existence

within every person of this inner dualism is a paradoxical phenomenon, for, on one side, we contain qualities "more or less like an
animal, on the other side . . . the final embodiment of an age-old
and endlessly complicated sum of hereditary factors" (Jung 1948,
par. 97). These contrasting inner forces "emerge from the same
root and yet are opposites engaged in a more or less constant
tension with one another" (Progoff 1973, p. 81).

However, when these otherwise distinct areas converge, this
becomes "one of the most fruitful sources of psychic energy"
(Jung 1954, par. 414). Sporting events provide a catalyst for this
inner fusion to occur and settings for this psychic energy to be
made manifest in the physical realm. These are the times when
the last-second basketball shot from half court swishes through
the net to win the game, or the home run is hit with bases loaded in
the bottom of the ninth. Bridging the gap between the instinctual
and the archetypal is what creates these electrifying performances. Athletes feel it, fans witness it. This is the energy of athletes, and these are the moments that make them heroes.

Heroic Allies

What better incites the instinctual side of our psyches than the
influence of symbols? "The boundless profusion of animal symbolism in the religion and art of all times does not merely empha-
size the importance of the symbol; it show how vital it is for men to
integrate into their lives the symbol's psychic content—instinct"
(Jung et al. 1964, p. 265). Historically, art and religion have played
a primary role in providing an outlet for the expression of symbols,
particularly those depicting animals. Symbols are undoubtedly
necessary for the evolution of mankind, and yet, today, symbology
has lost this traditional exposure and availability within our culture. To compensate for this loss, one place that symbols have
managed to emerge is in the sports arena in the form of team
mascots.

Teams identify themselves with animals—dolphins, tigers,
colts—hoping to emulate the characteristics associated with the
animal. Each athlete on a team becomes identified with the animal, not only in namesake, but also through attire. Athletes wearing helmets displaying ram's horns or jerseys depicting wolver-

ines come to resemble more closely the animal, the animal's qualities, and their own animalistic nature.

This is most expressively the case for American football. Given the amount of equipment that must be worn, players' original human forms become distorted and take on animal-like proportions and shapes. Similar to the use of masks in other cultures, the uniform "transforms its wearer into an archetypal image," which, in turn, manifests through them (Jung et al. 1964, p. 263). Like actors and actresses that become their character once in costume, athletes in uniform can be effectively raised to heroic heights, in part through the unconscious impact of symbols.

Within the animal symbols found in fairy tales, Marie-Louise von Franz distinguishes between two types (1982, p. 168). One type of animal symbol is the animal that is portraying his or her true form. These animals represent their own instinctual characteristics and personify the unconscious impulses of the heroes and heroines within the stories. The other type of animal often included in fairy tales are those animals that are actually humans confined in beastly form through the work of a curse or spell. The frog who was really a prince under a spell is one such example. These "human-animals" represent the spiritual impulse, or a repressed archetype waiting to be released.

The animals chosen for sports teams are a combination of both of these types. The mascots are in themselves animal totems representing their own characteristic qualities, for instance, the boldness of bears, the aggressiveness of tigers, the wild, untamable energy of colts. At the same time, these "animals" that we see on the field are humans masquerading in costume, unconsciously driven by their spiritual drive to transcend through physical excellence.

The animal spirit is lent to the human, and the human, through this compelling impulse, is elevated to the archetypal. The athlete reaches down one hand to borrow from the animal, and hence his own instinctive nature, while raising up the other to pull himself into the realm of the heroic archetype.

Similarly the animal symbolism included in the form of team mascots, takes on a much greater dimension for the fans than merely as a means of identifying teams names. When a fan adopts a favorite team, then each match becomes a competitive question of endurance, skill, and strength mounted against the other team or, more specifically, against the other mascot. For instance, it would not strike the listener odd to hear a coach say, "My boys are taking on the Rams this weekend." On a deeper level, this generalizing creates a contest between the qualities that these mascots represent, whether they be an animal mascot or an archetypal one, such as the Giants, and the other team of human players. While fans are discussing how their athletes will best defend against the latest running play of the Lions or the impenetrable defense of the Bears, they are unaware of the effect that these symbols have on their unconscious.

Heroic Tales

No one can argue the fact that today's athletes take on heroic proportions. The amount of time, energy, and money that goes into televising, coaching, and paying professional athletes and the amount of time people spend engaged in watching sports is indicative of this fact. ESPN provides around-the-clock sports coverage. Baseball is associated patriotically with apple pie. Football draws more viewers than a presidential State of the Union address. And basketball greats such as Michael Jordan and Larry Bird bedeck billboards and commercials selling us much more than just their athletic performances.

There is little question that we need heroes in today's life. When the news worldwide is full of human atrocities and tragedies, sports heroes can remind us all of the spark of greatness within each of us. Similarly, when so few people are truly satisfied and challenged in their working lives, it comes as no surprise that sports occupy the after-hours "escape" time. The popularity of treating the "Monday morning blues" with Monday night football is one case in point. But beyond this, tales of heroic deeds and achievements have always been incorporated into all cultures because there exists an innate and insatiable appetite for these stories.

As previously discussed, these athletes access the energy released from their unconscious and, for a moment, perform in near-transcendent ways. This fuels the heroic performances and weaves the threads that become our modern-day fairy tales. In this way, today's athletes provide their fans with an accessible version of the much needed contemporary hero.

Fans become inspired by the heroic qualities they witness in their favorite athletes and hope to find within themselves. Heroes "are characterized by a vocation which is carried through without any doubts" (von Franz 1982, p. 74). These sports stars display a single-pointed focus and determination. No quarterback says, "I feel a little anxious about the game today, I think I'll just sit this one out." The star basketball guard does not ask to be taken out of the game in the final minutes of play even though his breathing is labored and his muscles ache all over. These athletes have a job to do, and they long to do it well, to the utmost of their ability. This fortitude and commitment is one reason why fans become equally dedicated.

Heroic myths traditionally contain "a universal pattern" (Jung et al. 1964, p. 101), that is, there exists a generally similar story line for fairy-tale heroes based on a number of common denominators. Looking in more detail at some of these aspects, there are numerous parallels that can be drawn between the universal hero and a star athlete.

To begin with, storybook heroes typically emerge from a "miraculous but humble birth." Likewise, many star athletes come from modest backgrounds and have had to triumph over otherwise hindering situations. These modern-day myths tell of heroic athletes rising out of obscurity and poverty to become some of the country's most popular figures.

"Early proof of superhuman strength" is another characteristic of the mythic hero. Similarly, our heroic athletes-to-be are usually sighted early for their "gifted" talents. Definitely detected by the time they play for the high school scouts, but more often noticed much sooner through the after-school and park district sports programs, they are seen as displaying outstanding abilities and a special aptitude not present in others.

A "rapid rise to prominence or power" is the continuing saga of the storybook hero. This is reminiscent of those athletes who are sought out by the professional teams before the completion of their collegiate eligibility. Or even more dramatically illustrated in the cases of Shawn Kemp and Moses Malone, both drafted straight out of high school. Given large monetary offers and recognition, they were seen as ready to rise to the country's highest league play, skipping over the more usual career steps in the process.

A fairy-tale hero also displays a "triumphant struggle" over the "arduous tasks with which life confronts him" (Jung et al. 1964, p. 101). This is the tale of "a powerful man . . . . who vanquishes evil in the form of dragons, serpents, monsters, demons, and so on" (ibid., p. 68). The animal and archetypal mascots of today's sports teams now take the place of the beasts of the old tales. Modern-day heroes no longer face battles with dragons and serpents but instead meet their challenges on the field against Lions, Vikings, and Bears. The old quest was for the dragon to be slain, the curse removed, or the boon collected. The new quest is that the touchdown be thrown, the final showdown won, the trophy recouped.

The "fallibility to the sin of pride" is another common characteristic in fairy tales and often leads to the demise of the storybook hero. This quality of hubris has likewise been the downfall of many an athlete. The gambling behavior of Pete Rose is one case in point. His actions led not only to being thrown out of baseball, but also to being purposefully overlooked as a hall of fame candidate. Similar instances include the reckless driving charges incurred by basketball player Dale Ellis or the numerous drug charges received by all-pro Dexter Manly, which ultimately led to his eviction from the N.F.L. Such athletes behave off the field as if they were somehow beyond the legal ramifications of their actions or above the human weaknesses that exist for others. This overstepping of boundaries soon brings them face to face with their own vulnerabilities.

Just as each hero rises to the highest pedestal, so too must each hero eventually fall. The "death" of an athlete is either a tragic reality, as in the case of Brian Piccolo, or a symbolic ending as occurs in necessary retirement. Former heroes who are overshadowed by youthful, up and coming athletes also experience symbolic death, which can likewise be sorrowful. Seeing Steve Largent retire from the Seahawks or Magic Johnson from the Laker's brings an end to an era. This serves to remind all of us of our own fallibilities and the inevitable process of aging. Perhaps this was part of the immense fan support that followed Jimmy Connor's unlikely Wimbledon winning streak of 1991. Everyone loved seeing a once-sparkling athlete rise again from the ashes of near retirement. It gave hope that the end need not be so close at hand and the illusion that one can triumph over the aging process. Alas, he was not to be the trophy winner, but everyone enjoyed the fantasy for a time. Sad as it is to witness the fall of a heroic figure, it also heralds a new beginning. This provides an opening which will be filled by another equally stunning athlete and maintains the continuing and cyclical manifestation of the heroic archetype.

Marie-Louise von Franz discusses the "old-fashioned heroic" heroes as compared to the more "modern" heroes (1982, p. 75). The former were unwavering protagonists with a task to accomplish. Along with the more recent fairy tales came the heroes that were more reluctant, who found themselves having to act in situations that they did not choose to undertake and who met their battles full of doubt and hesitancy. In one sense, we want our sports heroes to be the caliber of the earlier hero, completely heroic in the "classical" sense. Perhaps in light of these uncertain times, we want our sports heroes to show none of the qualities of doubt and reluctance but rather only to display expertise and excellence with confidence and unfailing victory.

There are, of course, those moments within a sporting event where some athlete fumbles a well-thrown pass, misses an easy basket, kicks a field goal badly, or drops a fly ball. We all shake our heads in disgust: How could he (or she)? This is not the fairy tale we want to be told. We would demand a replay if only we could. Here it seems we don't want to be reminded of our own fallibility, our own propensity to err, our own humanness. We want fairy tales with happy endings.

But the drama unfolds regardless of our wishes. And like life, not everything happens in the way that we desire or with the control that we wished we had. Rather it is often the case that our team does not make it to the bowl game or become the world series winners, or that a heroic athlete suffers from a bad day, becomes injured, fouls out. However, in a contrasting sense, if these athletes ever make a comeback, we are even more elated, for this points to our potential to overcome our own weaknesses and faults and to triumph in the end. So, despite this similarity to life or perhaps, deep down because of it, sports fans persist with the making of fairy-tale heroes.

Like paint to an artist, sports becomes a medium through which the inner creative energy of an athlete can become realized. For the fans, sports offer a chance to witness this transformation through displays of legendary excellence. Whether it be the story of Gilgamesh or Babe Ruth, humankind has a hearty appetite for these heroic stories, and with this, the sports arena has indeed become a modern-day setting of fairy tales. In our contemporary culture, these athletic highlights of greatness are not forgotten but are told and retold with the same fervor with which folklore was conveyed in days past. These are the stories of physical agility and amazing feats, the stories of heroes risen from obscurity to fame and the great inner and outer contests they have won.

References

Jung, C. G., Marie-Louise von Franz, Joseph L. Henderson, Jolande Jacobi, and Aniela Jaffe. 1964. *Man and His Symbols.* New York: Dell Publishing Co., Inc.

Jung, C. G. 1948. On psychic energy. In *CW* 8:3–66. Princeton, N.J.: Princeton University Press, 1969.

_____. 1954. On the nature of the psyche. In *CW* 8:159–234. Princeton, N.J.: Princeton University Press, 1969.

Progoff, Ira. 1973. *Jung, Synchronicity, and Human Destiny.* New York: Julian Press.

von Franz, Marie-Louise. 1982. *Individuation in Fairy Tales.* Dallas: Spring Publications.

***Carol F. Odell**, M.S.W., is a psychotherapist in private practice and a medical school counselor at the University of Washington.*